Attentiveness to Vulnerability

Attentiveness to Vulnerability

A Dialogue Between Emmanuel Levinas,
Jean Porter, and the Virtue of Solidarity

DANIEL J. FLEMING

☙PICKWICK *Publications* · Eugene, Oregon

ATTENTIVENESS TO VULNERABILITY
A Dialogue Between Emmanuel Levinas, Jean Porter, and the Virtue of Solidarity

Copyright © 2019 Daniel J. Fleming. All rights reserved. Except for brief quotations in critical publications or reviews, no part of this book may be reproduced in any manner without prior written permission from the publisher. Write: Permissions, Wipf and Stock Publishers, 199 W. 8th Ave., Suite 3, Eugene, OR 97401.

Pickwick Publications
An Imprint of Wipf and Stock Publishers
199 W. 8th Ave., Suite 3
Eugene, OR 97401

www.wipfandstock.com

PAPERBACK ISBN: 978-1-5326-0663-2
HARDCOVER ISBN: 978-1-5326-0665-6
EBOOK ISBN: 978-1-5326-0664-9

Cataloguing-in-Publication data:

Names: Fleming, Daniel John, 1986–, author.

Title: Attentiveness to vulnerability : a dialogue between Emmanuel Levinas, Jean Porter, and the virtue of solidarity / Daniel J. Fleming.

Description: Eugene, OR : Pickwick Publications, 2019 | Includes bibliographical references and index.

Identifiers: ISBN 978-1-5326-0663-2 (paperback) | ISBN 978-1-5326-0665-6 (hardcover) | ISBN 978-1-5326-0664-9 (ebook)

Subjects: LCSH: Vulnerability (Personality trait). | Lévinas, Emmanuel. | Porter, Jean,—1955–.

Classification: BF698.35.V85 F57 2019 (paperback) | BF698.35.V85 (ebook)

Manufactured in the U.S.A.   04/16/19

To my wife, Rachelle, and my parents, Richard and Barbara, for encouraging and supporting me throughout this project, and for being the most profound examples of response to the ethical call.

Contents

List of Abbreviations | xi

Introduction | 1
　Preamble and Background to the Book | 1
　Phenomenology and Emmanuel Levinas | 4
　Natural Law and Jean Porter | 6
　Virtue Ethics | 9
　Catholic Social Teaching and the Virtue of Solidarity | 11
　The Possibility of Dialogue | 12
　Limitations | 13
　Methodology and Structure | 15
　Stylistic Features of the Book | 18

1　The Philosophy of Emmanuel Levinas | 21
　Introduction | 21
　Emmanuel Levinas—Biography of a Man and an Idea | 21
　Phenomenology, Edmund Husserl, and Martin Heidegger: The Background to Levinasian Thought | 23
　The Phenomenology of Emmanuel Levinas: Foundations | 33
　Grasping, Totalization, and the Limitations of Philosophy | 41
　Otherwise Than Being or Beyond Essence | 46
　Ethics as First Philosophy | 51
　The Levinasian Insight Regarding Human Subjectivity | 54
　Conclusion | 59

2　Nature in the Natural Law: The Foundations of Jean Porter's Approach | 60
　Introduction | 60
　Why Natural Law and Why Porter? | 61
　Nature in the Natural Law | 76

Intelligibility: Porter's Understanding of Nature | 84
Natural Intelligibility and Teleology in Porter's Theory | 87
Human Nature, Teleology, and Flourishing in Porter's Theory | 89
Initial Links between Porter and Levinas | 96
Conclusion | 99

3 Prerational Nature, Happiness, Virtue, and Jean Porter's Approach | 100

Introduction | 100
Well-being, Flourishing, and Happiness | 101
Virtue ethics | 108
The Foundations for a Thomistic Account of the Virtues: Porter and Others | 113
The Virtues of the Passions: Temperance and Fortitude | 123
The Virtue of Justice | 128
Conclusion | 135

4 An Anthropological Vision Informed by the Catholic Tradition | 137

Introduction | 137
A Paradigm of Justice within a Roman Catholic Framework | 138
Justice and the Personalist Criterion | 160
Vulnerability | 163
Sin | 167
Conclusion | 174

5 The Virtue of Prudence and the Importance of Attentiveness for Moral Reasoning | 176

Introduction | 176
Practical and Speculative Reason | 177
The Virtue of Practical Reason: Prudence | 189
Prudence as Attentiveness | 195
Conclusion | 197

6 The Virtue of Solidarity and Attentiveness to Vulnerability | 198

Introduction | 198
The Virtue of Solidarity: Background and Foundations | 199
The Virtue of Solidarity | 204
Vulnerability as Such and Vulnerability in Relationship | 215
The Vices Associated with the Virtue of Solidarity | 222
Conclusion | 228

Conclusion | 229

Purpose and Structure of the Conclusion | 229

Findings—Plausibility of the Hypothesis | 229
Findings—Other Implications of the Argument | 236
Possibilities for Future Research | 239
Concluding Remarks | 243

Bibliography | 245

List of Abbreviations

PRIMARY TEXTS

THE WORKS OF EMMANUEL Levinas and Jean Porter feature heavily and consistently in this book as primary texts. Where it references these texts, the following abbreviations apply:

TI   Levinas, Emmanuel. *Totality and Infinity: An Essay on Exteriority.* Translated by Alphonso Lingis. Pittsburgh: Duquesne University Press, 1969.

OB   Levinas, Emmanuel. *Otherwise Than Being or Beyond Essence.* Translated by Alphonso Lingis. Pittsburgh: Duquesne University Press, 1998.

NDL   Porter, Jean. *Natural & Divine Law: Reclaiming the Tradition for Christian Ethics.* Rapids: Eerdmans, 1999.

NR   Porter, Jean. *Nature as Reason: A Thomistic Theory of the Natural Law.* Grand Rapids: Eerdmans, 2005.

Where documents of the ecclesial magisterium of the Roman Catholic Church and Thomas Aquinas have been referenced in the book, the following abbreviations apply.

CHURCH DOCUMENTS

All translations used have been taken from the online Vatican archives— www.vatican.va.

RN   Pope Leo XIII, *Rerum Novarum* (1891)

QA   Pope Pius XI, *Quadragesimo Anno* (1931)

PT   Pope John XXIII, *Pacem in Terris* (1963)

GS	Vatican II Council, *Gaudium et Spes: The Pastoral Constitution of the Church in the Modern World* (1965)
DH	Vatican II Council, *Dignitatis Humanae* (1965)
OT	Vatican II Council, *Optatam Totius: Decree on Priestly Training* (1965)
PP	Pope Paul VI, *Populorum Progressio: On the Development of Peoples* (1967)
HV	Pope Paul VI, *Humanae Vitae* (1968)
OG	Pope Paul VI, *Octogesima Adveniens* (1971)
PH	Congregation for the Doctrine of the Faith, *Persona Humana: Declaration on Certain Questions Concerning Sexual Ethics* (1975)
SRS	Pope John Paul II, *Sollicitudio Rei Socialis* (1987)
CA	Pope John Paul II, *Centesimus Annus* (1991)
VS	Pope John Paul II, *Veritatis Splendor* (1993)
CCC	Congregation for the Doctrine of the Faith, *Catechism of the Catholic Church* (1994)
EV	Pope John Paul II, *Evangelium Vitae* (1995)
CS	International Theological Commission, *Communion and Stewardship: Human Persons Created in the Image of God* (2004)
CDSC	Pontifical Council for Justice and Peace, *Compendium of the Social Doctrine of the Church* (2006)
CV	Pope Benedict XVI, *Caritas in Veritate* (2009)

DOCUMENTS OF ST THOMAS AQUINAS

ST	*Summa Theologica*
SCG	*Summa Contra Gentiles*

Introduction

PREAMBLE AND BACKGROUND TO THE BOOK

THIS BOOK IS AN attempt to develop a dialogue between the philosophy of Emmanuel Levinas, Jean Porter's Thomistic theory of the natural law, and the virtue of solidarity as expressed in Catholic Social Teaching. It seeks to explore the implications that such a dialogue would have for our understanding of moral reasoning.

The book rests on the hypothesis that it is possible to develop a set of robust links between these thinkers and bodies of thought—markedly different as they are in terms of philosophical disposition and framework. Such links specify the ethical implications of Levinas's thought and develop Porter's theory in an original way. This work requires further specification through a developed anthropology, which allows for expansion within the tradition of Catholic theological ethics. Further, the inclusion of Levinas and a focus on the virtue of solidarity allows for an advancement of virtue theory and theological ethics, to the extent that the virtue of solidarity becomes a key aspect of any ethical reasoning.

Some Personal Notes

All academic work has its basis and, to a greater or lesser extent, its bias, in the lives of those who undertake it. The topic at hand is no exception and so I would like to give a brief explanation of the factors which led me to believe that exploring the possibility of dialogue between Emmanuel Levinas, Jean Porter and the Virtue of Solidarity would be worthwhile. I trust that these reflections will be helpful for those who read the book inasmuch as they place it within the context of the personalities, concerns and questions out of which it arose. I supplement them by explaining the more theoretical concerns out of which the topic arose below.

First, I write from the perspective of Catholic theological ethics, and my concern is largely to advance thinking in that field. However, as will be made clear below, the scope of this book is broad, and I hope that its insights will be valuable to those outside of this tradition. At its best, Catholic theological ethics draws on the best insights available to it—regardless of where they come from—and allows those insights to develop its thinking. This book will aim to exemplify that through the sources on which it draws.

Second, in relation to the specific sources on which the book focuses: Emmanuel Levinas, Jean Porter and the Virtue of Solidarity, there is a brief story behind each. I begin with Porter, because chronologically my exposure to her theory of the natural law came first. During my honors year, Porter's text *Nature as Reason: A Thomistic Theory of the Natural Law* was suggested to me by my supervisor, Professor Robert Gascoigne, as a possible lead for the topic I was pursuing.[1] So impressed was I by Porter's theory, which Robert rightly described as a "top shelf work," that it became a central part of my honors thesis which set the foundations for it to be included in the PhD. Porter's theory synthesizes what I see as the best in current Thomistic thought, and also provides avenues through which to integrate current trends and insights in virtue theory. Hence, my use of her work should be seen as a touchstone for other relevant work in this area. That Porter's theory is central does not mean that the book's insights apply to followers of hers only—they will be of interest to anyone engaging with moral theories that focus on virtue, natural law, and human flourishing.

During my honors year, I also had the opportunity to do an in-depth study of the virtue of solidarity, based on previous studies of the body of thought known as Catholic Social Teaching (CST). This led to the germination of a number of the key ideas in this text. I have continued to be impressed and inspired by the holistic anthropological vision upon which CST is based and how it gives rise to solidarity as a principle and a virtue. It, and the work done on it throughout this text, now underpins much of my current work in healthcare ethics.

Third, and moving now to Levinas, focus on his work also resulted from a suggestion by Robert, one for which I will be forever grateful. My original plan for the book was to develop something of an ethics for interpersonal relationships and, when I mentioned this to Robert, he immediately suggested that I read some of Levinas's work. I bought the first book I could find by Levinas, *Otherwise than Being or Beyond Essence*, and

---

1. Porter, *Nature as Reason* (Hereafter *NR*)

attempted to get through it.² In retrospect, I realize that this was a foolish move—*Otherwise than Being* is a particularly dense and confusing work, deliberately so in fact, a point to which I return in chapter 1. Nevertheless, I persevered with Levinas and read countless commentaries and articles on his work in an attempt to grapple with his big idea. When the "penny finally dropped," I understood why Jacques Derrida described the philosophy of Levinas as so powerful that it would "make us tremble."³ Immediately I was left wondering whether the "Levinasian Insight," as I refer to it throughout the book, could be linked with the research I had done before and how such links might help to develop existing theories. After some fairly deep contemplation, I decided that I would set out to explore the links between the three areas that had aroused my curiosity: Emmanuel Levinas, Jean Porter and the Virtue of Solidarity. In so doing, I would also be integrating virtue ethics which was another area that had caught my attention through my study of Porter's theory and contemporary trends in moral theology.

Admittedly choosing to link these four areas together and explore the implications of such a link was not the path of least resistance. When it comes to theoretical framework, the distance between Levinas's phenomenology and the visions of human flourishing held by Porter and CST seem vast, at least at first. Nevertheless, I pursued it and have produced what I think is a convincing dialogue between Levinas, Porter and the Virtue of Solidarity, a dialogue which has important implications for understanding attentiveness and vulnerability as key categories in moral discernment.

Having said something of the story behind the drawing together of these thinkers, I turn now to consider their theoretical work in more detail.

Academic Preamble—Introduction

What do Emmanuel Levinas's insight into human subjectivity, Jean Porter's theory of the natural law, and the virtue of solidarity have in common? Even though this is not the start of a joke pitched at a gathering of Levinasians, natural lawyers, virtue ethicists and social ethicists, the image of such a meeting is a helpful way of understanding the concurrent areas of study which I aim to bring into dialogue in this book. In this introductory chapter, I will consider each area of study in isolation. In so doing, I would like to point out that the purpose of this exercise is to set the context of the material that the book will draw into dialogue in its later chapters. I am therefore necessarily brief in my explanation of each study area.

2. Levinas, *Otherwise than Being* (Hereafter, *OB*).
3. Derrida, *Writing and Difference*, 101.

PHENOMENOLOGY AND EMMANUEL LEVINAS

Before considering the philosophy of Levinas himself, it is important to situate it within the discipline of phenomenology, given that Levinas referred to his project as a phenomenological one.[4] Phenomenology, as is well known, was one of the major philosophical movements in the twentieth century—a list of any of the major philosophers of this period includes a significant proportion of phenomenologists.[5] Whilst the origins of phenomenology are at times loosely associated with the work of Kant and Hegel, there is broad agreement that this specific way of doing philosophy was formally introduced by Edmund Husserl (1859–1938), whose aim was to lead the practitioner of phenomenology to a situation of pure transcendental subjectivity at which point the foundations of consciousness, and therefore the possibility of all philosophy, would become apparent.[6]

Whilst Husserl is credited with being the founder of phenomenology, this way of doing philosophy is not constituted by one agreed method, and its practitioners are not dogmatic in their adoption of Husserl's philosophy. Rather, as Paul Ricoeur has pointed out, "the history of phenomenology is the history of Husserlian heresies."[7] As such, those who are identified as practicing the method are as diverse as Martin Heidegger, Emmanuel Levinas, Hannah Arendt, Jean-Paul Sartre and Jacques Derrida.[8] Nevertheless, it is possible to identify a number of common features in the approach. To begin with, phenomenology is more a way of practicing philosophy than it is a body of philosophical knowledge.[9] Phenomenology is concerned with human experience, specifically the experience of consciousness and the way that things appear, or "give themselves," as phenomena in consciousness.[10] The task of the phenomenologist is to attend to this giving and describe these experiences from within, without imposing prior explanations onto them.[11]

---

4. See *OB*, 183.

5. Glendinning, "What Is Phenomenology?," 30.

6. Moran, *Introduction to Phenomenology*, 1; Solomon, "Phenomenology," 1754. Husserl's phenomenology is explained in more detail in chap. 1.

7. See Moran, *Phenomenology*, 3.

8. Dermot Moran provides a helpful commentary on each of these philosophers in terms of their use of phenomenology. See, respectively, Moran, *Phenomenology*, 192–247; 287–319; 354–90; 435–74.

9. Ibid., 4.

10. Solomon, "Phenomenology," 1757.

11. Flood, "Understanding Phenomenology," 9. Further explanation of the methods of phenomenology, including how these were developed by Husserl, Heidegger and Levinas, is included in chap. 1.

The precise way in which this task is done is dependent on the philosopher who is undertaking it, hence the diversity of phenomenological approaches. It is out of this background that Levinas can best be understood.

Levinas saw his philosophy as a phenomenology, but readily admitted that he was faithful to the spirit of Husserl's work rather than his specific conclusions.[12] As will be shown in chapter 1, Levinas used phenomenology to challenge the conclusions of those who had used it before him, with a specific focus on his teachers, Edmund Husserl and Martin Heidegger. Whilst Levinas covers a vast array of topics on his work, those who study Levinas concur that all of it orbits around one "big idea."[13] In simple terms (although as we will discover in chapter 1, there is nothing simple about the approach), Levinas can be understood as pointing out that consciousness never arises in isolation, but rather always-already in relationship with the mysterious human Other who calls consciousness into existence and also at once calls it into question by throwing light on its spontaneity and capacity for violence.[14] Hence, it is not consciousness that is primary for human experience, but rather the experience of being called by the Other and, specifically, the experience of being called into question by the Other. Given that Levinas understands this experience as giving rise to the capacity for consciousness, he sees consciousness as constituted by this call and thus fundamentally responsible for the way it answers. This is why he understood ethics as "first philosophy." Nonetheless, Levinas is not optimistic about the form that the response to the Other typically takes, which he sees as manifested most clearly in a tendency toward "totalization," understood as the violent reduction of the Other to an object over which consciousness can claim control.

As an important figure in twentieth century continental philosophy, the phenomenological insight of Levinas has received attention in disciplines as diverse as philosophy, theology, politics, psychoanalysis, law, education, art and literature.[15] Phenomenology's "turn to the subject" more broadly considered has also found its way into theology through the likes

---

12. *OB*, 183. See also Burggraeve, *The Wisdom of Love*, 34. On the continuing influence of Husserl's methodology in Levinas's work, see Davis, *Levinas*, 8–9.

13. Critchley, "Introduction," 6. Cf. Burggraeve, *The Wisdom of Love*, 28; Cohen, "Emmanuel Levinas: Judaism and the Primacy of the Ethical," 235; Derrida, *Writing and Difference*, 312; Putnam, *Jewish Philosophy as a Guide to Life*, 99. The specific ways in which each of these authors expresses Levinas's "big idea" are noted in chap. 1.

14. See chap. 1.

15. Among contemporary works, see for example Caygill, *Levinas and the Political*; Harold, *Prophetic Politics*; Manderson, ed., *Essays on Levinas and Law*; Marinos, *Levinas, Law, Politics*; Peperzak, ed., *Ethics as First Philosophy*; Purcell, *Levinas and Theology*.

of figures such as Karl Rahner, and specifically into moral theology through the increased focus on the human person and human experience that can be seen in the discipline today.[16] Hence, there are precedents for drawing work from Levinas's broad phenomenological school into theological ethics, however the implications of Levinas's particular approach for this field are not entirely clear. In my research, I have uncovered very few in the field of theological ethics, at least in the English-speaking world, who have attempted to explore the implications of Levinasian phenomenology for the discipline, and none who have linked it explicitly with natural law.[17]

Apart from a lack of prior work in this area, the possibility of linking Levinas with the other aspects of this work which have to do with the moral life is made all the more challenging in light of the fact that Levinas himself was not concerned with the specific practical implications of his philosophy. Instead, his focus is on the constitution of human subjectivity-in-relationship which exists behind practical morality "no matter how poorly or weakly this relationship is perceived or acted upon."[18] As such, Levinas leaves the door open for a consideration of the practical implications that his theory might have, without providing any more than clues as to the direction this should take.

NATURAL LAW AND JEAN PORTER

The second area of study which the book draws into dialogue is focused on natural law. Contemporary discussions of natural law theory are characterized by sharp divisions on a number of fronts. A primary reason for this

16. On the influence of phenomenology, specifically that of Martin Heidegger, on Karl Rahner, see Coolman, "Gestimmtheit: Attunement as a Description of the Nature-Grace Relationship in Rahner's Theology"; Marmion and Hines, "Introduction," 2. One of the most famous and influential figures to incorporate phenomenology into theology and moral theology was the late Pope John Paul II, see Leahy, "John Paul II and Hans Urs Von Balthasar," 36; O'Collins, "John Paul II and the Development of Doctrine," 4. In terms of the increased focus on human experience in the discipline of moral theology today, see Salzman, *What Are They Saying About Catholic Ethical Method?*, 48–79; Lawler and Salzman, "Human Experience and Catholic Moral Theology."

17. Rather, the use of Levinas tends to be confined to systematic and practical theology. See for example McArdle, "Levinas and Responsibility for the Other"; Morrison, "Good Teaching, Spirituality and the Philosophy of Emmanuel Levinas"; Purcell, "The Mystery of Death"; Purcell, *Mystery and Method*; Purcell, *Levinas and Theology*; Rigby, "Levinas and Christian Mysticism after Auschwitz"; Veling, "For You Alone"; Zimmermann, *Levinas and Theology*. However, it should be pointed out that the Leuven moral theologian Roger Burggraeve has written extensively on Levinas and moral theology. I draw on his work a number of times throughout this work.

18. Egéa-Kuehne, "Introduction," 16.

is that there is a suspicion of a certain conception of natural law, held by a number of contemporary moral theologians, which they take as aligned with the twentieth-century neo-scholastic manuals of moral theology, and which has been utilized in some of the Roman Catholic magisterium's strongest statements on sexual ethics.[19] Frequently, this approach is criticized for its reliance on a static physicalism which lacks an awareness of historical consciousness, as well as for falling prey to the naturalistic fallacy.[20] In response, the role of "nature" in Catholic moral theology has frequently been put to one side in favor of a turn to reason or to a focus on the human subject.[21] Whilst this "turn to reason" is distinct from the neo-scholastic version of natural law, some authors have still identified this approach broadly with a natural law framework inasmuch as the capacity to reason is natural to the human person and a focus on the subject implies a focus on its nature, understood in an holistic way to include more than its physical nature.[22]

Other authors have chosen to continue with a more explicit discussion of natural law, albeit upon different foundations to the physicalist approach noted above. Perhaps the most well-known is what is known as the New Natural Law Theory (NNLT), which has been developed primarily by Germain Grisez, John Finnis and Joseph Boyle.[23] This approach begins by arguing that practical reason is able to acknowledge the self-evident existence of certain "basic goods" and, following from this recognition, is able to determine specific, and universally applicable, moral norms.[24] Despite the deliberate attempt to distance itself from the physicalist approach to natural law, NNLT has been criticized on similar grounds to those directed at the

---

19. See Porter *Natural and Divine Law* (hereafter, *NDL*), 15–34, especially 29–34; *NR*, 1–44. Cf. Salzman and Lawler, *The Sexual Person*. In terms of the magisterium's specific statements on sexual ethics, see *HV*, no. 3 and *PH*, 3.

20. *NDL*, 29. Cf. Keenan, *A History of Catholic Moral Theology in the Twentieth Century*, 174; Pope, *The Evolution of Altruism and the Ordering of Love*, 3. See also Richard Gula's discussion of these points: Gula, *Reason Informed by Faith*, 231–40. These issues are analyzed in more detail in chap. 2 .

21. Richard Gula's treatment of the natural law is paradigmatic of this shift. In his *Reason Informed By Faith*, Gula includes a table that contrasts the "Order of Nature" approach to natural law with the "Order of Reason" approach. Gula, *Reason Informed by Faith*, 239–40.

22. On the former, see for example Curran and McCormick, *Readings in Moral Theology No. 7*, 1. On the latter, see for example Janssens, "Artificial Insemination: Ethical Considerations," 4. Further discussion of these approaches takes place in chap. 2.

23. This approach, which is also known as the Basic Goods Theory, is summarized by these three theorists in Grisez, et al., "Practical Principles."

24. See Grisez, et al., "Practical Principles," 106; 108; 121–27. See also *NR*, 128.

physicalist approach for failing to take into account historical consciousness and the development of moral norms.[25]

Whereas NNLT focuses on reason in order to distance itself from the physicalist approach to the natural law, a number of authors have "returned to nature" in response to a renewed interest in the relevance of nature for moral theology (and moral philosophy also), albeit understood in a more comprehensive manner than the physicalist approach noted above.[26] Mindful of the problem of the naturalistic fallacy, these authors are attempting to engage seriously with the many new insights we have into the human person thanks to modern scientific research, and with exploring the implications of these for ethics.[27] Jean Porter's approach to the natural law aligns itself with these concerns and with a retrieval of the natural law tradition. This takes her beyond the neo-scholastic manuals of natural law and into dialogue with the scholastic lawyers and theologians of the Middle Ages.[28] Her aim is to provide a convincing approach to natural law which incorporates the tradition's best features, including its legitimate concern for a consideration of nature in moral discourse, whilst avoiding the problems typically associated with some of the approaches to natural law theory noted above.[29] The strength and clarity of Porter's theory in this regard has seen it receive widespread critical praise.[30]

---

25. These and other critiques are made by a number of authors. For an overview, see Pope, *Human Evolution and Christian Ethics*, 51–54; Porter, "Basic Goods and the Human Good in Recent Catholic Moral Theology"; Salzman, "The Basic Goods Theory and Revisionism." Salzman has also written extensively on NNLT in Salzman, *Catholic Ethical Method*. I return to NNLT and critique it a number of times throughout the book, especially in chap. 2 and chap. 5.

26. In terms of moral theology, such a renewal is evident in Clark, *Biology & Christian Ethics*; Pope, *The Evolution of Altruism*; Pope, *Human Evolution and Christian Ethics*; NR. In terms of moral philosophy, this interest can be seen as a consequence of what Anthony J. Lisska suggests is a return to the ethical naturalism of Aristotle and Aquinas. As paradigmatic of this shift, he points towards the works of Alasdair MacIntyre, John Finnis, Henry Veatch, Ralph McInerny, Martha Nussbaum, and Paul Sigmund. Lisska, *Aquinas's Theory of Natural Law*, 46–54.

27. See for example Pope, *Human Evolution and Christian Ethics*.

28. This point is explored in more detail in chap. 2.

29. As one example, Porter makes a considered effort to show that her theory does not fall prey to the naturalistic fallacy. I explain Porter's argument on this point and develop it further in chap. 2.

30. See Fout, "Nature as Reason: A Thomistic Theory of the Natural Law by Jean Porter"; Jeffreys, "Nature as Reason: A Thomistic Theory of the Natural Law"; Magidon, "Nature as Reason: A Thomistic Theory of the Natural Law"; McCormick, "Review of *Nature as Reason: A Thomistic Theory of the Natural Law* by Jean Porter." See also my extended appraisal of and commentary on Porter's theory, Fleming, "Intelligibility in the Natural Law." Not all responses to Porter's theory have been as positive: see for

Porter's theory is most clearly articulated in her book, *Nature as Reason: A Thomistic Theory of the Natural Law*, which builds on the insights of her earlier work, *Natural & Divine Law: Reclaiming the Tradition for Christian Ethics*.[31] *Nature as Reason* begins by proposing an argument for the significance of "nature as nature," understood as the prerational nature of the human person, for moral discourse. In this, she draws heavily on the scholastics as well as contemporary philosophers, scientists and theologians to develop her argument, taking care to show that it does not fall prey to the naturalistic fallacy and to distinguish it from NNLT.[32] She proceeds to argue that the prerational nature of the human person is expressed in its most excellent form by means of the virtues, and develops her understanding of these in dialogue with Thomas Aquinas and a number of contemporary virtue ethicists.[33] After this point, Porter situates the human capacity for reason within the argument she has developed throughout and demonstrates its links with the specific virtue of prudence.[34]

VIRTUE ETHICS

As noted above, Porter's integration of virtue into her theory of the natural law, as well as the project's aim to include the virtue of solidarity, aligns this work with another contemporary area of study pertaining to the discipline of virtue ethics, one of the three major approaches to ethics in contemporary moral philosophy.[35] The so-called "return" to virtue ethics is frequently traced back to Elizabeth Anscombe's 1958 article "Modern Moral Philosophy," in which she argued that modern ethical theories needed to move away from a consideration of right and wrong actions and towards a consideration of the character dispositions of moral agents.[36] Proponents

---

example Rhonheimer, "Nature as Reason: A Thomistic Theory of the Natural Law (Review Article)." Rhonheimer's main concern with Porter's theory is that it misrepresents the Thomistic understanding of the natural law and is prone to relativism. Porter has provided a convincing response to Rhonheimer's critique: see Porter, "A Response to Martin Rhonheimer,."

31. See *NDL*; *NR*. The implications of these works for the specific issue of legal authority are explored by Porter in a more recent book, which has been referred to where relevant throughout this work. See Porter, *Ministers of the Law*, esp. 83.

32. See further exploration in chap. 2.

33. See further exploration in chap. 3.

34. See further exploration in chap. 5.

35. The other two being deontology and consequentialism. See Hursthouse, "Virtue Ethics," 2421.

36. Anscombe, "Modern Moral Philosophy." See also Battaly, "Introduction: Virtue and Vice."

of the virtue ethics approach argue that it is a helpful alternative to other dominant theories for a number of reasons, including: that it has the capacity to provide a more comprehensive vision of the moral life; it has received attention from both the continental and analytic schools of philosophy and as such provides a bridge between them; it can respond to postmodernism's critiques of the Enlightenment's "meta-narratives" while retaining a critical distance from the former's nihilistic tendencies; and, it provides a framework within which to consider the relationship between an analysis of moral action and an ongoing and sensitive attentiveness to the ethical dimensions of everyday life.[37] It has also been suggested that, from an educational point of view, virtue ethics has more potential for facilitating moral education than do the deontological and consequentialist approaches.[38]

The rise of virtue ethics has been understood as a "return" rather than a new phenomenon because reflection on virtuous character traits is something that can be found in the work of, among others, Confucius, Plato, Aristotle and Aquinas.[39] The common features of the approach, as it has been manifested over the ages, consist in understanding a virtue as a stable and good character disposition which expresses itself in the way a moral agent is motivated and/or acts in a diversity of circumstances.[40] The philosopher Stuart Rachels has provided a set of criteria as an outline of a virtue ethics approach:

> A theory of virtue should have several components: (a) an explanation of what a virtue is, (b) a list specifying which character traits are virtues, (c) an explanation of what these virtues consist in, and (d) an explanation of why these qualities are good ones for a person to have.[41]

I will return to these criteria later in the work to situate Porter's theory, and CST, within the context of virtue ethics.

---

37. Becker, "Virtue Ethics, Applied Ethics and Rationality Twenty-Three Years after *After Virtue*": 268; 270; Hursthouse, "Virtue Ethics," 2422; Spohn, "The Return of Virtue Ethics": 60. Each of these points are explored in detail in chap. 3.

38. See for example Dent, "Virtue, *Eudaimonia* and Teleological Ethics," 28; 30; Kupperman, "Virtues, Character and Moral Dispositions," 206–10. It should be noted that virtue ethics has also received significant criticism. I note this in chap. 3.

39. Hursthouse, "Virtue Ethics," 2421.

40. See Battaly, "Introduction: Virtue and Vice," 3; Rachels, *The Elements of Moral Philosophy*, 176. These points are explored in more detail in chap. 3.

41. Rachels, *The Elements of Moral Philosophy*, 175.

CATHOLIC SOCIAL TEACHING AND THE VIRTUE OF SOLIDARITY

The next area that the book engages with relates to Catholic Social Teaching (CST). It is widely agreed that this body of thought had its beginning in Pope Leo XIII's 1891 encyclical *Rerum Novarum*.[42] From this time CST would develop significantly and be well poised to deal with the emergence of globalization in the middle of the twentieth century, and onwards to continue as an important source of social guidance for the twenty-first century.[43] Methodologically, current manifestations of CST (here I include the more recent social encyclicals, as well as scholarly work in the area) stand in sharp contrast to the physicalist approach to the natural law discussed above.[44] Charles Curran has identified three major areas of difference. The first is that CST tends to be historically conscious, which means that it is aware of the possibility of development in moral thought and, correlatively, the necessary limitations of solutions to moral issues proposed at a particular period in time.[45] Second, Curran points out that CST has a clear personalist focus and emphasizes freedom, equality and participation.[46] Further, it places a high degree of importance on a developed and holistic concept of human dignity which is founded in the theological anthropology of documents such as Vatican II's *Gaudium et spes*.[47] Finally, Curran argues that CST embodies a relationality-responsibility ethical model, as distinct from a deontological one, which he defines as seeing "the human person in terms of one's multiple relationships with God, neighbor, world and self and the call to live responsibly in the midst of these relationships."[48]

---

42. *RV*. For a consideration of the context out of which the encyclical arose, see Aubert, *Catholic Social Teaching*; Sniegocki, *Catholic Social Teaching and Economic Globalization*, 106; 108.

43. These points are explored in more detail in chap. 6.

44. Compare, for example, Pope Paul VI's encyclical *Populorum Progressio* with his *Humanae Vitae*.

45. See Charles Curran, "Catholic Social and Sexual Teaching," 427–430. I would add here that CST is also contextually sensitive, by which I mean that it acknowledges the complexity of ethical situations and the corresponding need to pay careful attention before suggesting a particular response. See for example *OA*, no. 4. These points are explored in more detail in chap. 4.

46. Curran, "Catholic Social and Sexual Teaching," 430–2.

47. These points are explored in detail in chap. 4.

48. Curran, "Catholic Social and Sexual Teaching," 432. The specifics of this kind of ethical model are explored in more detail in chap. 4.

It is out of this background that the virtue of solidarity can be understood.[49] Beginning with an acknowledgement of the necessity of human relationality, the observation that we are radically interdependent creatures, and with a focus on interdependence between social groups, CST notes that there are equal and unequal forms of this interdependence.[50] Where the latter exists, relationships are characteristically damaging and violate, rather than promote, human dignity and flourishing. Inspired by a concern for the common good, solidarity requires that careful attention be given to situations of unequal interdependence by means of each party standing in solidarity with, and being attentive to, the other in order to develop an understanding of a method of response which promotes, rather than violates, the human dignity and flourishing of all.[51] Furthermore, given CST's foundational interest in a personalist approach which values the active participation of all human subjects, any such response would need to involve the participation of all, and cannot simply be a case of more powerful or wealthy individuals or groups imposing solutions on others.[52] Finally, a necessary aspect of solidarity is the recognition that some parties are more vulnerable than others and that, because the violation of their human dignity is a more immediate threat, they should receive priority of attention. The terminology used for this prioritization is the "preferential option for the poor."[53]

THE POSSIBILITY OF DIALOGUE

The four areas of study introduced thus far have distinctive methodologies and areas of focus. What hope is there, then, for bringing them into dialogue with one another and responding to the questions raised above? In the conclusion to his book, *A History of Moral Theology in the Twentieth Century*, James Keenan points out that moral theology in the current time is heading towards what he refers to as a "Global Discourse on Suffering and Solidarity," and proceeds to show how moral theologians from around the

---

49. Even though it does not arise from CST, but was adopted and adapted by it, a point which is explained in chap. 6.

50. For a more thorough explanation of this point, see Fleming, "Understanding Trade," 11–13. See also Hollenbach, *The Common Good and Christian Ethics*, 188.

51. See *SRS*, no. 38. Curran, *Catholic Social Teaching 1891-Present*, 31; O'Neill, "Christian Hospitality and Solidarity with the Stranger," 150; Sniegocki, *Catholic Social Teaching*, 144.

52. Curran, Himes, and Shannon, "Commentary on *Sollicitudo Rei Socialis*," 129; Hollenbach, *The Common Good and Christian Ethics*, 188.

53. *SRS*, 42; Curran, *Catholic Social Teaching*, 186.

world are united and in dialogue as they grapple with issues of suffering and seek to provide ever more adequate theoretical, and practical, responses.[54] I concur with Keenan that this is a positive move and I would add that it needs to be supplemented with a moral theology that is global in a theoretical sense—that is, that it can dialogue with, be challenged by, learn from and integrate insights from a diversity of disciplines as well as with and from the diversity that exists within its own. Hence, I think there is great hope for bringing the diverse conversations that stimulated this book into dialogue with each other. Not only that, I would suggest that the discussion that ensues will produce important insights that none of the areas of study would have produced were they to remain isolated and inwardly focused. The "devil is in the detail" of course, as the common expression warns, and the work of dialogue involves more than placing ideas alongside one another. Instead, authentic dialogue involves understanding each position clearly, bringing it into critical conversation with other perspectives, and seeing how this mutual engagement might lead to better insights overall. It is the task of the remainder of this book to undertake this project. Before doing so, some comments about the work's limitations and style are in order.

LIMITATIONS

Limitations are necessary for any work which has a completion date and a word limit. These represent a combination of self-imposed limitations, which assist in retaining focus on the topic, and others that are consequences of the approach taken. I limit my focus in the book to Levinas's philosophical work, especially as it is expressed in his two most famous and widely read volumes *Totality and Infinity* and *Otherwise than Being or Beyond Essence*. As such, it does not include a discussion of his Talmudic commentaries which form a significant and distinctive body of work in their own right.[55] Furthermore, given that its focus is on the philosophy of Levinas, the commentators whom I engage are largely philosophical commentators, rather than theologians who have explored the implications of Levinas for systematic or practical theology.

Given the specific focus of the topic, my consideration of natural law is primarily concerned with Jean Porter's articulation of this approach, a choice which I have given reasons for above and defend further in chapter 2. As a consequence, when I consider the authors Porter bases her work on, Aquinas most notably, I do so through the lens of Porter's work in order to

54. Keenan, *A History of Catholic Moral Theology*, 197–240.
55. This point is revisited in the conclusion to the book.

see how they are used in her theory. In future research, it will be possible to further this investigation with an independent analysis of the texts Porter uses and their relevance for the project. Nevertheless, where such investigation is called for either by gaps in Porter's theory or the need to explore a point more fully, I engage with a broader array of sources that move beyond her specific work.

In terms of the sources with which the book dialogues in the area of moral theology, namely Catholic anthropology and Catholic Social Teaching, these are largely Roman Catholic in their background. However, the insights of important figures outside the Catholic tradition have been incorporated where appropriate, and the inclusion of Levinas as a possible dialogue partner with natural law is significant in this regard. It is my hope that this work may encourage future research that seeks intersections with sources and worldviews outside of those incorporated within it.

Furthermore, it should be noted that whilst the book incorporates a significant discussion of Catholic Social Teaching, specifically in regard to the virtue of solidarity, its focus is not on social ethics as such, even though I will suggest in the conclusion that it has implications for this area.[56] Rather, it tends towards a foundational moral theology which is grounded in a natural law approach. Specific examples that have been used throughout the book tend to focus on ethical issues that arise between individuals, or within the complex matrix of close interpersonal relationships. This should not be taken as a suggestion that these are the only areas of focus that are important for this work, and this point is made strongly in chapter 6 and is revisited in the Conclusion.

Finally, as a work that is aligned with Catholic moral theology, a significant limitation of this work concerns a lack of detailed attention to Sacred Scripture, although—had space permitted it—this would have been desirable in light of Vatican II's call for the renewal of moral theology.[57] Initially I had planned to include a foundational chapter which focused on Scripture, specifically the Parable of the Good Samaritan, but quickly realized that the space needed to give this the exegetical attention that would allow it to inform the topic in a way that did justice to the Scriptural text would be greater than the book could accommodate.[58] My hope is that future research

---

56. Indeed, Porter's most recent work *Ministers of the Law* seeks to explore the implications of her theory in a sociopolitical context. This provides the possibility for future work, which includes her approach to the natural law in this area.

57. *OT*, 16.

58. On the importance of this kind of careful use of Scripture for all disciplines of theology, see O'Collins, *Rethinking Fundamental Theology*, 331–32.

will be able to draw in Scripture as yet another dialogue partner for this topic, a point which is also revisited in the Conclusion.

METHODOLOGY AND STRUCTURE

In order to achieve the goals stated above, I integrate a diversity of methodologies which include those unique to phenomenology, natural law, virtue ethics and Catholic Social Teaching. The book builds its own methodology out of this, and follows the component parts introduced above, beginning with a discussion of each part on its own terms and then bringing it into dialogue with the rest of the work and proposing arguments for the implications of the links created. This methodology is best demonstrated by way of an outline of the content of the chapters, which also reveals the way in which the remainder of the text is structured.

Chapter 1—The Philosophy of Emmanuel Levinas

Chapter 1 begins the book by developing an understanding of the philosophy of Emmanuel Levinas. Methodologically, the chapter explains Levinas's phenomenology in detail on its own terms and summarizes its key feature. When positioned within the book's argument as a whole, the chapter can be understood as providing the foundation for developing a robust link between Levinas and Porter.

Chapter 2—Nature in the Natural Law: The Foundations of Jean Porter's Approach

Chapter 2 marks a shift from the consideration of Levinas's phenomenology in chapter 1 to a close analysis of natural law theory and, more specifically, Jean Porter's approach, which becomes a central part of the rest of the argument. This allows me to begin developing an understanding of Porter's theory which enables the robust links between her and Levinas to be made. In its relationship with the book considered as a whole, this chapter focuses specifically on situating Porter's theory within contemporary discussions surrounding natural law and with analyzing her argument regarding the significance of nature in the natural law. This allows for an articulation of the first links between Porter and Levinas toward the end of the chapter.

Chapter 3—Virtue in the Natural Law

Chapter 3 continues with my detailed exploration of Porter's approach, moving from her consideration of nature and natural law to the integration of virtue ethics into her theory. Methodologically it thus marks a movement into a consideration of virtue ethics and how Porter's theory aligns with contemporary thought in this area, and also creates the possibility for an integration of the virtue of solidarity later in the book. When seen in relationship to the book's argument considered as a whole, it continues to build up an understanding of Porter's theory and create links with Levinas where possible. Furthermore, its consideration of Porter's development of the virtue of justice notes that she explicitly suggests engagement with a developed anthropology in order to refine an understanding of what is "due" to the human person. This enables me to move to the next part of the argument, namely its appeal to an anthropological vision informed by the Catholic tradition. This takes place in chapter 4, and provides a further point of linkage with the virtue of solidarity which draws heavily on this anthropological vision in chapter 6.

Chapter 4—A Paradigm for Justice: The Human Person Integrally and Adequately Considered

Chapter 4's turn to an anthropological vision informed by the Catholic tradition marks a further methodological shift. In so doing, it engages with a number of sources to develop a Catholic understanding of the human person. These include official Church teachings and the personalist methodology of Louis Janssens, frequently referred to as "the human person integrally and adequately considered," which arose out of Janssens's reflection on the theological anthropology of the Vatican II document *Gaudium et spes*. This has the capacity to fulfil the understanding of justice developed in chapter 3 in order to specify what is due to the human person. Furthermore, it opens up the possibility for considering the virtue of solidarity and its links with the Catholic vision of the human person in chapter 6. This chapter is an integrative part of the book in that it carefully and consistently links and refines the anthropological vision it develops in view of the content of chapters 1, 2, and 3, while providing significant material on which chapters 5 and 6 will build.

Chapter 5—The Virtue of Prudence and the Importance of Attentiveness for Moral Reasoning

Chapter 5 returns to a focus on Porter's theory and so, methodologically, marks a shift from the anthropological vision developed in chapter 4 back to a consideration of Porter's theory which is more akin to the methodology used in chapters 2 and 3. The reason that this chapter was included after chapter 4 can be understood in terms of Porter's argument that the virtue of prudence acts in dialogue with the other virtues. When considering the virtue of justice, this also means drawing from the anthropological vision to which this virtue appeals, the development of which was the purpose of chapter 4. When considered in relationship to the argument as a whole, chapter 5 thus represents a continuation of my focus on Porter's theory with the aim of continuing to provide the possibility for linking hers and Levinas's thought in a more robust way. Its discussion of prudence also introduces the importance of attentiveness in moral discernment which provides the book with a foundation upon which to consider the virtue of solidarity in detail in chapter 6.

Chapter 6—The Virtue of Solidarity and Attentiveness to Vulnerability

Chapter 6 marks the final substantive chapter of the book. Methodologically, it moves from the consideration of Porter's understanding of practical reason and prudence in chapter 5 to the introduction of the virtue of solidarity into the book's argument. In so doing, it carefully and critically integrates insights from the five previous chapters with its discussion of solidarity in order to propose an argument for its relevance in the context of the developed argument. Out of this framework, it argues that solidarity has the capacity to direct the attentiveness of prudence by means of its preferential concern for the most vulnerable and demonstrates that such a position can emphasize the importance of attentiveness to vulnerability in moral reasoning, while at the same time avoiding what Levinas refers to as "totalization."

Conclusion

The book ends with a conclusion intended to draw together the threads of its argument and reveal its findings.

STYLISTIC FEATURES OF THE BOOK

Use of First Person Pronouns

The book uses the first person pronoun a number of times in both its singular and plural forms. The former is used less frequently and only where necessary to indicate a specific point that I am making. The latter is used more frequently to develop an invitational style of writing that involves the reader in the development of the book's argument, as distinct from an overly abstract style that—for all intents and purposes—may be written for no one to read. In this, I follow the invitational style used by Porter in all three of her books that focus on the natural law.[59]

Inclusive Language

A considered effort has been made to avoid gender-exclusive language in the book. As far as possible, inclusive language has been used in place of gender-exclusive terms. However, given the book's fundamental interest in the human person, at times the consistent use of gender-neutral terms is difficult to sustain. As such, I have chosen to alternate between the masculine and feminine pronouns throughout the work.

In some cases, primary texts (especially those of Emmanuel Levinas, Louis Janssens, and Vatican documents) use gender-exclusive language extensively in their English translations. No provision has been made for inclusive language where I have quoted from these texts.

Specific Terminology

In this book I draw heavily on a number of authors who use common language in highly specific ways. An example of this can be found in Levinas's use of the personal pronoun "I," which refers to his understanding of the human ego and its capacities for violence. Where these so-called *terms of art* have been used, I have indicated them with quotation marks.

Apart from these terms of art, there are three specific terms that will be used frequently throughout the book and which require some clarification from the outset. The first is Levinas's use of the terminology "the Other," the second is my own use of the terminology of "the Levinasian insight" and the third is Porter's use of the terms "morally significant" and "morally relevant."

59. *NDL*; *NR*; *Ministers of the Law*.

First, Levinas is well known for his philosophy of "the Other," which we will explore in detail in chapter 1. Given the frequency with which this term is used in the book, it is important to point out an issue of translation which can be missed in the English versions of Levinas's texts. That is, Levinas speaks of two kinds of "other." The first refers to anything that is other than one's self: a rock; a cat; or a bookcase, for example. For these "others," Levinas typically uses the French *l'autre*. English translators of the Levinasian texts tend to use the lowercase "o" when translating this, e.g., "other." The second refers to the other who is human. Levinas uses the term *autrui* in his works for this other, and this is frequently (although not consistently) capitalized.[60] Most English translators choose to capitalize *autrui*—the Other—in order to show that here Levinas is referring to the one who is "radically Other."[61] I follow the same conventions in the book when I am referring to the human Other.

Second, the book has a foundational interest in the philosophy of Levinas, particularly his major insight regarding human subjectivity. After exploring this insight and the process that led Levinas to it in chapter 1, the book summarizes it under the title of *The Levinasian Insight Regarding Human Subjectivity*. After this point, the book's argument frequently refers back to this insight, both in general and to specific aspects of it. When it refers back to the general insight, it does so by way of the shorthand "Levinasian insight." When it refers to specific aspects of this insight, it revisits them in greater detail.

Third, Porter's theory of natural law consistently emphasizes the relevance of nature, understood as the prerational nature of the human creature, for moral discourse. In Porter's theory, this is frequently couched in terminology that refers to nature as "morally relevant," "morally significant," or "freighted with moral significance."[62] By this, she means that the way in which we understand the nature of the human person has an influence on what we consider as morally normative. An example of this can be framed with reference to prohibitions against harm and injunctions to do good, which are necessarily related to our understanding of human nature because of the kinds of harms to which the person is typically vulnerable (in the case of prohibitions) and, correlatively, our understanding of the needs which the human person has (in the case of injunctions to do good). So, for example, the medical doctor's response to the injunction "do no harm"

---

60. See Davis, *Levinas*, 43.

61. See for example the translator's note in Levinas, *Totality and Infinity* (hereafter, *TI*), 24.

62. See for example, *NR*, 53; 147.

will necessarily be related to her understanding of what constitutes harm to her patient on the level of the latter's natural existence. As we will see, however, there is a clear distinction between moral relevance understood in this way and moral normativity. In the book, I have used the terminology of "moral significance" to avoid the unnecessary confusion that can arise from alternating between the terms and, where I do, I also mean it in the sense described above.

1

The Philosophy of Emmanuel Levinas

INTRODUCTION

IN THIS CHAPTER I begin by situating Levinas's work in its historical, biographical, and phenomenological contexts, which includes some discussion of the phenomenologies of the two greatest influences on Levinas's thought: Edmund Husserl and Martin Heidegger. Out of this background, I then explore the unique phenomenology of Levinas with a consideration of his book *Totality and Infinity*. Jacques Derrida's strong criticism of *Totality and Infinity* is introduced further on, and leads in to my analysis of Levinas's second major work, *Otherwise Than Being Or Beyond Essence*, which commentators on Levinas largely agree is a response to Derrida's critique. I then tie together the chapter's commentary on Levinas by turning to, and analyzing, his argument that ethics is "first philosophy." This allows for a summary of the Levinasian insight regarding human subjectivity, which becomes foundational for the remainder of the book.

EMMANUEL LEVINAS—BIOGRAPHY OF A MAN AND AN IDEA

Emmanuel Levinas was born on January 12th, 1906, in Lithuania.[1] His studies in philosophy began in 1923 and took place at the University of

---

1. Cohen, "Emmanuel Levinas," 234.

Strasbourg in France.[2] In the academic year spanning 1928–9, he studied under the two philosophers whose thought would constitute the grounding for his own unique theory: Edmund Husserl (1859–1938) and Martin Heidegger (1889–1976).[3] After this, Levinas took up residence in Paris where he would live until he died in 1995, leaving behind a rich body of publications. The most widely known and notable of these are *Totality and Infinity: An Essay on Exteriority* and *Beyond Essence Or Otherwise Than Being*.[4] When and where Levinas lived is significant for understanding his theory. Simon Critchley explains that his lifespan:

> traverses and connects many of the intellectual movements of the twentieth century and intersects with some of its major historical events, its moments of light as well as its point of absolute darkness—Levinas said that his life had been dominated by the memory of the Nazi horror.[5]

Indeed, it was this horror—and Heidegger's continual association with it—that would give Levinas reason to develop his own form of phenomenology.[6] Whilst his work is possessed of a great richness and deals with a wide variety of topics, as I noted earlier, commentators on Levinas's work agree that underlying all of his musings is one "big idea."[7] Derrida, for example, compares Levinas to the "infinite insistence" of a wave on the beach which continues to renew and enrich itself, crashing on the shore as the same body of water with a gradually deepening influence each time.[8] Hilary Putnam understands Levinas as a hedgehog who knows "one big thing" as opposed to a fox who knows "many small things."[9] Levinas's entire body of work is an attempt to explain this big idea. So what is it?

Simon Critchley suggests that Levinas's foundational idea is his understanding of our infinite responsibility for the other person, formulated

---

2. Ibid.
3. Ibid., "Emmanuel Levinas."
4. Ibid., 235. Critchley, "Introduction"; *TI*; *OB*.
5. Critchley, "Introduction," 1.
6. Burggraeve, *The Wisdom of Love*, 35. For more background information on the man behind the theory we will be dealing with, see ibid., 21–39; Hand, *Emmanuel Levinas*, 9–22.
7. Critchley, "Introduction," 6.
8. Derrida, *Writing and Difference*, 312.
9. Putnam, *Jewish Philosophy as a Guide to Life*, 99. Here Putnam acknowledges that this comparison originally came from Isaiah Berlin's well known division of thinkers into the categories of "foxes" and "hedgehogs" in his *The Hedgehog and the Fox: An Essay on Tolstoy's View of History*.

in his thesis of ethics as the "first philosophy."[10] Richard Cohen notes that Levinas's philosophy is an expression of the imperative to "love your neighbour as yourself."[11] Roger Burggraeve argues that the "whole of Levinas's thinking can be interpreted as an immense effort to bring to light the roots of violence and racism, and as an attempt to overcome this in principle by *thinking otherwise*," understood as thinking about the Other.[12]

Levinas himself often said that his theory could be summarized in the words, "*Après vous, Monsieur!*" (After you, sir!).[13] Such a philosophy invites us to reconsider ethics. Levinas's foundational idea is that ethical responsibility is not, as is commonly suggested, something that proceeds from our understanding of what it means to be human but rather that it is the very structure out of which the possibility for this understanding arises. Levinas's challenge is that our encounter with the other person precedes consciousness: because of this it also precedes the meaning we make of the encounter, the meaning we make of ourselves and the rational activity of making decisions regarding the nature of our response to this other person.

PHENOMENOLOGY, EDMUND HUSSERL, AND MARTIN HEIDEGGER: THE BACKGROUND TO LEVINASIAN THOUGHT

The Phenomenological Approach

Lest we get ahead of ourselves and draw premature conclusions about the point Levinas was making, we should take some time to consider the thought out of which his theory was born: phenomenology. Levinas referred to his project as a phenomenological one but admits being faithful to the spirit of phenomenology's founder and his teacher, Edmund Husserl, rather than concerning himself solely with Husserl's specific conclusions.[14] This point should be underscored because it is a common position amongst phenomenologists who frequently acknowledge the great value of Husserl's

10. Critchley, "Introduction," 6.
11. Cohen, "Emmanuel Levinas," 235.
12. Burggraeve, *The Wisdom of Love*, 28.
13. Critchley, "Introduction," 27.
14. *OB*, 183. See also Burggraeve, *The Wisdom of Love*, 34. Although, as Davis notes, Husserl's work remains a consistent influence on Levinas both in terms of philosophical methodology and through ongoing reference to key texts and notions. Davis, *Levinas*, 8–9. This faithfulness to the methodology of Husserl over and above his specific conclusions is a common feature in the phenomenological movement. See Moran, *Phenomenology*, 3.

vision and methodology, but do not subscribe to his way of engaging with the discipline and do not reach the same conclusions. This underpins Paul Ricoeur's comment, noted earlier, that "the history of phenomenology is the history of Husserlian heresies."[15]

It might therefore be prudent to speak of *phenomenologies* rather than *phenomenology*. However, it is possible to identify some key characteristics of the phenomenological approach and these will serve us well as a background for considering the approach of those who influenced Levinas directly (Husserl and Heidegger) and also Levinas's own theory.

To begin with, we should note that phenomenology is less a body of philosophical knowledge or a philosophical system and more a practice—it is a way of doing philosophy rather than a theory in and of itself; this can account for the diversity of ways in which it has been done.[16] The phenomenological way of doing philosophy emphasizes the human experience of consciousness, especially the way things appear to us in consciousness or "give themselves" as phenomena, and attempts to describe that experience from within.[17] Phenomenology seeks to begin this exploration without presuppositions, on the premise that if an experience is to be truly understood from within it must be experienced in a pure way without having prior explanations imposed on it.[18] This means that the phenomenological approach attempts to be descriptive and reflective which is distinct from a philosophy that engages in causal explanation.[19] This is not to say that phenomenology is in conflict with such approaches. The point is that phenomenology is concerned with the things themselves, understood as a description of the *a priori* conditions which allow for the possibility of causal explanations in the first place.[20]

An example will be helpful here. Let us imagine the following situation:

A theologian sits in wonder and awe at the spectacle of a sunset. With a tremble in her voice, she remarks: "Surely God is a poet, for who but a poet could create such a marvelous view?"

Where a scientific approach might look to a causal explanation for the theologian's experience of the sunset, and other philosophical approaches might look to the claim about God that the theologian makes, phenomenology asks the question *what are the conditions of consciousness which*

---

15. See Moran, *Phenomenology*, 3.
16. Ibid., 4.
17. Cf. Solomon, "Phenomenology," 1757.
18. Moran, *Phenomenology*, 4–5.
19. Ibid., 5, 7, 9.
20. Ibid., 9.

made this claim possible in the first place, and how are they experienced by the person who is experiencing it? For the phenomenologist, naming this experience is equivalent to naming the ultimate *a priori* because it is the naming of the condition which makes the pursuit of all other knowledge possible. As such, the focus of phenomenology is on the human subject and on the experience of being conscious of a world that is perceived as existing outside of consciousness.[21]

In a moment, we will turn to a brief analysis of the phenomenological method found in Levinas's most influential teachers, Husserl and Heidegger. The philosophies of both Husserl and Heidegger are profound in their complexity and insight and it would be impossible for us to consider their approaches in depth here. However, an in-depth analysis of these two great philosophers is not the purpose of this work and their approaches will be engaged with only inasmuch as they provide a foundation for our exploration of the Levinasian approach below.[22]

Edmund Husserl's Phenomenology

Whilst the name "phenomenology" has its origins in the philosophy of Immanuel Kant (1724–1804), it became fundamental in the work of Georg Wilheim Friedrich Hegel (1770–1831) and came to maturity with Edmund Husserl in the twentieth century.[23] Husserl's agenda was to provide a response to the perspectivism/relativism which had entered philosophy in his time, especially as a result of psychologism's suggestion that philosophical truth was simply a product of the make-up of the human mind in such a way that a different make-up would produce different truth.[24] Having produced a strong logical argument against the suggestion that philosophical truth was simply "in the eye of the beholder," Husserl argued that phenomenology was the theory necessary to uncover the universal and essential truths that underlie all philosophical inquiry.[25] In essence, Husserl's phenomenology

21. As Moran notes, the phenomenological approach seeks to reinvigorate philosophical discourse by turning back to the human subject and "lived human experience in all its richness." Ibid., 5.

22. As such, the research drawn upon here is primarily introductory in terms of Husserl and Heidegger's approaches. For the reader's convenience I have indicated the primary sources on which each resource is drawing where relevant.

23. Crosson, "Phenomenology," 230.

24. Crowell, "Husserlian Phenomenology."

25. Husserl employed the well-known logical response to relativism, which shows that, if all truth is held to be relative, the theory relativizes its own truth claim. Crowell, "Husserlian Phenomenology." See also Solomon, "Phenomenology," 1755. Husserl's original argument appears in Husserl, *Logical Investigations*, 135.

follows the basic definition we have given above: it is the attempt to understand and define the essential structures of consciousness—the basic framework which enables human consciousness to achieve its purpose of knowing the world.[26] The ability to acknowledge this structure would allow the phenomenologist to discover an *a priori* framework out of which all consciousness stems. According to Husserl, phenomenology's role is to describe and clarify the reality of phenomena as they appear to consciousness, as distinct from an approach which seeks to theorize about and explain these.[27]

Husserl's core insight was that the condition of all human experience is the reality of consciousness itself and that, without this, the possibility of experience, philosophical reflection and scientific discovery would not exist. In addition, he noted that the activities of consciousness were such that they went by largely unnoticed and are therefore difficult to describe.[28] This leads Husserl to distinguish between what he terms the "natural standpoint" and the "phenomenological standpoint." The natural standpoint is our ordinary viewpoint. It can be understood as our ability to describe the natural world, the events which we encounter, and all manner of objects towards which our attention is directed. It is the position from which we come to an understanding of ourselves and the world around us. The natural standpoint therefore seeks to grasp and make meaning of what we encounter.[29]

In contrast, the phenomenological standpoint is the viewpoint achieved when the philosopher employs the method of phenomenology in order to turn not to the objects of consciousness but to consciousness itself. This allows the phenomenologist to make a key distinction between what is being perceived by consciousness (the object of consciousness) and the consciousness doing the work of perception (noticing the object; analyzing it; interpreting what is seen; drawing on past experiences to do so; and, amidst all this, bringing meaning to the experience).[30] Such a distinction was a further response to Husserl's contemporaries who were collapsing the

---

26. Solomon, "Phenomenology," 1755. Cf. Moran, *Phenomenology*, 61. See Husserl, *The Crisis of European Sciences and Transcendental Phenomenology*, 5.

27. Crowell, "Husserlian Phenomenology." See Husserl, *Logical Investigations*, 262, 264, 265.

28. Moran, *Phenomenology*, 61.

29. Crowell, "Husserlian Phenomenology."; Husserl, *The Basic Problems of Phenomenology*, especially 2–3. See also Husserl, *Ideas Pertaining to a Pure Phenomenology and to a Phenomenological Philosophy*, 51–52.

30. Crowell, "Husserlian Phenomenology." See Husserl, *The Crisis of the European Sciences*, 118.

object of consciousness into consciousness itself and thus subjecting the meaning of the former to the laws of thought.[31]

An acknowledgement of the difference between the natural and phenomenological standpoints enables the philosopher to engage with the phenomenological method.[32] This method primarily involves what Husserl called the *epoché*, or bracketing, which F.J. Crosson defines as "the setting aside of all philosophical presuppositions about reality, the world, man, the distinctions of primary and secondary qualities, the exterior and interior worlds, etc."[33] This bracketing is the technique that the phenomenologist must use to begin her description of experience from the presuppositionless starting point which allows access to the experience of consciousness in and of itself, without any meaning imposed onto this.[34] The purpose of this bracketing is achieved in its pinnacle moment when that which is naively and unconsciously accepted as existing (the human ability to search for and find philosophical and scientific truth, for example) is bracketed in order to discover the grounding structure out of which consciousness is able to arise.[35] It is important to note that such a methodological tool does not actually change anything; it simply draws our attention to an aspect of ourselves that we would not have recognized otherwise.[36]

Intentional Consciousness

This leads Husserl to his phenomenological insight. His suggestion is that—at a level prior to the moment of meaning-making—the human subject is

---

31. Crosson, "Phenomenology," 230. However, Husserl did not solve the philosophical problem of whether such objects of consciousness were in fact real objects or simply projections of consciousness itself. For further discussion, see Moran, *Phenomenology*, 186–91.

32. This method is important for us to understand given that it is what Levinas used to take Husserl's theory further.

33. Crosson, "Phenomenology," 231. Cf. Moran, *Phenomenology*, 4. See for example Husserl, *The Idea of Phenomenology*, 4.

34. Husserl's idealist perspective on this point is fairly clear and would not stand up to the postmodern awareness of socially and historically conditioned nature of consciousness. This would rightly query whether it is possible to bracket all presuppositions in order to achieve the unconditioned access to experience that Husserl is seeking. Indeed, Husserl's most eminent disciple Martin Heidegger would begin such a critique. For a helpful exploration of his and others' criticisms see Moran, *Phenomenology*, 160–61.

35. Crosson, "Phenomenology," 231.

36. Moran, *Phenomenology*, 149. On the methodology noted above, see Husserl, *Psychological and Transcendental Phenomenology and the Confrontation with Heidegger*, 493–97.

characterized by an intentional, directed consciousness. The person is an outwardly focused and signifying consciousness out of which the more specific abilities of consciousness arise. Since this is the case at an *a priori* level (and therefore prior to the specific work that consciousness does, e.g. when it engages with philosophical or scientific exploration), it is taken for granted in the very function of consciousness and therefore not accessible to the natural viewpoint.[37] Moran explicates this point in terms of the phenomenon of doubting:

> For Husserl, when I try to doubt everything, I come up against the bedrock fact that I cannot doubt that I am doubting, I cannot doubt or wish away my very conscious act of doubting. Not only is the "I am," as experienced by me, always immediately certain, but so also is any mental experience just as it is experienced.[38]

It is, in an analogous sense, similar to the way one can remain ignorant of the force of gravity and yet sustain the ability to remain ignorant (or develop an understanding of gravity) whilst being conditioned by gravity itself. To take the analogy further, a bracketing of mistaken (or otherwise) assumptions about gravity would eventually lead one to recognize the impossibility of floating from the earth. When it comes to consciousness, such an approach leads Husserl to argue that our conscious activities are always-already absolutely self-given in the form of intentional, directed consciousness.[39] If this were not the case, according to Husserl, I would not be writing this book and you would not be reading it.

The value of Husserl's phenomenological viewpoint is that it allows us to see that we—at a level taken for granted, a horizon of being not recognized—are structured in a way that allows us to make meaning out of that which we encounter. Cohen provides the following helpful illustration of the uniqueness of Husserl's phenomenological conclusion. He illustrates the "correspondence theory of truth" (the model Husserl was reacting against that suggests that the meaning/description that consciousness creates in encountering an object corresponds directly to the meaning of that which is encountered) in this way:

Meaning/description → refers to—signified/thing itself

---

37. Cf. Crowell, "Husserlian Phenomenology"; Husserl, *Psychological and Transcendental Phenomenology*, 493.

38. Moran, *Phenomenology*, 129.

39. Ibid., 129. See Husserl, *Ideas Pertaining to a Pure Phenomenology and to a Phenomenological Philosophy*.

Husserl's suggestion is that the underlying structure necessary to make this event possible is that we are an outwardly focused, intentional, signifying consciousness which makes the correspondence model possible:

> Intentional consciousness/signifier (meaning/description → refers to—signified/thing itself)[40]

There is thus a distinction between what Husserl would call the *noesis* (understood as the act of thinking which is made possible by intentional consciousness) and the *noema* (understood as the meaning/description which is thought by this consciousness). This model allows Husserl to suggest that the origins of all meaning are born out of the intentional consciousness framework and that it has a necessary influence on the way in which meaning is made, even though its activities go by unnoticed until we move to the phenomenological standpoint. For this reason, Levinas referred to Husserl's phenomenology as the dis-covering of our naiveties. He describes intentional consciousness, and Husserl's unique discovery, in this way:

> Intentional analysis is the search for the concrete. Notions held under the direct gaze of the thought that defines them are nevertheless, unbeknown to this naïve thought, revealed to be implanted in horizons unsuspected by this thought; these horizons endow them with a meaning—such is the essential teaching of Husserl.[41]

Levinas described consciousness as the "overflowing of objectifying thought by a forgotten experience from which it lives" and he understood the task of phenomenology as naming this forgotten experience.[42] It is clear that Levinas agreed with Husserl on this point—however, as we will see, he used Husserl's phenomenological method to show that his teacher's conclusion did not go far enough. Another of Levinas's teachers, Martin Heidegger, also noticed this and made several changes to Husserl's theory which would influence the thought of Levinas deeply. We will consider his work in a moment. Before we do, however, it is helpful to turn to the example I used earlier which will provide us with some clarification on what has been discussed thus far.

A theologian sits in wonder and awe at the spectacle of a sunset. With a tremble in her voice, she remarks: "Surely God is a poet, for who but a poet could create such a marvelous view?"

---

40. Cohen, "Emmanuel Levinas," 242.
41. *TI*, 28.
42. Ibid.

Whereas the correspondence theory of truth would suggest that the philosophical truth claim of this situation is largely epistemological and lies in the meaning that the theologian has made of the sunset, Husserl's phenomenology turns its attention to *why* the theologian can formulate this meaning. As such, Husserl's phenomenology says nothing of the truth of the meaning created, but simply invites the philosopher to consider that which is taken for granted in this situation—namely, that the theologian is able to make meaning of her situation in the first place. In this case, Husserl would argue, the theologian is *a priori* an intentional consciousness—an outwardly focused signifier who is capable of creating meaning—and this structure underlies all capability for conscious thought, theory, judgment, and so on. Our naivety in this situation would be to acknowledge the theologian's assessment of the meaning of the sunset without noticing the structure that underlies this.[43]

Heidegger's Challenge to Husserl

Heidegger recognized the importance of Husserl's phenomenological method, but drew into question his emphasis on the signifier/consciousness model as the structure of the meaning-making subject.[44] To Heidegger, this was far too Cartesian and dualistic. This, he argued, revealed that Husserl had adopted the horizon of Descartes' primary understanding of the world despite his suggestion that philosophical enquiry should begin without such presuppositions.[45] For Heidegger, Husserl's beginning with the assumption that the mind was the primary focus of phenomenological investigation undermined the phenomenological method itself and so, whilst abandoning the former, he remained true to Husserl's formulation of the latter which led him to several new insights about the structure out of which the ability to describe the world is born. Heidegger turned away from questions of signification and consciousness to a focus on the existential reality of the being out of which such questions arise. His is a theory concerned with ontology.

Heidegger was so concerned to distance himself from the Cartesian influence he perceived in Husserl's phenomenology that he created a new

---

43. We will return to this narrative after our explorations of Heidegger and Levinas to illustrate how their formulations of phenomenology differ from Husserl's.

44. Moran, *Phenomenology*, 194.

45. Solomon, "Phenomenology," 1756. See Heidegger, *Being and Time*. Some authors have called Heidegger's critique of Husserl into question, suggesting that he confused Husserl's neglecting the question of ontology with an implicit (but unacknowledged) acceptance of a particular ontology. See for example Hickerson, "Neglecting the Question of Being: Heidegger's Argument against Husserl," especially 591–94.

term for the "being from whose perspective the world is being described."[46] This term was *Dasein* which translates literally as "being-there."[47] For Heidegger, the *Dasein* was the fundamental ontology which made all further questions about ontology (as well as consciousness, meaning, and so on) possible. Heidegger's most important book *Sein und Zeit (Being and Time)* is the attempt to describe what exactly the conditions of this fundamental ontology are. The question Heidegger seeks to answer is: what are the fundamental structures of the *Dasein* out of which the question of being arises? One quickly notices the phenomenological method in action here—Heidegger is bracketing Husserl's intentional consciousness and searching for the conditions which make it possible.

The Dasein

In Heidegger's own words, the *Dasein* is the "horizon in which something like being in general becomes intelligible."[48] To understand this horizon, we must not turn immediately to what we think about ourselves (this is a product of the *Dasein*, not the *Dasein* itself), but to what we are before we think about ourselves. His attention is focused on how we exist when we are caught up in the practicalities of our existence.[49] Heidegger's observation is that:

> humans are primarily caught up in living their lives, wrapped up in moods and emotional commitments, in cares and worries, falling into temptation, projecting themselves into possibilities, seeking to make themselves whole. Cognition and intellectual activity emerges out of the engaged structures of everyday life where we are on top of things, we are "up for it," able to cope.[50]

Heidegger's suggestion is that a phenomenology of "everydayness" helps us to discover the fundamental ontology that makes our interaction with the world intelligible.[51] What he points out is that our relationship with the world and our ability to make meaning presuppose our existing in

---

46. Solomon, "Phenomenology," 1756.
47. Guignon, "Introduction," 5. Cf. Moran, *Phenomenology*, 193; 206–7; 238–39. See Heidegger, *Being and Time*, 274.
48. Heidegger, *Being and Time*, 274.
49. Guignon, "Introduction," 6.
50. Moran, *Phenomenology*, 228. See Heidegger, *Being and Time*, 7; 28; 50; Heidegger, *History of the Concept of Time*, 20; 161.
51. Guignon, "Introduction," 6.

the world. This fundamental ontology is the *Dasein* in its very be-ing (verb): the *Dasein* is a Being-in-the-World before anything else. Heidegger uses the image of a craftsman who "knows his stuff" to clarify this suggestion.[52] Whilst the craftsman might not be able to explain and articulate his craft, he nevertheless knows how to do it and reveals this by simply doing it.[53] This knowing *how* to interact with his tools and materials comes before the craftsman's knowing *that* he is doing it, *why* he is doing it and *what* he is doing. Furthermore, it is not as if the craftsman is somehow separated from his craft—he is intimately and necessarily involved in it.[54]

To return to a previous analogy, we could say that a person knows *how* to live with gravity (she knows she will not float away into space, for example) before she knows *that* she is held on the earth by a force, that the force which is holding her down is gravity and that this force has particular properties, and so on. The point is that the activity of intentional consciousness, the conscious engagement with the tools, or with gravity, or whatever, is a *subsequent* moment. It is not primary as it was for Husserl.[55] Of course, this phenomenological reduction also leads us to note that the *Dasein* is a Being-in-the-World before even being able to act. More specifically, then, the *Dasein* is not so much a thing or an object as a *happening*, an unfolding of life that occurs in between birth and death.[56] In this way, the *Dasein* is necessarily historical in that it is characterized by having a past, a present and a future, all of which are oriented towards the mystery of death.[57] What is more, the *Dasein* is always *mitsein*, or *with others*. The Being-in-the-World encounters that world and eventually makes meaning of it from within the context of shared existential concern.[58]

Let us return to our narrative about the theologian's encounter with the sunset to make clear the difference between Husserl and Heidegger. Whereas Husserl would posit the theologian as a signifier on an *a priori* level, Heidegger would look past this to the theologian as a *Dasein*. The theologian's *Being-in-the-World* is presupposed in this event and, without this fundamental ontology, not only would the conditions required for meaning be lacking but no experience would be possible in the first place

52. Solomon, "Phenomenology," 1756.
53. Heidegger, *Being and Time*, 98–99.
54. Moran, *Phenomenology*, 233.
55. Ibid. Heidegger refers to these moments as inauthentic (i.e., automatic) and authentic (i.e., reflective) being. See Moran, *Phenomenology*, 239–40.
56. Heidegger, *Being and Time*, 427. This point is also noted in Guignon, "Introduction," 7.
57. Indeed, this why Heidegger's book is entitled *Being and Time*.
58. Moran, *Phenomenology*, 242. See Heidegger, *Being and Time*, 153–54.

and there would be no history of being upon which she could draw in order to make meaning, nor a future for which the theologian is concerned that would motivate action. The meaning-making within the situation is therefore not simply a consequence of a signifying consciousness, but the overflowing of the *Dasein*'s Being-in-the-World. In this way, Heidegger is primarily existential—he begins with existence as it is and posits Husserl's signifying consciousness as the result, not the origin, of this existence.[59]

Levinas saw great value in Heidegger's fundamental ontology, especially given that it was a critique of Husserl's apparent intellectualism and that it began by locating the human being within the reality of everyday life. However, Levinas would use the phenomenological method to bracket Heidegger's insight and propose yet another radically new structure out of which the intentional consciousness, Heidegger's *Dasein* and all other philosophical theory, arises.[60]

THE PHENOMENOLOGY OF EMMANUEL LEVINAS: FOUNDATIONS

The Idea of Infinity

For Levinas, the forgotten experience out of which the possibility for intentional consciousness arises is an encounter with the Other who is always radically beyond the capabilities of the objectifying thought which attempts to comprehend his presence. Levinas's radical insight is that the ability to conceptualize and make meaning arises not primarily out of an *a priori* structure like Husserl's intentional consciousness or Heidegger's *Dasein*, but rather out of an *a posteriori* experience of encountering something radically different from oneself which has an insatiable impact on the constitution of consciousness and its operation.[61] It is the task of this section to explore this encounter. I will begin by discussing Levinas's understanding of infinity, particularly as it relates to the Other human person.

Levinas's argument for the infinity of the Other relies on the phenomenon of the thought that thinks more than it can think—the thought of infinity. In his philosophy, this resembles the relationship between consciousness

---

59. Guignon, "Introduction," 6.

60. This point should be noted carefully. Levinas is not fundamentally concerned with undermining Heidegger and Husserl (although his rhetoric can, at times, lend itself to this interpretation). He is, rather, *adding* a new level of depth to their phenomenology, which has a necessary impact on how their theories are to be understood.

61. Davis, *Levinas*, 39; *TI*, 54. Cf. Davis, *Levinas*, 21.

and the infinity of God in René Descartes' (1596–1650) Third Meditation which Levinas understands as one of the "boldest moments" in Western philosophy.[62] The motivation for this Cartesian meditation is the question of whether or not the subject can consider herself the source of all of her ideas. Descartes answered the question by arguing that an effect cannot be greater than its cause and that a subject was therefore unable to produce ideas which are beyond the capabilities of her own intentional consciousness.[63] Bearing this in mind, Descartes sought to analyze the subject's idea of God, an idea of infinity which is inherently transcendent, in surplus of itself and that could not, he suggested, be understood as constituted by consciousness on its own.[64]

For Descartes, the reality of this idea and the impossibility of its constitution within the subject pointed towards a far greater reality outside of the self: God, whose relationship with the subject was the cause of the idea. In the Third Meditation, Descartes uses this idea as evidence of God's existence. Levinas, however, is less interested in Descartes' discovery for its proof of God than for its consequences for phenomenology (which he admits that Descartes himself may not have understood).[65] Following Descartes, Levinas argues that the idea of infinity cannot come from within the self.[66] For Levinas, the value of Descartes' argument lies in the observation that "the idea of infinity is exceptional in that its *ideatum* surpasses its idea" and points to something beyond itself.[67] Levinas uses this insight as a proof that the primordial condition for consciousness cannot be Husserl's understanding of intentional consciousness, nor Heidegger's *Dasein*, because both remain focused on the self and, given that the idea of infinity must come from a source outside the self, neither of these theories can account for it.[68] This means that both remain naïve to the idea of infinity and, furthermore, it points towards the presence of a horizon beyond which neither philosopher turned his focus and thus remains un-dis-covered by phenomenology. For

62. Critchley, "Introduction," 14; *TI*, 48.

63. Davis, *Levinas*, 39. Of course, Descartes himself did not use the language of intentional consciousness. It has been employed here for consistency and clarity of thought.

64. Ibid.

65. Ibid. Indeed, the question of God's existence is of little concern in the work of Levinas. As such, he utilizes the formal structure of Descartes's argument rather than its specific conclusions. See Critchley, "Introduction," 14; Davis, *Levinas*, 97. He does make it clear, however, that he understands the primary mode of the self's encounter with God as through the other person. See *TI*, 78–79. Cf. Robbins, "Tracing Responsibility in Levinas's Ethical Thought," 181.

66. This point is developed in more detail below.

67. *TI*, 49.

68. Ibid., 209–11.

Levinas, Descartes' great contribution is his discovering within the subject a horizon beyond intentional consciousness and the *Dasein*, "a relation with a total alterity irreducible to interiority."[69]

Levinas gives various names to this alterity, including exteriority, infinity and transcendence, all of which attempt to point towards something that is beyond what was named by Husserl and Heidegger. From this observation, he takes two of the cornerstones of his approach.[70] The first is that the presence of an idea of infinity which "overflows the thought that thinks it" presupposes a relationship with a transcendence that exists outside of the self.[71] The second, proceeding from the first, is that phenomenology's task is finding and describing the forgotten phenomenon of this relationship which makes the idea of infinity possible and is prior to, and therefore constitutive of, the operations of consciousness.[72] Turning to the latter of these, Levinas builds on the Cartesian idea of infinity and suggests that the human person finds himself "always already" in relationship with exteriority. This is a relationship with something that is radically Other, completely exterior to the self and unable to be contained by intentional consciousness. Such a relationship is expressed most adequately through metaphors of remoteness and separation rather than connection and grasping, given that the latter would imply that otherness could be reduced to an object for the self and thus not truly "Other."[73] This leads Levinas to call the relationship with otherness "metaphysical," and he frequently refers to the self as the metaphysician.[74] So who is this Other and how do we encounter her? This question leads us to explore the mode by which the human person encounters Otherness.

The Face of the Other

For Levinas, the transcendent encounter is an encounter with any other human person: in Levinasian terminology, the Other.[75] Core in Levinas's

69. Ibid., 211. Whilst this statement appears as anachronistic given that Descartes was writing well before Husserl and Heidegger, it should be remembered that Descartes himself did not develop the *phenomenological* concerns of his argument. In fact, Levinas argues that Descartes may have underestimated the importance of this discovery. *TI*, 48.

70. Peperzak, *Beyond*, 11.

71. *TI*, 25.

72. Peperzak, *Beyond*, 32.

73. *TI*, 34.

74. Ibid., 36.

75. Peperzak, *Beyond*, 136–37. Cf. Waldenfels, "Levinas and the Face of the Other,"

approach is that all encounters with the Other are saturated by mystery. Common experience of our encounters with other persons reveals that they are rarely easily, and never fully, understood.[76] In Burggraeve's words, "that the Other is radically Other comes simply from the fact that she is incomparable with anyone or anything else."[77] This means that there is always an aspect of surprise, transcendence, and infinity in an encounter with an Other.[78]

In *Totality and Infinity*, the way in which one is encountered by the Other, always "exceeding *the idea of the other in me*" (as per the Cartesian idea of infinity) is named *face*.[79] This is not a literal use of the word "face."[80] Levinas is not referring to a person's physical face as such, but rather to the transcendent presence which the self encounters when the Other draws near.[81] As Bernhard Waldenfels notes, the Levinasian understanding of face points towards both transcendent *and* immanent qualities. He cautions that a failure to recognize this by way of understanding the face as "something too real or too sublime" can lead to a misunderstanding of the magnitude and force of the encounter with the Other.[82] Waldenfels distinguishes between the narrow, common meaning of "face" and a wider, more emphatic meaning. The former is understood as the frontal view, being-face-to-face with another human, as well as that part of the human body which contains the eyes, ears and nose and has a primary role in communication. The latter

---

67. While Levinas himself did not entertain the possibility of the Otherness of other life forms—animals and plants, for example—contemporary commentators have begun to explore this area. See for example Waldenfels, "Levinas and the Face of the Other," 68. The analysis below follows closely Fleming, "Ethics is an Optics."

76. Cf. *GS*, no. 21.

77. Burggraeve, *The Wisdom of Love*, 89.

78. Peperzak, *Beyond*, 33.

79. *TI*, 51. Cf. *OB*, 88; 158. It is worth noting that Levinas links the appearance of the face to the biblical notion of the neighbor for whom the self is responsible in *Otherwise Than Being*. It is also to be noted here that the face is no longer the central focus of *Otherwise Than Being*, which becomes more concerned with the entanglement between self and Other that occurs in "proximity." As Waldenfels notes, *Otherwise Than Being* presents a recasting of Levinas's thought that moves away from an apparent dualism between self and Other in *Totality and Infinity* and toward a more refined phenomenology of the interpersonal relationship; see Waldenfels, "Levinas and the Face of the Other," 73. However, *Totality and Infinity* is the necessary foundation for this move and the details of the change in Levinas's thought need not constrain us here, although we will consider them briefly inasmuch as they influence this work below.

80. As we will see, this caution applies to many of Levinas's key terms.

81. *TI*, 269. See also Roger Burggraeve, "Violence and the Vulnerable Face of the Other," 29; Raffoul, *The Origins of Responsibility*, 185.

82. Waldenfels, "Levinas and the Face of the Other," 63, cf. 68.

is the "corporeal self-presence" of the Other that one is exposed to in the encounter with exteriority and reflects the Levinasian usage of the term.[83] As such, the face is the mode through which the Other's transcendence is communicated through any part of his person. The face therefore refers to the way the whole human body expresses its presence—hands, feet and arms as well as the face understood in its common sense.[84]

What differentiates the face from anything else that the human person encounters is that it communicates transcendence. In the same moment it is encountered as some*thing* which the self experiences and can grasp by way of the function of intentional consciousness and, at the same time, as a transcendence which escapes.[85] It is, therefore, not a static reality which could be contained by thought, but rather always escapes the self's ability to grasp and understand.[86] It is "essentially beyond every typology, characterology, diagnosis and classification, in short, every attempt to know and comprehend."[87] These points are illustrated by Levinas in *Totality and Infinity*:

> The face of the Other at each moment destroys and overflows the plastic image it leaves me, the idea existing to my own measure and to the measure of its *ideate*—the adequate idea.[88]

And later:

> The face is present in its refusal to be contained. In this sense it cannot be comprehended, that is, encompassed. It is neither seen nor touched—for in visual or tactile sensation the identity of the I envelops the alterity of the object, which becomes precisely a content.[89]

In view of this, the face is encountered by the self as an "epiphany"—something that is surprising and shocking.[90] Since this encounter between the self and the face is always surprising and shocking, and hence characterized by the new, Levinas suggests that before the self can speak *about* the face (which would correspond with the activity of intentional consciousness),

---

83. Ibid., 64–65.
84. *TI*, 262. Cf. Waldenfels, "Levinas and the Face of the Other," 65.
85. Hand, *Emmanuel Levinas*, 36; Robbins, "Tracing Responsibility," 175.
86. Hutchens, *Levinas*, 50.
87. Burggraeve, *The Wisdom of Love*, 90.
88. *TI*, 51. Cf. Waldenfels, "Levinas and the Face of the Other," 67.
89. *TI*, 194.
90. Ibid., 171, 212.

"the face speaks."[91] When the self encounters the face, it finds itself in a position of being addressed, of being called to by something from outside.[92] As Waldenfels notes, "this simple truth changes the whole situation."[93] What we have now is not a case of yet another object which was already on the horizon of intentional consciousness, but rather an Other who addresses the self before any objectification can occur. For Levinas, the communication of the face is best understood in the imperative mood. In its calling to the self, the face forces a situation wherein the self's first reaction cannot be to decipher or theorize about what is encountered in its own isolation, but rather where it must respond.[94] As such, this experience is prior to and constitutive of what Husserl referred to as intentional consciousness.

The Encounter with the Face of the Other as an Affective Intentionality

Andrew Tallon provides some clarity on Levinas's approach here by pointing out two "moments" that occur in the encounter between the self and the face. By way of background, Tallon points out that what Levinas is highlighting is a preconscious and prerational experience of encounter with the face.[95] By this he means that such an encounter:

> is not something first understood in concepts or reached as a conclusion in judgements, nor is it freely chosen or decided on after deliberation. Rather, one is affected by meaning, one is commanded by proximity, held hostage by an experience, not after representation but before it, in presence, presentation, vulnerability, embodiment, in affectivity as its own kind of intentionality, its own access to meaning.[96]

Tallon refers to the self which can experience such an encounter as constituted by an "affective intentionality," the capacity to experience meaning on the level of embodiment before it is thought about. He links this with the observation that persons are constituted by "our created solidarity as one

---

91. Ibid., 66.
92. Ibid., 66.
93. Waldenfels, "Levinas and the Face of the Other," 67.
94. Ibid., 69. See also Hutchens, *Levinas*, 47.
95. Cf. Levinas's suggestion that intentional consciousness is a surplus of a nonintentional consciousness, which acts as its foundation in Levinas, "Ethics as First Philosophy," 79.
96. Tallon, "Nonintentional Affectivity," 108.

species."[97] That we can have such an encounter is distinguished by the second "moment" when the self encounters the face, which is the self's capacity for thinking about and expressing the meaning of that encounter. Tallon sees this as the work of "intentional consciousness."[98] Levinas's philosophical writings are an expression of this second moment which, incidentally, has been the cause of some of the critiques of his theory to which we will return below. However, Tallon rightly notes that Levinas's philosophy would remain largely inaccessible and unintelligible unless it found resonance in the common human experience of being simultaneously fascinated, bewildered and affected by others.[99] This experience, Levinas argues, is reflected still further in the human person's insatiable desire for it.

The Curvature of Intersubjective Space

For Levinas, the self's encounter with the face reveals *the* constitutive dimension of the human person, a dimension which he believes we have forgotten, but which still defines us. Levinas argues that the encounter with the face reveals the self's essentially outward focus: before we undertake the work of intentional consciousness, we are constituted in such a way as to be attentive to the Call of the Other. Levinas names this "desire." According to Levinas, in desire, we thirst for what is irreducibly Other, that which is unfamiliar and strange.[100] Desire reflects the same two moments that we explored above in the encounter with the face—it is oriented on a preconscious level and reflected on only after the fact.[101] Desire is Other-focused and juxtaposed in Levinas's theory with "need." In contrast to desire, need seeks to fill a void in the self, for example hunger with bread, thirst with

---

97. Ibid., 109.

98. Tallon, "Nonintentional Affectivity," 109. Cf. Levinas's comments that the "intentional consciousness of reflection, in taking as its object the transcendental ego, along with its mental acts and states, may also thematize and grasp supposedly implicit modes of non-intentional lived experience. It is invited to do this by philosophy in its fundamental project which consists in enlightening the inevitable transcendental naivety of a consciousness forgetful of its horizon, of its implicit content and even of the time it lives through." Levinas, "Ethics as First Philosophy," 80. Cf. Husserl's understanding of intentional consciousness above.

99. Tallon, "Nonintentional Affectivity," 109.

100. TI, 33. Cf. Gibbs, "Height and Nearness: Jewish Dimensions of Radical Ethics," 16.

101. Cf. Tallon's points above with Peperzak's description of desire as "oriented before one can discover it." Peperzak, "Transcendence," 187.

water, or isolation with company.[102] Need thus has its focus on the self. In contrast, desire is an orientation towards Otherness that cannot be filled. There is no satisfaction in desire, only deepening:

> metaphysical desire does not long to return, for it is a desire for a land not of our birth, a land foreign to every nature, which has not been our fatherland and to which we shall never betake ourselves. The metaphysical desire does not rest upon any prior kinship. It is a desire that can not be satisfied. . . The metaphysical desire has another intention; it desires beyond everything that can simply complete it. It is like goodness—the Desired does not fulfill it, but deepens it.[103]

In an enduring critique of Greek philosophy, Levinas shows what he means by desire in contrasting the character Ulysses, whose life is characterized by traveling the world only to return home again, with Abraham, who seeks after an unknown destination which he never reaches: the Promised Land.[104] The example is instructive in terms of the self's movement and the catalyst for that movement—for Abraham and for the self of desire, the journey towards Otherness is a response to a revelation from the outside, in the case of desire it is the encounter with the face.[105]

Furthermore, for Levinas desire in the encounter with the face opens a dimension of height between the self and the other, understood in the Platonic manner of the result of knowledge of the unseen. When this is combined with Levinas's insight, the dimension of height is no longer the result of gazing into the heavens, but instead the experience of infinity that the self has in its encounter with the face.[106] These observations lead Levinas to one of his most well-known observations: there is an inherent curvature in intersubjective space.[107] He returns to Descartes in order to observe what might be the most appropriate response to the encounter with infinity in the face, noting that the contemplation of the idea of infinity, according to Descartes, turns into "admiration, adoration, and joy."[108]

102. *TI*, 62.

103. Ibid., 33–34. Cf. 117; 179.

104. Or, as Raffoul expresses it, "to escape, exit or go beyond the same, toward an other that does not return to a same, that does not come back, and to that extent is infinite." Raffoul, *The Origins of Responsibility*, 168. See also Hutchens, *Levinas*, 43; Peperzak, *Beyond*, 104. Cf. *TI*, 27.

105. *TI*, 62.

106. Ibid., 34–35. See also Burggraeve, *The Wisdom of Love*, 97; Raffoul, *The Origins of Responsibility*, 191.

107. *TI*, 291.

108. Ibid., 211. See also Raffoul, *The Origins of Responsibility*, 191.

GRASPING, TOTALIZATION, AND THE LIMITATIONS OF PHILOSOPHY

At Home with One's Self

Levinas contrasts the experience of the infinity of the face of the Other with the experience of being-at-home-with-one's-self. His observation is that whilst we can acknowledge that the self is in relationship with an Other, we must also acknowledge that it is an "I" that is concerned not only with the experience of transcendence, but also with the survival of itself. Levinas uses various words throughout his work to refer to this experience of the "I," including the ego and the being-at-home-with-oneself.[109] The latter is a helpful metaphor—Levinas's reflection on the "I" is mainly concerned with self-consciousness that builds itself up in isolation, surrounds itself with secure walls, and brings home to itself what it needs for its survival.[110] As such, for Levinas, the "I" is that part of the human person that is concerned with gathering together and bringing home the "gear consisting of things necessary" for life itself.[111]

In order to build such a home, the "I" is impelled beyond itself to take what is other and bring it home: the analogy can extend to a builder who needs to leave the place on which a home will be built in order to gather materials together that he needs to build with. In *Totality and Infinity*, Levinas's paradigmatic example of this is eating bread, an activity wherein the self takes something that is exterior and incorporates it into its own interiority—the self takes the bread home, so to speak.[112]

As such, the "I" takes objects from outside of itself, those things that it needs, brings them home, and then deals with them as objects that it can "observe, handle, and transform by labour and study within the framework of scientific theories."[113] To illustrate this activity, Levinas uses the image

---

109. *TI*, 39; Note that this corresponds with the understanding of need that was developed above.

110. As such, Levinas sees the "I" as developing "from inside out, and not from the outside in." Burggraeve, *The Wisdom of Love*, 45.

111. *TI*, 152.

112. Ibid., 33. Cf. 111. There is a subtlety in the French text when Levinas is describing this phenomenon that is not clear in the English translation. The word for the "other" that is taken into the self, the bread in this case, is the French *l'autre*, which is contrasted with the word for the human Other, *autrui*. Davis, *Levinas*, 43. Most English translators choose to capitalize *autrui* (as "Other") in order to indicate the difference and this is the method that will be followed throughout the book. Cf. Translator's note in *TI*, 24.

113. Peperzak, *Beyond*, 9. See also Hutchens, *Levinas*, 42–43.

of a hand which reaches out to, and grasps at, what is around it, always returning to the self. He refers to this action of the "I" as *labor*.[114] With this in mind, we can observe a correlation between the distinction between the "I" and the encounter with the Other and the distinction between need, as an activity of the "I" in securing its home and desire. If the appropriate "object" of desire is the Other, then the appropriate object of need is that which is required to fill a void within the self.[115] The motivation for a need is distinct in that its origin and destination are the same.

As such, the activity of labor is appropriate when directed towards objects which Levinas names *elements*. Such objects are independent to the self but are not the Other (they are other only in the sense of *l'autre*).[116] When the "I" takes an element into itself, its element becomes "fixed between the four walls of the home" and a possession.[117] Given the nature of the element possessed, Levinas sees this drawing of an element into the self as unproblematic and states that "in the last analysis labour cannot be called violence: it is applied to what is faceless, to the resistance of nothingness."[118]

Such labor is a necessary condition for human activity, but given the analysis above it cannot be the final word.[119] As such, labor is not an end in itself, nor the most primary moment for the human person, instead it should be seen as a means of securing the basic necessities for human existence. This leads Levinas to issue a challenge to any theoretical framework which exults the "I" to a level at which it is given permission to treat the encounter with the face as an element, to overcome it through labor, and to draw it in to the four walls of the self.[120] Any activity which falls into this trap Levinas calls a totality, and it is to his exploration of this idea that we now turn.

Violence and "Totalization"

It would not be an exaggeration to call Levinas's understanding of the violence of totality the most challenging part of his theory. Underlying his argument is the conviction that Western philosophy—from Ancient Greece

---

114. *TI*, 159. See also Burggraeve, *The Wisdom of Love*, 52.
115. Ibid., 62.
116. Ibid., 158.
117. Ibid.
118. Ibid., 160.
119. Ibid., 152.
120. Ibid., 38.

until the twentieth century—has been dominated by "totalization."[121] By this, he means that philosophers have been too quick to assume that a particular theory or philosophical method can encapsulate and express reality, and especially the reality of the human person, in its fullness. For Levinas, such an approach is an extrapolation of the human "I" to a level beyond its capabilities as it attempts to "reduce the universe to an originary and ultimate unity by way of panoramic overviews and dialectical syntheses."[122] Such a disposition is referred to in his work as "totalization," and it reveals a fundamental aversion to mystery, especially in the face of the Other, and a need to dominate and control. When such a philosophical system is posited, the Other receives his identity not from the inherent infinity that he is, but according to a prescription applied to him by the totality.[123] This constitutes a violence because it forces the Other to fit into a system which cannot account for his infinity. It is as if the "I" had taken possession of an Other who, by his nature, cannot be possessed and reduced to an object for the "I" to master.[124] This leads to another important word in Levinasian philosophy: the *same*. For Levinas, the same refers to anything which has its origin in the "I" and is reduced to the part it plays in reference to the "I." Turning to Levinas's critique of Husserl and Heidegger will help to explicate these points further.

As I noted earlier, Levinas found Husserl's phenomenological method attractive but did not think his conclusions about intentional consciousness went far enough, and it is now possible for us to understand why. Levinas, with Heidegger, argued that Husserl's positing of intentional consciousness as the *a priori* horizon out of which consciousness arises simply turned that horizon into another object for intentional consciousness to master.[125] Intentional consciousness is therefore both a product of consciousness and an object for its overcoming.[126] The human Other is then expected to fit into this framework, as would an element fit into the self when it is possessed by labor. Meaning here begins with the self and returns to the self.[127] For Levinas, this approach is inadequate because it cannot account for Des-

---

121. Ibid., 22.

122. Peperzak, *Beyond*, 4. Cf. Hutchens's description of this disposition as "an often horrific propensity to reduce everything fortuitous, foreign and enigmatic to conditions of intelligibility." Hutchens, *Levinas*, 14. See also Raffoul, *The Origins of Responsibility*, 169.

123. *TI*, 21.

124. Burggraeve, "Violence and the Vulnerable Face of the Other," 35–37.

125. *TI*, 28.

126. Ibid., 123.

127. Ibid., 29.

cartes' idea of infinity and therefore cannot take into account the infinity of the Other.[128] The Other is assigned a role and held within the gaze of a thought that is incapable of comprehending her, which means that an act of violence is committed.[129] Levinas leveled the same argument at the work of Heidegger—*Dasein* was yet another attempt to fit the Other into a linear framework, posited by consciousness and objectified by consciousness, in which transcendence is destroyed.[130]

The central concern of Levinas is that each of these philosophies, in trying to discover the essential structures out of which the ability of consciousness arises, has confused the name they have given these structures with the structures themselves and has therefore paved the way for reducing something that is wholly transcendent to yet another object for the "I" to master and bring home to itself. He compares such approaches to the metaphor of the hand which grasps and understands and he sets this up in clear contrast with the appropriate response to the transcendence of the Other noted above.[131] In "totalization," everything is subordinated to a universal law and, as a consequence, the reality of infinitude is excluded—no Other is her or his self, they are reduced to the anonymity of an element.[132] This is the action of an "I" who seeks to become master of itself and of the universe, illuminating each and every darkness.[133] Peperzak makes this point still more strongly, arguing that in a "totalization," the following occurs:

> Everything that exists appears as an element of the self-constitution of an ego dominating the world, in such a way that the Other can emerge only as a beautiful and intelligent animal, an animated tool, a slave or a cherished object.[134]

Levinas's argument that most of Western philosophy can be understood as "totalization" leads him to consider it largely as an economy, understood in the etymological sense of the word as a "law of the home."[135] The most obvious examples of this would of course be psychological and ethical

---

128. Ibid., 209–11.

129. Ibid., 53.

130. Ibid., 45–46. Cf. Peperzak, *Beyond*, 10; 51; Raffoul, *The Origins of Responsibility*, 171.

131. It should be noted that this is not an attack on the intellectual capacity of particular philosophers: "It is not the insufficiency of the I that prevents totalization, but the Infinity of the Other." *TI*, 80.

132. Waldenfels, "Levinas and the Face of the Other," 66.

133. Levinas, "Ethics as First Philosophy," 79.

134. Peperzak, *Beyond*, 122.

135. Peperzak, *Beyond*, 9.

egoism wherein everything is reduced to its function for the self although, as Patricia Werhane notes, even more subtle self-referential philosophical theories would find it difficult to break away from this understanding of economy if the return to the self is an essential part of their cycle.[136]

This is not to say that "totalization" does not have its place. Before we consider this point, however, consider how Levinas's own words provide a summary of some of the major points we have explored in the last two sections—I have added emphasis on the key Levinasian terms we have been discussing:

> The Other—the absolutely other—paralyzes *possession*, which he contests by his *epiphany in the face*. He can contest my possession only because he approaches me not from the outside [as would an *element*] but from *above*. The *same* cannot lay hold of this other without suppressing him.[137]

Where "Totalization" Fits

Levinas suggests that the move away from "totalization" begins when the "I" remembers this primordial experience of being affected by the encounter with the face of the Other. This insight allows the philosopher to realize that the Other will always elude thematization and that "the relation with the Other breaks the ceiling of the totality."[138] It encourages a move which takes phenomenology beyond "totalization" and toward the *a posteriori* encounter with the face.[139] Levinas argues that the way to understand the encounter with the face is not through the means of comprehension, given that this would reduce it to yet another totality, but *discourse*, understood as the situation wherein the "I" welcomes the transcendence of the Other's face and is addressed by her revelation. Intentional consciousness and all of its objects are constituted not prior to this discourse, but after it, and we will return to this point below. What is most important at this stage is that the phenomenological insight of Levinas, which he suggests is the condition of possibility for consciousness, is a *relationship* which involves an Other and thus cannot be reduced to thematization, rather than a particular *theoretical work* such as intentional consciousness or the *Dasein*.

---

136. Werhane, "Levinas's Ethics: A Normative Perspective without Metaethical Constraints," 60.
137. *TI*, 118. Parenthesis in original; emphasis added.
138. Ibid., 171.
139. Cf. *TI*, 24.

In spite of the above, it would be a mistake to over-interpret Levinas here and suggest that he sees no role for a thematized understanding of the human person. As Peperzak notes, "Levinas explicitly recognizes the positive and necessary aspects of the practical and theoretical totalizations produced by all people in every civilization."[140] Indeed, he frequently notes their value in obtaining justice and ordering society and, as a philosopher, enters into the practice of what he calls "totalization" (a point to which we will return in a moment). What Levinas cautions against is the absolutization of totality at the expense of the infinity of the Other.[141] Totalities must therefore be subordinated to the infinity of the Other and, as much as possible, respect and respond to his unique dignity as an infinity. A totality should always, in other words, constitute the *second* movement—response will always be the first given that it constitutes the possibility of the second.[142] As an example of how seriously Levinas took this task, we turn now to Jacques Derrida's critique of *Totality and Infinity* and the method of Levinas's response.

OTHERWISE THAN BEING OR BEYOND ESSENCE

The Shift Toward an Otherwise than Being

Three years after the release of *Totality and Infinity*, Jacques Derrida published a respectful but critical response to the work of Levinas entitled *Violence and Metaphysics* which points out a number of flaws in Levinas's approach.[143] There is no academic pride in Derrida's critique—he does not claim to know more than Levinas and he presents his critique as a series of questions rather than answers, suggesting that the shortfalls of Levinas's work are likely a result of the challenging nature of the task he has set himself, rather than oversight or carelessness.[144] Derrida points out two kinds of problems in the work of Levinas: the first, a series of misrepresentations of the work of others; and, the second, an inconsistency in thinking and formulation in his philosophy.[145] The specifics of the former of these need not

---

140. Peperzak, *Beyond*, 12. See also Hutchens, *Levinas*, 36.

141. Peperzak, *Beyond*, 12–13.

142. See Burggraeve, *The Wisdom of Love*, 141–42.

143. The English translation of *Violence and Metaphysics* can be found in Derrida, *Writing and Difference*, 97–192.

144. Hand, *Emmanuel Levinas*, 46.

145. Davis, *Levinas*, 64; Hand, *Emmanuel Levinas*, 46–47. These misrepresentations of others' thought include the critiques of Husserl and Heidegger noted above. Given that the precise nature of the disagreements Levinas had with Husserl and Heidegger is not our focus we will leave this issue aside here.

concern us here inasmuch as we are focusing on Levinas's body of work in and of itself, rather than how he deployed others' work. However, a consideration of the inconsistencies Derrida found in the work of Levinas will help us to track the development in his thought between *Totality and Infinity* and his second major work, *Otherwise than Being or Beyond Essence* and show how this is relevant for the task at hand.

The focus of Derrida's questions on the inconsistency of Levinas's work is leveled at the fact that, while Levinas is highly critical of the use of terms, categories and philosophical language to describe and "totalize" the metaphysical relationship with the Other, his work itself utilizes these tools in order to make its point.[146] Derrida notes that this problem is to be expected of a work which is trying to break out of the tradition of "totalization" within philosophy, whilst building on that very tradition's language and ideas.[147] In *Violence and Metaphysics*, Derrida shows that Levinas's attempt to speak about the Other is inevitably expressed in the language of the Same and thus becomes a victim of the very problem it seeks to critique.[148] The crux of Derrida's argument is that in an encounter with transcendence, all language will eventually falter, and that Levinas has not acknowledged this in his own work. It is hard to overestimate the influence that Derrida's critique had on Levinas. While never explicitly acknowledging it, most commentators agree that his second major work, *Otherwise than Being*, is a "sustained and critical response to Derrida."[149] In it, Levinas seeks to break open the confines of philosophical language and draw his reader into the mystery of transcendence. In a move away from *Totality and Infinity*, Levinas explicitly acknowledges the limitations of this task given that it must, of necessity, draw on the very language that its conclusions seek to undermine.[150]

Language in Otherwise than Being

One of the deepest questions that *Otherwise Than Being* seeks to answer is whether or not such a move is possible given that the use of language will always involve an element of betrayal when it seeks to express something that is, by its nature, beyond expression.[151] In addressing these concerns, Levinas

---

146. Davis, *Levinas*, 64.
147. Ibid., 66.
148. Hand, *Emmanuel Levinas*, 46–47.
149. Davis, *Levinas*, 69.
150. *OB*, 7. Cf. 185.
151. Ibid., 6–7.

gives a subtle nod to Derrida, noting that these "are familiar objections!"[152] However, he remains consistent with *Totality and Infinity*'s affirmation that some "totalization" is necessary and argues that language itself is indispensable in the task of undermining its own exaltation.[153] The deeply paradoxical nature of *Otherwise than Being*, in its attempt to go beyond the confines of philosophical language by using that language, makes it a deeply self-conscious text that, even as it expresses itself, seeks to undo that expression:

> In simply letting these words stand, Levinas confronts the attentive reader with a dilemma. It is an unsettling but exemplary moment: one in which this complex text is not allowed to close in on itself; one in which it is obliged to lose something of its authority, to be unsure of how it is to see or to present itself.[154]

Indeed, it is the self-consciousness of this paradox which makes *Otherwise than Being* such a difficult text with which to engage—its arguments are hardly linear, and Levinas's use of language seems to disorient the reader deliberately.[155] Levinas himself notes the difficulty of his task and the resulting complexity of his text with a touch of humor: "Perhaps the clarity of the exposition does not suffer here only from the clumsiness of the expounder."[156] Indeed, it seems to come as a result of Levinas's attempt to take language beyond its own limits and to ensure that it does not "close in on itself."

While the focus of *Otherwise than Being* is directed at the proper place and use of philosophical language, it is instructive that the reason for Levinas's intense concern with this problem remains the transcendental encounter with the Other who cannot be contained by language. In this way, the work remains consistent with *Totality and Infinity* whilst at the same time developing its central insight through the language used to express it. What Levinas continues to argue is that the encounter with the Other is something that is always beyond, or otherwise than, an ontology and that there is a transcendental quality to meaning that exists beyond and before the work of consciousness.[157] In a reframing of *Totality and Infinity*'s encounter with

---

152. Ibid., 155. See also Hand's introduction to *Otherwise than Being* in which he emphasizes this point, Hand, *Emmanuel Levinas*, 51–52.

153. *OB*, 6.

154. Davies, "On Resorting to an Ethical Language," 104.

155. See Davis, *Levinas*, 71–72. On the complexity of Levinas's use of language, see also Hutchens, *Levinas*, 3–5.

156. *OB*, 19.

157. Levinas writes that one of the purposes of *Otherwise than Being* is to ask "if all meaning proceeds from essence." Ibid., 176.

the face, the underlying argument of *Otherwise than Being* is that *saying* always precedes *said*.

The 'Saying' and the 'Said'

We noted earlier that, in *Totality and Infinity*, Levinas argued that the "I" finds itself always already in a state of discourse. That the subject begins to think about itself and the world from a position of being addressed by an Other is also of central concern in *Otherwise than Being*. Levinas moves away from the word "discourse" to describe this encounter and employs the word "Saying" instead.[158] The observation which underlies this is simple but surprisingly radical: discourse is always addressed by someone to someone—interpersonal meaning always has an *accusative* dimension.[159] He argues that this action of communicating the revelation of transcendence between persons in the proximity of one another is always prior to and outside of the conceptualization that is made of it—language is primordially communication between the Other and the "I" before it is expression and articulation.[160] For Levinas, the Saying is:

> Antecedent to the verbal signs it conjugates, to the linguistic systems and the semantic glimmerings, a foreword preceding languages, it is the proximity of the one to the other, the commitment of an approach, the one for the other, the very signifyingness of signification.[161]

Levinas contrasts this Saying with what is *Said* about it, understood as all expression wherein the meaning of the Saying is verbalized or written.[162] The use of the past tense "Said" appears to be deliberate in that it is always the attempt to capture a transcendence that has inevitably escaped from its grasp.[163] In a now familiar turn, he argues that philosophy has been concerned mostly with the Said, and has naively glanced over the Saying that is the condition for the Said's possibility. *Otherwise than Being* thus seeks to go beyond ontology (the Said) and recapture something of the experience

---

158. Werhane suggests that translating the French *dire* as "to say" captures Levinas's intended meaning more adequately because the infinitive expresses both the act of saying and the one who underlies the act. See Werhane, "Levinas's Ethics," 63.

159. Levinas, "Ethics as First Philosophy," 81; *OB*, 85. Cf. Cohen, "Emmanuel Levinas," 243; Peperzak, *Beyond*, 61.

160. Peperzak, *Beyond*, 62.

161. *OB*, 5.

162. Peperzak, *Beyond*, 60.

163. *OB*, 10; cf. 152.

of the Saying that precedes it.[164] For Levinas, this movement beyond the Said and toward the Saying is what is uncovered by the phenomenological *epoché*.[165]

One can notice here the formal relationship between the *Saying* as distinct from the *Said* and *Infinity* as distinct from *Totality* in Levinas's earlier work. However, *Otherwise than Being* is far less dualistic about this distinction and seems to express a recognition that the two cannot be separated so easily. Levinas now argues, for example, that the Saying is oriented towards expression in the Said (even though the latter acts as its demise); that language is "ancillary and thus indispensable" in the task of pointing to the Otherwise than Being; and that the Said has its "hour and time" as a phenomenon that arises in the Saying.[166] However, his project of "attempting to speak about" (or make a Said of) the Saying is still problematic, given that the Said cannot encapsulate the transcendence of the Saying.[167] Thus Levinas remains critical of the Said, but expresses this as an ongoing revision and undoing of the Said by the Saying rather than Infinity's complete undermining of Totality.[168] As Colin Davis notes,

> [the resulting] textual disturbances which characterize the language of *Otherwise than Being* are the surface effects of deep tensions within the work. It is as if the text were trying to shake off its own propositional structure, whilst remaining aware that the success of such a project would be disastrous for the philosophical ambitions that the text continues to entertain.[169]

164. Ibid., 38. Cf. Peperzak, *Beyond*, 71; 93.

165. "The movement back to the saying is the phenomenological reduction." *OB*, 53. Levinas's attempt to go beyond ontology is the reason for the full title of *Otherwise than Being or Beyond Essence*, which is a double translation of Plato's definition of the Good as that which is beyond essence.

166. *OB*, 37; 6; 46 (respectively). Cf. Davis, *Levinas*, 76: "Saying is never fully present in the Said, yet the Said also constitutes the only access we have to it; it leaves a trace on the Said but is never revealed in it; it (Saying) is not a theme, but can only be discussed in terms of themes"; parenthesis added.

167. Peperzak, *Beyond*, 93.

168. *OB*, 152. Peperzak points to a link between Levinas's task and that of apophatic/negative theology that seeks to avoid propositional statements about God given that God cannot be contained adequately by language. Davis disagrees with this point, suggesting that even stating what God is not allows for an implicit conception of what God is which falls back into the problem with ontology. Given Levinas's move away from the extremes of totality versus infinity and toward the more subtle and necessary relationship between Saying and Said, Peperzak's argument is more convincing. See Davis, *Levinas*, 99; Peperzak, *Beyond*, 62. Burggraeve also raises the same point, see Burggraeve, *The Wisdom of Love*, 90.

169. Davis, *Levinas*, 75. Cf. Waldenfels, "Levinas and the Face of the Other," 75.

As a further consequence of his ongoing concern about the role and limitations of philosophy, Levinas revisits *Totality and Infinity*'s concern about infinity being overcome by totality by way of warnings about the Saying being subordinated to Said. This leads Levinas to acknowledge the important role of philosophical skepticism which follows philosophy "like a shadow" and consistently casts a critical eye over what is posited as *a priori* truth.[170]

An appropriate skepticism is therefore a tool which reminds philosophy of its rightful place and its responsibility for its own ongoing renewal in the face of an encounter that will always elude any form of restrictive comprehension. This, of course, can also be understood as another approving nod in the direction of Derrida's earlier critique. For Levinas, an adequate philosophy is now one which is honest about its limitations, and expresses this honesty by honoring the transcendence of the Other rather than "totalizing" her, or absolutizing what is Said about her. As Paul Davies notes, such a philosophy "only gets going by never quite getting going."[171] It has mystery at its core and does not express the tidiness and linear coherence that is often expected of a philosophical theory.

The reason for this is the return to the encounter with the face of the Other, the experience of Saying in which the Other communicates a revelation of transcendence to the "I" which precedes and eludes conceptualization and can never adequately be Said. With this in mind, we turn now to the core of Levinas's "big idea." We have delayed our consideration of it until now in order that it can be heard with full force in light of an understanding of the Infinity of the Other, the Totality and Violence of the Same, the Saying in which the "I" is caught up before it realizes and the Said which can never grasp it entirely. We turn now to the insight that Derrida said would "make us tremble" if properly understood: Ethics as First Philosophy.[172]

ETHICS AS FIRST PHILOSOPHY

Foundational Arguments Revisited

> The relationship between the same and the other, my welcoming of the other, is the ultimate fact, and in it the things figure not as what one builds but as what one gives.[173]

---

170. *OB*, 168. See also Hutchens's chapter on Levinas and skepticism, Hutchens, *Levinas*, 55–66. Cf. Burggraeve, *The Wisdom of Love*, 91.
171. Davies, "On Resorting," 99.
172. Derrida, *Writing and Difference*, 101.
173. *TI*, 77.

As we have seen, for Levinas the "I" always finds itself in relationship with the Other. The primordial fact of the human person out of which consciousness arises, the conclusion of Levinas's phenomenology, is the mystery of this encounter. The core of Levinas's phenomenological insight is therefore that a person is never a person in isolation: we always find ourselves in the midst of responsibility-laden relationships which are prior to understanding. Beyond and before we can think about it, we are held to ethical responsibility by the face of the Other. This insight has enormous consequences for the way we see philosophy, for if ethics is an optics, as Levinas suggests, it changes the manner in which we see the discipline in the first place.

The major consequence of this primordial call to responsibility is that ontology (or epistemology) is *not* the first philosophy. We have seen that Levinas argues against the positing of an ontological philosophy as the essential framework into which our conception of the Other must fit. Since it is impossible for such an approach to create the idea of infinity, as per Descartes observations noted above, it cannot be the first movement of philosophy—the "I" does not create the idea of infinity, it receives it.[174] If Levinas's suggestion is correct, to be a person is in the first instance to be the one who is addressed by the Saying of transcendence by the Other. The first movement of consciousness is therefore not some form of spontaneous thought or conceptualization. Instead, the first movement of consciousness is *response* to the call of the Other. It is as if the "I" finds itself in the middle of a conversation that it did not begin, in which it is being questioned. The beginnings of philosophy are an attempt at how Being answers when it is addressed by the Other.[175]

Why Ethics is the First Philosophy

According to Levinas, as the "I" encounters the face of the Other its urge towards continuing its own free and spontaneous operations which reduce the Other to self-referential "totalization" are fundamentally questioned:

> We name this calling into question of my spontaneity by the presence of the Other ethics. The strangeness of the Other, his irreducibility to the I, to my thoughts and my possessions, is precisely accomplished as a calling into question of my spontaneity, as ethics.[176]

---

174. Ibid., 204.
175. Levinas, "Ethics as First Philosophy," 86.
176. *TI*, 43.

This articulates why Levinas refers to *ethics* as the first philosophy. The "I" of consciousness always-already finds itself as called into question in this way—never after the thought that reflects on this question, but before it. Levinas's use of the word "ethics" here is peculiar when held up against modern conceptions of the same. Ethics, for Levinas, does not refer to a framework for moral decision-making or a system for evaluating the merits of moral actions or dispositions. Rather, he is pointing toward a constitutive responsibility that precedes the human person's capacity for any such activities—a constitutive sense of being questioned that animates such activities rather than directs them. The "I" is always conditioned by the fact of this responsibility, even before it can grasp this fact.[177] For Levinas, this *must* have an influence on how we go about philosophy:

> the comprehension of Being in general cannot *dominate* the re-lationship with the Other. The latter relationship commands the first. I cannot disentangle myself from society with the Other, even when I consider the Being of the existent he is.[178]

Hence, for Levinas, ethics refers to a way of *seeing*—in his own words, "ethics is an optics."[179] Peperzak notes that "ethical" in this Levinasian usage is akin to "animation" or "inspiration"—ethics is what calls the "I" into itself.[180] The "I" never simply says "I am," as per the Cartesian *cogito*; it can only say "here I am" in response to the Other who stands before it.[181]

This means that questions of how the "I" responds in the presence of the face of the Other are fundamental to all expressions of thinking. They cannot be suspended until the "foundational" questions of philosophy (or theology, or anthropology or any other discipline) are resolved.[182] To take Levinas seriously here would mean that any such attempt is based on a "false understanding of reality."[183] To acknowledge that any activity of the "I," including philosophy, happens in response to the ethical call of the face is to reframe philosophy: all philosophy is already ethics, because all philosophy is a response to this call.[184] This declares as violence any philosophical

---

177. Peperzak, *Beyond*, 13. Cf. Davis, *Levinas*, 47–48.

178. *TI*, 47. See also Levinas, "Ethics as First Philosophy," 84.

179. Ibid., 23.

180. Peperzak, *Beyond*, 109.

181. *OB*, 114. Cf. Hutchens, *Levinas*, 49; Raffoul, *The Origins of Responsibility*, 164; 194.

182. *TI*, 23. Cf. Peperzak, *Beyond*, 207.

183. Peperzak, *Beyond*, 205.

184. "Even the philosopher that speaks of it (the encounter with the Other), over and beyond the universality in which the subjectivity that is *said* appears, remains a subjectivity obsessed by the neighbour." *OB*, 84; parenthesis added.

framework which establishes itself against the call of the Other, by positing a product of the "I" as a "totalization" into which all otherness must fit.[185] The ethical demand here holds that philosophy—and all other articulations of what it means to be human—must not fall into the comfort of particular conceptualizations, but rather attend to the implications of responding to the call in the face of the Other.[186]

THE LEVINASIAN INSIGHT REGARDING HUMAN SUBJECTIVITY

Constituted by the Encounter with the Other

As we have seen, for Levinas the human person is not seen as a conscious *cogito*, an intentional consciousness, or a being-in-the-world. To posit any of these as the primordial fact of human subjectivity would be to focus only on the human person at-home-with-himself and to reduce the reality of a subject to an economy, a law of the home, and an element which labor is able to overcome and reduce to the same. For Levinas, the human subject is shocked out of the comfort of any such approach by the memory of the primordial experience of encounter with the Other. In the words of Perperzak:

> You surprise me by coming to me. Even if I invited you, your coming disturbs my world. Indeed, your entering into my dwelling place interrupts the coherence of my economy; you disarrange my order in which all things familiar to me have their proper place, function and time. Your emergence makes holes in the walls of my house. If I could see and treat you as a being amidst other beings, like a knot in the all-encompassing time flow, or as an element of a universe unfolding its riches before my mental eye, you would have been bereft of everything that justifies my calling you by the pronoun "you." You would be a particular part of my realm.[187]

The proximity and immediacy of this encounter is antecedent to the ability of the human "I" to question or articulate it.[188] As such, the human

---

185. See Raffoul, *The Origins of Responsibility*, 166.

186 As Levinas phrases it, "The relationship between the same and the other, my welcoming of the other, is the ultimate fact, and in it the things figure not as what one builds but as what one gives." *TI*, 77. Cf. Westphal, "Levinas's Teleological Suspension of the Religious," 154.

187. Peperzak, *Beyond*, 66. Cf. Hutchens, *Levinas*, 16.

188. Levinas, "Ethics as First Philosophy," 81, 83. Cf. Ciaramell, "The Riddle of the Pre-Original," 88; Tallon, "Nonintentional Affectivity," 116.

person is prerationally affected and constituted by the encounter with the transcendent Other. For Levinas this is the primary fact of subjectivity. It is therefore less a case of being *subject*, and more a case of being *subjected* to the fact of the ethical call of the Other. The "I" is itself a response, and this response is what constitutes human subjectivity.[189] Hence, as the "I" finds itself, it also finds the Other:

> The neighbour is nearer to me, so to speak, than I am to myself . . . My home, as it turns out, is already occupied, by the homeless, by the Guatemalan refugee, by the Jewish refugee.[190]

Human subjectivity is thus always an answer to the ethic call, even to say "No!" to it is still to respond.[191] As such, the subject is:

> Someone who, in the absence of anyone is called upon to be someone, and cannot slip away from this call. The subject is inseparable from this appeal or this election, which cannot be declined.[192]

Andrew Tallon and Preintentional Affective Attunement

Andrew Tallon has taken the Levinasian understanding of subjectivity into consideration from the perspective of philosophical anthropology.[193] His analysis is helpful for deepening our understanding of the Levinasian insight. Tallon suggests that Levinas can be understood as revealing that the human person is created with an affectability which is unintended by the subject, in the sense of chosen or decided upon, but nevertheless the essential identifying *characteristic* of her being.[194] Tallon refers to this constitutive affectability as a "preintentional affective attunement."[195] His argument is

---

189. *OB*, 46, 55. Or, as Hutchens phrases it, the primordial encounter with the Other causes "an 'upsurge' of consciousness." Hutchens, *Levinas*, 47. See also Burggraeve, *The Wisdom of Love*, 87, 99; Raffoul, *The Origins of Responsibility*, 196.

190. Miller, "Reply to Bernhard Waldenfels," 54, 57. See also Weber, "The Notion of Persecution in Levinas's *Otherwise Than Being or Beyond Essence*," 73.

191. Hutchens, *Levinas*, 20; cf. 23. *OB*, 25, 14.

192. *OB*, 53.

193. The following analysis builds upon my earlier publication, Fleming, "Ethics is an Optics: The Levinasian Perspective on Value as Primary."

194. Tallon, "Nonintentional Affectivity," 117.

195. Tallon, "Levinas's Ethical Horizon," 48. One could also look to Raffoul here, who describes the Levinasian insight as a "pre-originary openness to the other" or, more simply, a fundamental hospitality for the Other. See Raffoul, *The Origins of Responsibility*, 177–78.

that the human person is attuned to her responsibility for the other person at an affective level that is prior to intentionality. In Levinasian language, the person is constituted by an essential response-ability, which is exemplified in the interpersonal encounter.

Tallon suggests that the encounter between the "I" and the face should be understood as an "amplification event." When the "I" encounters the Other, it experiences a rise in its sense of responsibility. We might think of the moment when we walk past a vulnerable person in the street and our senses and attention toward the person are heightened, even where our response is to move away. Tallon points out that Levinas's language is at its most extreme when he seeks to describe this situation.[196] Indeed, it is the idea of an amplification event that leads Levinas to one of his most well-known formulas in which he describes the relationship between the "I" and the Other in terms of a curvature of intersubjective space.[197] Levinas uses this formula as a way of describing the experience of encountering value which, metaphorically, always calls the "I" to look *up* toward a source of value that lies beyond itself. The key insight here is that the experience of amplification is also an experience of the value of the Other who is encountered:

> This means that *whatever we feel is by that fact not flat*, but value (evaluation), or it would not affect us in the first place; we would not feel it; the vast majority of energies in our world produce no effect on our receptors at all because they are biologically (and/ or socially) irrelevant.[198]

This experience of value, Tallon argues, is analogous to the experience of gravity: it is prior to our existence, our capacities for rationality, choice, and so on, but conditions and shapes the very nature of these.[199] In the same way, the call that Levinas identified is prior to human subjectivity, but shapes the very nature of that subjectivity.[200] We experience a curvature in interpersonal space because of what we, as persons, *are*, and the value that we experience in the Other's face is an essential aspect of this. For Tallon, Levinas points out the mistake of any "totalization," philosophy or ethical theory that ignores this point and posits that this affectability is something that is learned and added to the human person after some appropriate framework of meaning is set up, rather than acknowledging that it is something that

---

196. Tallon, "Levinas's Ethical Horizon," 53.
197. See *TI*, 291.
198. Tallon, "Levinas's Ethical Horizon," 56.
199. The analogy of gravity used earlier was included to point clearly to Tallon's use of it here. Cf. Burggraeve, *The Wisdom of Love*, 87.
200. Tallon, "Levinas's Ethical Horizon," 58.

he is characterized by at the most fundamental level.[201] This observation will have several implications when it comes to the following chapters, in which we consider how Levinas's philosophy might align with Jean Porter's theory of the natural law. Before making that step, it is important to deal with several more aspects and implications of Levinas's thought.

Modes of Responsibility

At this stage of the chapter, it may be helpful to make a clear distinction between the understanding of responsibility developed to this point, understood as the human subject who is always already answerable to the ethical call of the Other, and a second, more common, understanding of responsibility, understood as the responsibility a human subject takes (or is able to take) in choosing to direct the precise form that their response takes. This distinction is not entirely clear in Levinas's writings, however turning to Waldenfels helps to clarify the distinction we seek here. Waldenfels notes that the traditional usage of the word "responsibility" falls into three categories. In the first instance, responsibility refers to something or other that one has done and for which he is responsible. In the second instance, responsibility describes the condition of being responsible to somebody, understood as an individual, forum or tribunal. In the third instance, responsibility refers to the state of someone who acknowledges responsibility and thus has to justify themselves.[202]

These understandings of responsibility are distinct from the Levinasian usage because, as we have noted, Levinas's concern is not with what the person *does* but with what the person *is*. This corresponds with the proper task of phenomenology, which, as we have also noted, is primarily concerned with naming the essential structures out of which the human person's unique ability for consciousness arises, rather than developing ethical frameworks. This is why Levinas can say that the human person is in a state of "infinite responsibility"—responsibility in his usage is never exhausted because it is an essential part of the nature of the human subject—as soon as the "I" is not responding to the Other it is no longer "I."[203] The reality that

---

201. Ibid., 60. Cf. Pope's comments about the value of the form of this insight, which has also been named by the personalist tradition in Catholic ethics, Pope, *The Evolution of Altruism*, 26.

202. Waldenfels, "Response and Responsibility," 40.

203. See *TI*, 244–45. See also Hutchens's explanation of the foundation of Levinas's ethics of responsibility, which accords with what we have said here, Hutchens, *Levinas*, 19.

Levinas points us toward thus permeates human subjectivity in an analogous way to gravity, as we noted above: one may ignore the fact, even though one is constituted by it, in the same way that one may choose to ignore the fact of gravity without floating into space.

The fact of the responsibility noted in the Levinasian insight does not necessarily mean, however, that the "I" will respond adequately. That the human person's subjectivity is constituted in a relationship of responsibility does not mean that this responsibility will be honored. Indeed, one finds in Levinas's writing a sense that the "I" can easily overcome its constitution by responding against the ethical call doing violence to the Other through "totalization." It is important, therefore, to distinguish between "the unavoidable of the situation we have to respond to, that is, the *necessary* in its literal sense—and the range of possible responses."[204] Peperzak provides an illuminating reflection on what this means in practice:

> Not being able to choose or reject my responsibility, I am therefore not free either to be or not to be responsible. The Good that chose me created me as already oriented, listening, looking up to the Other . . . In this sense everybody begins by already being good. Of course, when I become conscious of the enormous burden responsibility puts on me, I can decide to refuse further obedience.[205]

Still more succinctly, Burggraeve states that "*How* I answer depends on my freedom; *that* I answer does not."[206] Levinas's phenomenology is thus not deterministic, and he is not suggesting that the fact of responsibility will correspond with a willingness or ability to respond adequately.[207]

---

204. Waldenfels, "Response and Responsibility," 46. There is a similarity here between this reading of Levinas and the experience of conscience as an experience of goodness and a call to respond to goodness, cf. GS, 16. This is well captured by the first dimension of Timothy O'Connell's three-part understanding of conscience, which he names conscience/1, and which he distinguishes from conscience/2 and conscience/3. These latter dimensions of conscience refer to, respectively, the process of discovering what is objectively right and wrong, and the decision of conscience to commit to a particular action. I have explored this point in more detail in Fleming, "Primoridal Moral Awareness." O'Connell's understanding of conscience was first published in O'Connell, "The Theology of Conscience." O'Connell then developed the argument of this article in *Principles for a Catholic Morality*, 103–19. In a later work, O'Connell aligned his understanding of conscience with an impressive synthesis of information on the task of moral formation, see O'Connell, *Making Disciples*, especially 36–37.

205. Peperzak, "Transcendence," 190.

206. Burggraeve, *The Wisdom of Love*, 102.

207. In this sense another comparison can be made to Stephen Pope's understanding of "motivation" as an "emotional impetus for behaviour," which stimulates

This means that a consideration of the Levinasian insight is not sufficient material for a moral theory because the fundamental awareness of value can yield very different understandings of what it means to act in right or wrong ways.[208] Indeed, commentators on Levinas agree that his phenomenology is not concerned with providing a specific set of moral norms, and suggest that he points us toward some theory of morality without telling us exactly what this theory might look like.[209] As such, it is here that we must look beyond Levinas and toward a moral theory that can provide a framework for such specification, which, following from the direction set for the book, will be Jean Porter's theory of the natural law. What links this has with the Levinasian understanding of the human person, and how it will specify some of the ethical implications of his thought, will therefore be the focus of the next chapters.

CONCLUSION

In this chapter, we focused on the first part of the hypothesis which looks towards the philosophy of Emmanuel Levinas and, by situating Levinas in his historical and philosophical contexts, developed a picture of his understanding of the human person by tracing his thought through his major works, *Totality and Infinity* and *Otherwise than Being*, and drawing on the insights of a number of his commentators for further clarification. It is helpful to conclude by reiterating the two main concerns that Levinas leaves us with as we attempt to develop our understanding of moral truth in light of his phenomenology: the first is that any theory that posits itself as *a priori* and comprehensive, ignores the mystery of the other human person; the second is that the human subject is always in a state of responsibility. As we have noted in this chapter, Levinas has given us a starting point in telling us something about who we are, but his insight needs to be supplemented and specified in terms of what we should do. In the next chapter, we will begin this task by considering Jean Porter's theory of the natural law, which I will argue can specify some of the implications of Levinas's thought.

---

the human person and encourages a response but is largely indeterminate in terms of which *specific* response is chosen. See Pope, *Human Evolution and Christian Ethics*, 222–23, cf. 223–34.

208. O'Connell, *Principles for a Catholic Morality*, 110.

209. See for example Critchley, "Introduction," 27.

2

Nature in the Natural Law
The Foundations of Jean Porter's Approach

INTRODUCTION

THIS CHAPTER MARKS A shift in the book from consideration of the prerational call to goodness, to the process which searches for the ethical implications of this. It does this by moving from the phenomenology of Emmanuel Levinas to Jean Porter's theory of natural law, which becomes a central part of the remainder of its argument.

The chapter begins by situating Porter's approach to natural law within contemporary discussions and concerns about the theory. Noting that Porter places an emphasis of the role of prerational nature in her theory, the chapter then explores the extent to which we can hope to gain an understanding of nature in the current context. After this, it moves into a consideration of natural intelligibility and towards the development of a paradigm for human flourishing, whilst remaining aware of Levinas's warnings about 'totalization'. Revealing that Porter provides a convincing argument for the possibility of the development of a paradigm for human flourishing that is accountable to this Levinasian warning, the chapter notes that such a paradigm requires recourse to further knowledge and specification if it is going to provide a morally salient account of human flourishing, which becomes the focus of Chapters Three and Four. The chapter concludes by developing initial links between Levinas and Porter that focus on the relevance of prerational nature for moral reflection and ethics as a natural phenomenon.

WHY NATURAL LAW AND WHY PORTER?

Contemporary Discussion Around Natural Law Theory

It is to be acknowledged at the outset that, in the contemporary climate of moral theology and philosophy, natural law does not seem the most obvious choice for developing the ethical implications of Emmanuel Levinas's phenomenology. In this section I will name and respond to the reasons for this from the perspectives of both Porter and Levinas. I will then posit three arguments for engaging with natural law in order to show the validity of the ensuing study.

First and foremost of the concerns about natural law is a deep-seated suspicion of the theory amongst many moral theologians. Jean Porter begins both of her *magna opera* books by noting the need for what could only be described as an apologetic for natural law in light of the form of the theory which became prevalent in the neo-scholastic manuals of moral theology, and still holds a degree of authority in Catholic sexual ethics.[1] One of the consequences of the prevalence of this approach to natural law has been a widespread suspicion of the theory, and a tendency to read any reference to 'natural law' through the paradigm of this suspicion. Most often, this means that the generic term 'natural law' is understood to refer to a reductionist approach to morality which develops moral norms according to an understanding of the appropriate biological function of particular organs, on the premise that such an understanding reveals God's intention for their proper use.[2] Nowhere is such an approach more famously articulated than in the following sentence from Pope Paul VI's 1968 encyclical *Humanae Vitae*:

> An act of mutual love which impairs the capacity to transmit life which God the Creator, through specific laws, has built into it, frustrates His design which constitutes the norm of marriage, and contradicts the will of the Author of life.[3]

---

1. See *NDL*, 15–34, esp. 29–34; *NR*, 1–44. Cf. Salzman and Lawler, *The Sexual Person*, 48–57.

2. *NDL*, 29. Cf. Keenan, *A History of Catholic Moral Theology*, 174; Pope, *The Evolution of Altruism*, 3. Pope also sees a link between this suspicion of natural law and the recent "turn to the subject" in moral theology and notes that this turn has "been accompanied by an unfortunate tendency to avoid discussing human nature in all its dimensions." He goes on to argue that one negative consequence of this move has been a tendency toward what Margaret Farley has called a "disembodied" anthropology. Pope, *The Evolution of Altruism*, 2–3; 34. For a later work of Farley's that explores this in detail, see Farley, *Just Love*, 110–32.

3. *HV*, no. 13.

The arguments that challenge this understanding of natural law as the 'law of nature' (which, in this case, is reduced to a 'law of biology') are well known and it would take us too far afield to repeat them in detail here. Suffice to say that a number of authors have argued that such an account of natural law is unsustainable in light of our understanding of the complexity of the human person, a point which is further magnified when we come to consider the social and historical variability that exists in interpretations of what constitutes 'human nature.'[4] It has thus been termed 'classical,' 'rigid,' 'physicalist' and 'reductionist' and has not infrequently been condemned as falling prey to the naturalistic fallacy.[5] As a consequence, the role of 'nature' in Catholic moral theology has been put to one side in favor of a focus on reason as the natural ability for moral discernment.

Richard Gula's treatment of natural law is paradigmatic of this shift. In his *Reason Informed By Faith*, Gula includes a table which contrasts the 'Order of Nature' approach to natural law (his name for the approach which we have just been considering) with the 'Order of Reason' approach.[6] From this latter perspective, *reason*, which is a capacity to seek truth that is part of human *nature*, seeks to come to an understanding of reality, which can be understood as the true *nature* of things. The natural law approach thereby becomes a dynamic search for moral truth which can account for historical and social consciousness and focuses largely on the operations of practical

---

4. As McGrath notes, "once the importance of socially mediated ideas, theories and values is conceded, it is impossible to avoid the conclusion that the concept of nature is, at least in part, a social construction. If the concept of nature is socially mediated—to whatever extent—it cannot serve as an allegedly neutral, objective or uninterpreted foundation of a theory or theology. *Nature is already an interpreted category*." McGrath, *A Scientific Theology*, 113; emphasis in original. We will return to this point and develop it further below. For further discussion of these points, see Keenan, *A History of Catholic Moral Theology*, 173–75. Richard Gula's discussion of these same points is also worth considering, see Gula, *Reason Informed by Faith*, 231–40.

5. See Gula, *Reason Informed by Faith*, 234–5. A very thorough study and critique of the Roman Catholic magisterium's use of this approach to the natural law along these lines can be found in Salzman and Lawler, *The Sexual Person*. Charles Curran has also noted the methodological issues that exist in such an approach, see Curran, "Catholic Social and Sexual Teaching," 435–39. In *NDL*, 26, Porter points to what G. E. Moore, drawing on David Hume, called the naturalistic fallacy as a reason for the hesitation many contemporary theologians show in looking to the morally significant aspects of human nature. And indeed two of the greatest Catholic theologians of the twentieth century, Karl Rahner and Bernard Lonergan, echoed these very critiques. See *NDL*, 31. We will return to a detailed consideration and critique of the naturalistic fallacy below.

6. Gula, *Reason Informed by Faith*, 235; 239–40. Dolores Christie notes that, in a technical sense, this can be understood as natural law from the *metaethical* perspective. That is, it seeks to provide a foundation for the search for ethical truth by making a claim about the human capacity to seek and know the good. See Christie, *Adequately Considered*, 106–7.

reason.[7] On this view, as Charles Curran and Richard McCormick put it, "anyone who admits human reason as a source of moral wisdom adopts a natural law perspective."[8] Such a broad definition can cover a vast array of ethical approaches and, whilst it avoids the physicalism which was so problematic in the 'Order of Nature' approach, this breadth of the definition may itself be problematic. Indeed, one might observe that the approach is so inclusive that the term 'natural law' loses any form of meaningful contribution to moral theory. Notwithstanding this critique, there is also no intrinsic guarantee that the 'Order of Reason' approach will be any less susceptible to the reductionist critiques noted above, and a contemporary example of this lies with the so-called New Natural Law Theory.

The New Natural Law Theory

The New Natural Law Theory (hereafter, NNLT), which has been developed primarily by Germain Grisez, John Finnis, and Joseph Boyle, begins by arguing that practical reason is able to acknowledge the self-evident existence of certain 'basic goods'—components of human existence which are basic and necessary for human well-being—regardless of its social and historical context. Of itself, this is not a controversial claim, and many others take a similar approach in their discussions on natural law.[9] However, the NNLT theorists extend their version of the claim and suggest that practical reason is able to determine specific, universally self-evident, moral conclusions from its acknowledgment of basic goods. Underlying NNLT is the following claim:

> we have a rational grasp of certain basic goods, elemental enough to be regarded plausibly as self-evident to all and yet provided with enough content to provide an immediate basis for practical reflection.[10]

7. Gula, *Reason Informed by Faith*, 235–46.

8. Curran and McCormick, *Readings in Moral Theology No. 7: Natural Law and Theology*, 1. Cf. *NDL*, 66.

9. Robert Gascoigne, for example, argues that natural law points to the fact that "there are fundamental needs and purposes of human existence, that we can know them, and that we can know them in common through our shared humanity." Gascoigne, *Freedom and Purpose*, 31. However, Gascoigne cautions against taking this insight too far at the expense of what we know about social and historical consciousness. Thus, natural law has "the strength of pointing out basic and universal human characteristics, but the weakness of confusing these basic characteristics with certain historically conditioned social relationships." Gascoigne, *Freedom and Purpose*, 32. As we will see, the NNLT theorists fail to acknowledge such a weakness in their approach.

10. *NR*, 128. These arguments are summarized by the NNLT theorists in Grisez, et al., "Practical Principles," 108, 106, 121–27, respectively.

To exemplify the point of difference between NNLT and the 'Order of Nature' approach, we can return to *Humanae vitae*'s condemnation of sexual acts which are not naturally open to the transmission of life. Where *Humanae vitae* condemned such acts based on an observation of the biological functionality of the human person's sexual organs, the NNLT theorists posit the exigencies of practical reason as the methodology for coming to the same moral conclusion.[11] On their view, the reason that artificially contraceptive acts are immoral lies in a supposed undermining of the basic good of human life and thus committing such an act represents the same disposition in terms of the good it undermines as the act of murder.[12]

Again, the criticisms of NNLT are well known and we need not repeat them in detail here. It has been argued that the theory is problematic in similar ways to the 'Order of Nature' approach we noted above: it relies on a static understanding of practical reason and cannot take into account social or historical consciousness, and thus falls prey to the reductionist critique articulated earlier.[13] Furthermore, NNLT expects far too much specificity for the operations of practical reason alone, a point to which we will return in some detail when we come to consider Porter's understanding of practical reason later in the book. As such, as Porter notes, we need not expect that this 'reason alone' approach will be any more promising than the 'nature alone' approach mentioned earlier.[14]

'Totalization': A Levinasian Critique of the Physicalist Approach and the New Natural Law Theory

What we can add to the criticisms of both approaches, in light of chapter 1, is the Levinasian warning about 'totalization.' As noted, Levinas argues that human personhood is primarily characterized by a dimension of mystery—an infinity—which cannot be encapsulated in any particular philosophical

---

11. Porter suggests that they engage with this type of reasoning in order to avoid the naturalistic fallacy. See *NDL*, 93.

12. In their own words, the motivation underlying the use of artificial contraception "is like that of murderers." Germain Grisez and others, "'Every Marital Act Ought to Be Open to New Life,'" 374. The article itself does not overstate this particular point, but it is clear throughout that the argument against artificial contraception is really an argument against the undermining of the good of human life.

13. These and other critiques are made by a number of authors. For an overview of these, see Pope, *Human Evolution and Christian Ethics*, 51–54; Porter, "Basic Goods"; Salzman, "The Basic Goods Theory and Revisionism"; Salzman and Lawler, "New Natural Law Theory and Foundational Sexual Ethical Principles."

14. *NR*, 131.

system. Philosophy, as a creation of consciousness, cannot ever account for that which is prior to and foundational for consciousness: namely, the relationship with the infinity of the Other. For Levinas, the problem with most philosophy is that it has been too quick to assume that it is capable of providing such an encapsulating overview. Levinas names such an approach 'totalization.' He argues that totalization, rather than being a genuine search for truth in the face of mystery, reveals a need to dominate and control and leads to philosophical systems in which the Other is not identified by her infinity, but according to a prescription applied to her by the 'totalization.' For Levinas, this is a violence which represents the reduction of the human person, and so something which she is not. To avoid such violence, as we noted in chapter 1, we must turn away from prescriptive and deductive philosophies which are closed to infinity and responsibility that is implied therein, and towards approaches which are inherently open to it.

In view of this, I would argue that both the physicalist approach and NNLT fall into the category of 'totalizations.' This critical evaluation has less to do with the norms which these approaches develop, and more to do with the anthropological vision out of which such norms arise. In their suggestions that norms for moral action can be derived purely from the biology of the human person (the physicalist approach) or from the exigencies of reason alone (NNLT), both approaches reveal the kind of reductionist understanding, criticized by Levinas, of what counts as philosophical truth about the human person.

The resulting narrow vision of what counts as good for the human person is held up as a static metaphysical one into which all persons must fit and out of which moral conclusions are deduced and prescribed. As such, both approaches fail to include the elements of responsibility and inductivity which we noted were crucial in view of Levinas's warnings about 'totalization.' This critique is furthered by the arguments advanced against these approaches noted above, which point out their unacknowledged reliance on visions of the human person which ignore her transcendent and dynamic characteristics. From a Levinasian point of view, such approaches are violent, precisely because they do not allow the human person to be as she is.

These and other approaches like them are therefore not appropriate for our task. So, does this mean we should abandon natural law theory altogether? Not necessarily. In fact, I will now suggest that there are three compelling reasons for engaging with a natural law approach, as long as such an approach can avoid the extremes of the approaches we have just been considering.

Three Reasons to Retain a Natural Law Approach

The first of the reasons for engaging with a natural law approach is theological, and is reflected in the Catholic understanding of the goodness of creation and especially the goodness of the human person. From this perspective, something of the will of God can be discerned through reflection on God's good creation, and what is revealed has moral significance. Richard McBrien articulates this point by stating that "the presence and will of God are available in all created realities, because these realities come from the creative hand of God and have been redeemed by the Word-made-flesh."[15] Or, as Porter herself puts it:

> the God who has redeemed us in Jesus Christ is the very same God who created us, and while the fact of redemption transforms our understanding of creation, it cannot wholly obviate the order and intelligibility of created human existence. As Aquinas repeatedly reminds us, grace perfects nature; it does not destroy it.[16]

This argument can be furthered by understanding natural law in terms of Divine Providence and Wisdom, and humanity's call to share in this through the use of intelligence in the search for truth and the exercise of prudence. We thus have a theological reason to expect that a reflection on nature, and more specifically the nature of the human person, will be fruitful for our moral enquiry.

The second point is grounded in the first and incorporates Timothy O'Connell's argument that the process of moral discernment, with which we are now engaged, must draw on the most accurate information available in order to gain authentic moral knowledge.[17] To further this point, if it is true that reflection on human nature provides us with morally significant insights related to the will of God and what is truly good, all disciplines which provide genuine insight into the human person and the complex reality in which she lives will be valuable in our quest for moral insight. An approach which takes nature seriously can thus also take seriously the many insights of modern science, and of philosophical and historical enquiry.[18]

Such a grounding point means that moral theology must be intrinsically open to new insights as they are discovered and, correlatively, must

---

15. McBrien, *Catholicism*, 960.

16. Porter, "Natural Law as Scriptural Concept," 236.

17. O'Connell, *Principles for a Catholic Morality*, 112. Cf. Gula, *Reason Informed By Faith*, 131.

18. Keenan, *A History of Catholic Moral Theology*, 175.

show an awareness of a social, historical and scientific consciousness.[19] This point can also be framed as an important corrective to some of the deficiencies of current trends towards personalist and liberation approaches to moral theology which Stephen Pope has pointed out, and which could also be present if one were to take a 'purely' Levinasian approach. Whilst acknowledging the many valuable insights that these approaches have added to the discipline of moral theology, Pope argues that their focus on the human subject as an interpersonal being (personalist approaches) and an historical/intersubjective being (liberation approaches) has tended to happen at the expense of a focus on human nature more comprehensively considered, and thus leads to neglect of the legitimate contributions to moral reflection that are provided by the natural and human sciences.[20]

The third and final point arises out of the philosophy of Levinas. As we have seen, Levinas helps us to notice our prerational orientation towards the acknowledgment of the moral value of the other person. We have also seen, however, that he was not optimistic about our willingness to acknowledge this fact or take it seriously in the way we think or act, and he sees this as a common problem throughout the history of philosophy. Given that Levinas points us towards an observation about who we are as persons at a level prior to rationality, a natural law approach is valuable in that its starting point will inevitably be what we know about our nature as human persons. Furthermore, if we avoid the extremes of the NNLT theorists who suggest that our prerational nature should not have an influence on moral decision making, then our reflections on what constitutes us as human persons before our ability to rationalize will have an influence on how we develop moral norms and will inevitably influence our practical moral conclusions.

Jean Porter's Theory of the Natural Law as a Way Forward

Jean Porter's theory of natural law moves away from the extremes of both problematic variations on the theory noted above and provides a balance between the need for a moral theory which is grounded in a robust

---

19. This is an important move for any moral theology, and indeed theology in general, if it wishes to be taken seriously in an age in which a supposed correlation between religion and irrationality is becoming widely accepted in popular discussions on the topic. The so-called "new atheist" movement encourages such an understanding, the primary text of which is Richard Dawkins's bestseller *The God Delusion*. For a sustained, critical and convincing response to the new atheist movement's understanding of religion, see Beattie, *The New Atheists*.

20. See Pope, *The Evolution of Altruism*, 19–42. We will return to these critiques in chap. 6.

understanding of the human person and one which is also open to revision in light of new experiences and insights. Hers is a theory which acknowledges the moral significance of prerational nature and yet allows for the creative and dynamic role of human reason in developing concrete moral conclusions. The strength and clarity of Porter's theory in these regards has ensured that it has received widespread praise.[21] Porter's methodology is significant here, inasmuch as it allows her to stretch back into the wisdom of the natural law tradition as developed in the scholastic era and reach forward to the best insights that modern theology, science and philosophy have to offer. As we explore her theory over the next three chapters I will aim to show how she achieves this. At the end of this chapter, we will also begin to see how Porter's theory can take the Levinasian insight seriously and why it is in a position to begin to develop the practical implications of the Levinasian insight, whilst at the same time avoiding 'totalization.'

Before launching into this study I would like to note one significant criticism of Porter's approach to natural law which was not highlighted in any of the reviews consulted. That is, for a body of work which explicitly names itself *A Thomistic Theory of the Natural Law*, Porter's theory is firmly positioned as a philosophical approach which tends to avoid engaging with some of Aquinas' theological commitments in his theory of natural law. Apart from Porter's obvious grounding point in the doctrine of creation which was noted above, she tends not to situate her theory of natural law within the theological framework that Aquinas does.[22] As such, we will see that her theory lacks attention to the theological virtues of faith, hope, and

21. See Fout, "Nature as Reason"; Jeffreys, "Nature as Reason: A Thomistic Theory of the Natural Law"; Magidon, "Nature as Reason: A Thomistic Theory of the Natural Law"; McCormick, "Review of *Nature as Reason: A Thomistic Theory of the Natural Law* by Jean Porter." See also my extended appraisal and commentary on Porter's theory in which I argue that it is a more adequate approach to natural law than the problematic theories noted above, Fleming, "Intelligibility in the Natural Law."

22. This extent of this problem can be noted by observing that, for Aquinas, an analysis of the moral life was contextualized within a consideration of the gift of grace and a consideration of beatitude that begins with the theological virtues and leads to the cardinal virtues. This can be seen in the table of contents of *ST*, II-II. This leads Fergus Kerr to conclude that, rather than a virtue ethics or divine command ethics, Aquinas's ethics is best described as "an ethics of divine beautitude." Kerr, *After Aquinas*, 133. I do not share this concern, at least for the project at hand. As I show below, the relevant sections of Aquinas are congruent with the theory Porter develops and can be included without major adjustment to her theory. This would suggest that it has been a simple matter of leaving them out to focus on the more philosophical and temporal dimensions of Aquinas (for example, the cardinal virtues as distinct from the theological ones) without negating the possibility of the other dimensions being included. My one criticism of Porter in this regard is that she does not name this issue and thereby does not give an explanation of it.

love, that its conception of happiness focuses almost entirely on earthly happiness with no consideration of eschatological happiness, and that it includes a discussion of vice without a consideration of sin. Where appropriate, especially with regards to sin, I have turned to Aquinas and his commentators to fill out this account. However, I do so only where supplementing Porter's theory in this way will benefit the study at hand: this project is not focused on critiquing and correcting Porter's use of Aquinas.

As background to the study of Porter, it is worth considering in some detail one further potential objection to her theory that can be raised even before we engage directly with her. That is, given that Porter grounds a good deal of her argument in observations about prerational nature, to what extent is her theory vulnerable to the naturalistic fallacy?

The Naturalistic Fallacy

As Jan and Birgitta Tullberg note, the naturalistic fallacy still has a high degree of currency in philosophical discourse and yet, as we will see below, it is not immune from significant critical evaluation.[23] In this section, I will give a brief background to the naturalistic fallacy, name its core argument, and then point out three relevant critical appraisals of it. The first of these comes from the discipline of phenomenology and aligns closely with the argument we have been developing in dialogue with Levinas; the second is the response that Porter names in her own work, and the third is a cautionary critique which points out that an acceptance of the naturalistic fallacy opens up the possibility for what Tullberg and Tullberg refer to as the 'ideological fallacy.' Finally, I will turn to what can be understood as the legitimate concern of the naturalistic fallacy and show its relationship with the physicalist approach to natural law noted above, before explaining how Porter's approach avoids this problem.

The Naturalistic Fallacy: Foundations and Importance

It is widely recognized that the philosopher David Hume laid the foundation for the naturalistic fallacy in his *A Treatise on Human Nature*, in which he notes a subtle shift between the language of 'is' and 'ought' in moral discourse and proceeds to question whether the latter can be deduced from

---

23 And nor should it be. As Tullberg and Tullberg argue, "Simply because the current opinion favours the Naturalistic Fallacy Thesis does not make it right, or by default provide it with immunity from deliberation." Tullberg and Tullberg, "A Critique of the Naturalistic Fallacy Thesis," 165.

the former.[24] Whilst Hume was the first to point out this problem, it was the philosopher G.E. Moore who named the naturalistic fallacy and framed it as "the attempt to derive evaluations from natural matters of fact."[25] The argument is that a "deductive argument cannot contain anything in the conclusion that is not implicitly present in the premises" and, therefore, that "moral goodness cannot be defined in terms of non-moral qualities."[26] The implication of this is the well-known description of the naturalistic fallacy, namely, that one cannot derive an 'ought' from an 'is,' and this is commonly understood to mean that a consideration of the facts of nature cannot lead one to any normative moral conclusions.[27] In other words, even when we understand what 'is,' we must rely on another source or insight about value in order to determine what 'ought' to be done.[28]

Porter, and other contemporary writers in the Catholic moral tradition, recognize the importance of considering the naturalistic fallacy, especially as a cautionary tool to remind us not to move too quickly from statements about the way things 'are' to moral conclusions about the way they 'should be,' and this is especially true given our somewhat limited access to the nature of things as they are, the consideration of which we will return to below.[29] However, there are a number of arguments which challenge the naturalistic fallacy, and we will now consider three of them.

Phenomenology and Levinas as Response to the Naturalistic Fallacy

The first can be found in the 'phenomenological argument' which relates closely to the understanding of the human person that we developed in

24. Hume, *A Treatise on Human Nature*, 469. For further discussion, see Anthony J. Lisska's helpful comments on this aspect of Hume's thinking, Lisska, *Aquinas's Theory of Natural Law*, 57.

25. Svend, "Facts, Values, and the Naturalistic Fallacy in Psychology," 2.

26. *NDL*, 106. Cf. *NR*, 123; Salzman and Lawler, *The Sexual Person*, 48. Moore's original argument appears in Moore, *Principa Ethica*, 64. For further discussion of Moore's argument, see Lisska, *Aquinas's Theory of Natural Law*, 58–62.

27. As Todd Salzman articulates it, it is logically invalid to derive an "ought" (a value judgment or obligation) from an "is" (a fact)." Salzman, *Catholic Ethical Method*, 20.

28. Salzman and Lawler, *The Sexual Person*, 48. As Tullberg and Tullberg note, the naturalistic fallacy thesis would argue that "values and value judgments are generated by value premises, and there is no real opening for other influences." Tullberg and Tullberg, "A Critique of the Naturalistic Fallacy Thesis," 166.

29. See for example Pope, *The Evolution of Altruism*, 129; Pope, *Human Evolution and Christian Ethics*, 6; *NR*, 124; Salzman and Lawler, *The Sexual Person*, 48.

chapter 1.[30] As a phenomenological approach, this argument proceeds from the experience of being human which is necessarily related to the experience of perceiving value as something that is real and external to the subjective self. This means that "we experience ourselves being *moved* by values that are there independently of our subjective perspective."[31] This is at the heart of the Levinasian insight into human subjectivity that we have explored in chapter 1. Human consciousness, on Levinas's view, is constituted by its experience of value, especially in the presence of the Other. Recall also that for Andrew Tallon, commentating on Levinas, the core insight of this approach to phenomenology was to acknowledge that we do not experience the world as "flat," understood as value-less, but rather as value-full, and that this is best expressed in terms of 'amplification events' which stimulate the sense of value within us, most dramatically in the presence of the human person. In view of these observations, our experience of being human is such that our engagement with the facts of ourselves and the world around us is constituted in terms of value; "we not only see "what *is*" in our environments, but also often "what *ought* to be.""[32]

On this view, there are at least some facts which are related to value in such a way that the two cannot be separated. For example, I could describe my experience of the presence of another person as a factual account which refers to the measurement of distance between us, the words which are exchanged, and the language in which they are spoken. Nonetheless, to say that these *facts* can be recounted without an awareness of the *value* that is inherent in the encounter would be a mistake according to the view that we developed in chapter 1. Human subjectivity is constituted in such a way that there is an awareness that the fact of the other person's presence carries with it a sense of the value of that presence and the exchange that occurs because of it. Given that the Other *is* there, I am aware that I *ought* to respond.[33] If this is the case, then the is/ought distinction cannot be made as easily as the naturalistic fallacy would suppose. Human experience, and

---

30. In what follows I draw on the basic argument presented in Brinkmann Svend's article and then develop this specifically in terms of Levinas's phenomenology as described in chap. 1. See Svend, "Facts, Values, and the Naturalistic Fallacy in Psychology."

31. Ibid., 5.

32. Ibid., 4. A similar conclusion has been developed in the field of educational theory known as *values education* which has found, as Lovat notes, that "all knowing has an ethical component and is related in some way to human action, whether technical, communicative, or reflective." Lovat, "Synergies and Balance between Values Education and Quality Teaching," 494.

33. Although, it is likely that I will not be aware of exactly what this *ought* implies, which draws into our discussion the difference between facts as morally significant and facts as morally normative. We will return to this point below.

the phenomenological reflection on this, can remind us that there are some facts which carry value with them.

The Value of Facts as a Response to the Naturalistic Fallacy

The second response to the naturalistic fallacy develops a similar point regarding the value of facts but from a different direction. It rests on a presupposition about what counts as valuable in a moral system, and it is well expressed by Porter in the following:

> If we assume, as nearly everyone does, that morality is centrally concerned with human well-being and harm, then facts about human nature are morally relevant because we must take them into account in deciding what counts as either well-being or harm.[34]

From this perspective, facts are relevant precisely because they have an inherent relationship with what is of value for the human person. A simple example can illustrate this relationship. If we build from the presupposition that morality is concerned with human well-being, and we acknowledge the fact that a core condition of human well-being is that a person is fed enough to be able to live and continue living, then we draw an indelible line between value (what is *good* for the person) and a fact (what we can *know* about what is good for the person).[35] Roger Masters is helpful on this point:

> I am, of course, aware of the so-called naturalistic fallacy which has so often been condemned by logicians and methodologists. But when the doctor prescribes a treatment, we don't normally object that this practice bridges the logical distinction between the facts of diagnosis and the value of health.[36]

This response to the naturalistic fallacy argues, therefore, that an awareness of the relationship between human well-being and morality implies that an accurate understanding of what counts as human well-being

---

34. *NDL*, 107.

35. This aligns with what Svend terms the "functional" response to the naturalistic fallacy that follows Aristotle's argument that something of what a thing *ought* to be is presented in what it *is*. The Thomistic version of the argument, as developed by Porter, is considered in detail below as part of the overall argument of the book, and so will not be included here. Svend's description can be found in "Facts, Values and the Naturalistic Fallacy in Psychology," 5.

36. Masters, *The Nature of Politics*, xv. Quoted in Tullberg and Tullberg, "A Critique of the Naturalistic Fallacy Thesis," 170–71.

(and, correlatively, what counts as harm), which can be provided by empirical research into the facts of human nature, is morally significant.[37] Such a view suggests that the naturalistic fallacy is incorrect in its presupposition that there is an inherent, and impassable, divide that exists between what 'is' and what 'ought to be' precisely because what ought to be, when it is concerned with what is good for the human person, is accountable to what we can know about reality.[38]

The Problem of the Ideological Fallacy as a Challenge to the Naturalistic Fallacy

This last point regarding accountability is crucial, according to Tullberg and Tullberg, because it can reduce the instances of what they refer to as the 'ideological fallacy':

> A preoccupation with the naturalistic fallacy makes us vulnerable to the real fallacy—the ideological fallacy: to think that something exists because it is wished. When the "ought" is disconnected from the profane "is," the road is opened for illusions of positive thinking.[39]

Pope finds evidence for such a position in the work of the New Natural Law theorists who, in their staunch attempts to avoid the naturalistic fallacy, fail to show that their assertions are accountable to what we know about reality. Pope uses a specific example from John Finnis to illustrate the problem. In his book, *Aquinas: Moral, Political and Legal Theory*, Finnis argues that all same-sex relations fail to embody any intelligible goods in themselves, but offer only "bodily and emotional satisfaction, pleasurable experience, unhinged from basic human reasons for action and posing as its own rationale."[40] However, Pope points out that Finnis makes this claim without any recourse to evidence whatsoever.[41] This is reflective, Pope ar-

---

37. Cf. Pope, *The Evolution of Altruism*, 129; Pope, *Human Evolution and Christian Ethics*, 6.

38. As we have also seen, and will explore further below, Porter argues that there are explicitly *theological* reasons for understanding facts about nature as valuable in terms of their relevance for a concept of human flourishing.

39. Tullberg and Tullberg, "A Critique of the Naturalistic Fallacy Thesis," 173.

40. Finnis, *Aquinas: Moral, Political and Legal Theory*, 153, 151. Quoted in Pope, *Human Evolution and Christian Ethics*, 54.

41. This point raises the question of what kind of evidence would act as a corrective to this issue, which Pope himself does not comment on, although assumedly, given the context of the remark in his book *Human Evolution and Christian Ethics*,

gues, of the broader NNLT approach which attempts "to interpret natural law without giving any account of human nature itself."[42] As such, it is possible for the NNLT theorists to read into the operations of practical reason conclusions which—coincidentally or not—tend to align with the specific moral conclusions found in the *Catechism of the Catholic Church*.[43] The philosophical problem here is less with their specific conclusions, and more with the weakness of the methodology by which they are reached. As we have noted above, accountability to reality is necessary for moral discourse and it is here that NNLT provides an example of the problem of the ideological fallacy.

Concluding Remarks on the Naturalistic Fallacy and the Role of Nature in Porter's Theory

In view of the arguments developed above, we can acknowledge that there are some significant problems with the naturalistic fallacy, and state with confidence that it is both philosophically sound and desirable to acknowledge value in facts, and therefore to engage with a serious consideration of prerational human nature and the implications of this for our moral discourse. Nature is, in other words, morally significant. Such a consideration need not imply, however, that we can proceed directly from an acknowledgment of particular facts to highly specific moral norms in the way that the physicalist approach to natural law critiqued earlier does. This highlights an important issue regarding the extent to which a consideration of facts relates to moral normativity. Porter's approach to this issue will become clear over this and the next chapter. At this point, it is worth noting a number of features of this understanding for the sake of clarifying the discussion that will ensue below.

At the outset, we should restate that Porter sees a consideration of what we know about nature as integral to the task of moral reflection. In

---

he is referring to some form of scientific enquiry into human experience. Lawler and Salzman have analyzed some possibilities for such an enquiry into human experience and how it links with moral theology, with a special focus on the discipline of sociology. See Lawler and Salzman, "Human Experience and Catholic Moral Theology," especially 48–52. A further example of a hermeneutic of experience (specifically, suffering) in moral theology can be found in Gascoigne, "Suffering and Theological Ethics: Intimidation and Hope."

42. Pope, *Human Evolution and Christian Ethics*, 54.

43. Ibid., 53. We return to this critique in chap. 5 and explain it in more detail. At this point it is used for illustrative purposes only.

her own words, "nature is freighted with moral significance."[44] As we have seen above, such a consideration of the moral significance of nature can be desirable, and need not be condemned as falling prey to the naturalistic fallacy. There is still a risk, however, that we can proceed too quickly from facts about nature to normative judgments, the problems of which have been noted in regards to physicalism above.

As we will see, Porter's theory responds to this potential problem in two ways. First, whilst demonstrating the moral significance of nature, she also acknowledges the interpretive and historical limitations that are inherent in any study of nature and thus the care that needs to be taken in assessing what exactly the moral significance of nature might mean when it comes to considering what ought to be done, a point to which we will return below. Second, in what follows we will see that for Porter a consideration of nature of itself cannot lead to specific, and morally normative, conclusions about human action. This is because a consideration of nature reveals a multitude of ways in which human persons can act 'according to their nature,' but does not provide a simple or obvious way of evaluating these according to which are the most adequate or fully human. Hence, whilst a consideration of nature is morally significant, it is not immediately prescriptive in the sense of providing a clear, normative account of human morality.[45] In view of what has been developed here, we can turn now to a more specific focus on Porter's theory.

---

44. *NR*, 53.

45. A further observation can be made here and, while it is not central to the book's argument, may provide further clarification on this issue and the language of moral significance. That is, in Porter's observations about the moral significance of nature, she is building from an argument about the ontological goodness of creation. In this way, nature has the same moral significance as does the ontic or premoral good explored in the work of Louis Janssens. This term applies to those goods that are prior to an agent's free choice (for example, the nature of her human personhood and her historical context) but that are necessarily related to the way in which the agent acts given that they provide the condition of possibility (and perhaps limitation) for this action, a point to which we will return in chap. 4. As such, Janssens would argue that they cannot be called "moral" in the sense that the agent is responsible for them as the result of a free decision, but that a consideration of them is nevertheless important for understanding the condition of possibility for moral action, which makes them significant for moral reflection. For Janssens, the same would apply to what he terms ontic or premoral evil. Janssens's own exploration of these points can be found in Louis Janssens, "Ontic Good and Evil: Premoral Values and Disvalues." In this description I have also drawn from Christie, *Adequately Considered*, 67–69.

NATURE IN THE NATURAL LAW

Why Nature is Morally Significant

Porter's theory, then, grounds itself in a consideration of the moral significance of prerational nature and, in so doing, aligns with the three reasons for engaging with a natural law approach we have noted above. Now that we are engaging with her theory on its own terms, it will be helpful to develop her specific argument in more detail, and her response to the question of why nature is morally significant:

> In its primary sense, the natural law is identified with reason, which after all is the defining mark of human nature. But this way of construing the natural law does not imply that other aspects of human nature, including its prerational components, are empty of moral significance. On the contrary, "nature as nature" is freighted with independent moral significance, even though that significance must be discerned through rational reflection. Hence, the natural law reflects both the distinctiveness of the human creature and our more basic continuity with the rest of God's creation: distinctiveness, because only a rational creature can be said properly speaking to follow a law; continuity, because our participation in the natural law is one expression of the universal activity of God's provident wisdom, in which all things are created and through which all things are governed.[46]

Porter acknowledges that her focus on prerational nature will run up against resistance from many contemporary moral theologians who have distanced themselves from such appeals on the grounds noted above.[47] She also points out, however, that it is difficult to maintain such an aversion to considerations of prerational nature if only because of its association with problematic approaches in the past, and that this is especially so now that there has been a revival of interest in the significance of prerational nature

---

46. *NR*, 53. Porter finds support for this claim in the writings of Aquinas, for whom reason is the natural operation appropriate to the human person: "[A]ll those things to which the human person is inclined in accordance with his nature pertain to the law of nature. For everything whatever is naturally inclined to an operation appropriate to itself in accordance with its form; for example, fire is inclined to heat. Hence since the rational soul is the proper form of the human person, there is a natural inclination in each person to act in accordance with reason." *ST* I-II 94.3. Quoted in *NR*, 53.

47. *NR*, 54. As noted above, this has contributed to the reticence toward an engagement with the natural sciences among some prevalent approaches to moral theology. Stephen Pope provides a helpful overview of these approaches and some of the deficiencies that result from a lack of due attention to prerational nature, see Pope, *Human Evolution and Christian Ethics*, 32–55.

for moral discourse, albeit a more comprehensive understanding of what it means to talk about prerational nature, amongst moral theologians and philosophers. Further to the reasons stated in the previous section, this has also arisen out of a heightened awareness of the degree of continuity that exists between the human person and the rest of the created world: it is difficult to maintain a position which suggests that reason operates in complete isolation from the natural world which necessarily underlies its operational capacities, even if this does force us to acknowledge some of the limitations of our capacities for knowledge and autonomy.[48] What follows from this observation is that an understanding of the natural world can give us insight into ourselves. However, we must seek such an understanding under the awareness that it will come with its limitations and we need to ask the following questions: to what extent can we come to know the natural world out of which our rational abilities arise?[49] How much accurate and objective knowledge can we claim to have about nature in and of itself?

Approaching Nature with Alister McGrath

The questions raised above are of key importance for this work, given that we have started from Levinas's phenomenological viewpoint which argues that our use of reason is constituted by our orientation towards the Other, and that this will inevitably have an influence on the way in which we come to know the world around us. To add to Levinas's insight, we could also look to Heidegger's argument that the human person perceives the outside world in terms of its usefulness and that this necessarily reflects *how* the world is perceived. Porter adds to these concerns the question of the social construction of reality which challenges us to acknowledge the extent to which our understanding of 'nature' is a socially mediated understanding. She turns to the British theologian, Alister McGrath, who highlights this issue in his book *A Scientific Theology—Volume 1: Nature*.

McGrath frames his discussion of the issue by turning to the philosopher of science N. R. Hanson, who argued that any form of observation from a human standpoint is far from a neutral access to *a priori* facts.[50] Rather, all observation is "assumption-laden" observation.[51] For McGrath,

---

48. Denis Edwards explains these points and their implications for contemporary theology in a particularly inviting and helpful way. See Edwards, *Ecology at the Heart of Faith*.

49. As we saw in the last chapter, this question was one of Heidegger's concerns.

50. See Hanson, *Patterns of Discovery*.

51. McGrath, *A Scientific Theology*, 112. While aligning my focus here with the

this means that there is no neutral way of seeing the world. All attempts at observation are necessarily influenced by a complex pattern of cognition that is grounded in a system of thought that has inevitably been shaped by the society in which it operates.[52] In an attempt to illustrate this point, McGrath contrasts William Paley and Charles Darwin who each observed the same natural phenomena, but understood these in different ways, Paley attributing their cause to special creation, and Darwin to natural selection.[53] This leads McGrath to state the following:

> 'Nature' is thus not a neutral entity, having the status of an 'observation statement'; it involves seeing the world in a particular way—and the way in which it is seen shapes the resulting concept of 'nature.' Far from being a 'given,' the idea of 'nature' is shaped by the prior assumptions of the observer. One does not 'observe' nature; one constructs it. And once the importance of socially mediated ideas, theories and values is conceded, it is impossible to avoid the conclusion that the concept of nature is, at least in part, a social construction. If the concept of nature is socially mediated—to whatever extent—it cannot serve as an allegedly neutral, objective or uninterpreted foundation of a theory or theology. *Nature is already an interpreted category.*[54]

And, later on, he further specifies this observation:

> In pointing out that 'nature' is a socially mediated concept, we are noting that nature is necessarily viewed through a prism of beliefs and values, reflecting the historical and social location of the observer, which inevitably skews the resulting notion.[55]

If we follow Porter's lead and take McGrath's observations seriously, the question we must now ask is, how much does our 'prism of beliefs and values' skew our concept of nature? Ultimately, Porter agrees with McGrath's response to this question, which is that we must accept that our concept will be at least partially shaped by cultural and social forces.[56]

---

points Porter highlights in *Nature as Reason*, I have engaged with McGrath's original text in order to broaden the discussion of this issue and show how McGrath develops his argument.

52. To use McGrath's own metaphor for this phenomenon, we all "have spectacles behind our eyes." McGrath, *A Scientific Theology*, 112.

53. Ibid., 113.

54. Ibid., 113; emphasis in original. Also quoted in *NR*, 58.

55. McGrath, *A Scientific Theology*, 132.

56. Ibid., 133. In Porter's own words, "We cannot derive clear and uncontroversial starting points for theological speculation, much less a whole ontology, from our

However, the operative word in McGrath's and Porter's final assessments is that our concept of nature will be *partially*, not *totally*, shaped by cultural and social forces. After all, there would be no such thing as truly scientific knowledge if the process of scientific enquiry simply led to socially or culturally determined conclusions. For Porter, this is a very serious point, because she argues that even the theological starting point which understands nature as God's good creation must be accountable to the best and most accurate accounts of the natural world that are available.[57] So the question remains—to what extent will our understanding of nature be influenced by our starting point?

The Postmodern Challenge for Approaching Nature

Porter's answer to this question draws her into a brief analysis of the contrast between modern and postmodern perspectives on the question of knowledge, and the reader will have already noticed that these lie at the root of the issue that we have been discussing. Indeed, as we will soon see, the perspective McGrath takes is saturated with the clear influence of postmodernism. Very briefly, the modern perspective tended towards a philosophical position which argued that we could use reason to know the foundations of our knowledge with a high, if not complete, degree of certainty. Porter follows Alasdair MacIntyre in locating this movement within the broad socio-historical context of the Enlightenment project.[58] This work was largely carried out by philosophers and scientists who "attempted to establish perspicuous and universally accessible foundations for their claims, in the form of logical or mathematical principles, clear and certain ideas, empirical observations,

---

observation of the natural world. Our ideas about nature stem out of social processes of inquiry and reflection." *NR*, 59.

57. *NR*, 59. Stephen Pope shares Porter's concern about moral theology's accountability to the legitimate insights of modern science, and also argues that science "can make an important constructive contribution to Christian ethics, particularly with regard to our thinking about the natural law and the virtues. Science can help us understand the biological factors that allow for the human capacities that provide the basis for morality and religion." Further on he notes that "Christian ethics, especially as developed in the natural law tradition engaged here, gives moral significance to the central constituents of human nature, so it must take seriously the massive body of literature and significant discoveries about where we come from, who we are, and what we need and desire as human beings." See Pope, *Human Evolution and Christian Ethics*, 3–5, see also 35. I will develop many of the points Pope makes here as we engage with Porter's theory below. Given the nature of Pope's work, I will also note congruencies and differences between his and Porter's approaches throughout.

58. *NR*, 62.

or some combination of these."⁵⁹ Porter refers to this general movement as foundationalism, and I follow her usage of the term below.⁶⁰

As Porter notes, foundationalism eventually "began to break down in the twentieth century under the cumulative weight of philosophical, cultural, and literary attacks on its central presuppositions."⁶¹ This led to the movement we now know as postmodernism, which has widely discredited the foundationalist project and has tended towards an acknowledgment of the grounding of knowledge in context, the essence of which is captured in Jacques Derrida's famous argument that "no meaning can be determined out of context, but no context permits saturation."⁶² As such, the project of foundationalism is called into question, which forces us to ask again whether we can have any robust and reliable access to the nature of things, and whether it is ever possible to draw conclusions which are in any way thought of as universal. In response to this tension, Porter seeks to find a convincing middle ground. Whilst she argues that postmodernism was correct in drawing into question the form of foundationalism described above, an acceptance of the thrust of the critique, such as the one exemplified by McGrath above, does not necessarily lead to the epistemological relativism which is sometimes associated with it.⁶³

A Response to the Challenge: Alasdair MacIntyre

Porter finds her middle ground in Alasdair MacIntyre's theory of knowledge as 'tradition constituted and tradition constitutive enquiry.'⁶⁴ Ma-

---

59. Ibid.

60. The use of this term follows Porter's own. As she notes, the ideal of the Enlightenment project "is frequently described as foundationalism, and while this term can be misleading, taken as a shorthand way of expressing what early modern philosophers were after, it does no harm." Ibid. This description of foundationalism should be distinguished from a "weaker" form which would argue that "thought is impossible without some starting points which stand in need of no justification," a position Porter sees as reflected in the scholastic methodology and in the work of Alasdair MacIntyre, more on which below. Paul Moser refers to this weaker form of foundationalism as "modest foundationalism" and, like Porter, contrasts it with radical foundationalism of the kind that we have noted above. See Moser, "Foundationalism," 840.

61. *NR*, 63.

62. Derrida, "Living On," 81. We can also notice echoes of Levinas's critique of absolutization of ontology in the postmodernist concern. Cf. McGrath's acknowledgment of the influence social and historical context has on our understanding of nature above.

63. *NR*, 63. Porter's discussion of the points made above occurs between pages 61 and 63.

64. MacIntyre, *Whose Justice? Which Rationality*, 389. In what follows I draw

cIntyre developed this approach as a response to the risk of epistemological relativism that is inherent in the postmodern criticism of foundationalism and a corresponding desire to avoid finding an answer to this problem by returning to foundationalism itself.[65] Two important factors underlie MacIntyre's response: first, he does not expect to find a completely neutral and objective standpoint from which to engage in the search for knowledge; and second, he does not expect to arrive at an all-embracing truth which could be posited as an absolute.[66] Nonetheless, he does believe that we can come to accurate knowledge even in light of his more realistic expectations, and we do this through our participation in traditions.

Traditions, for MacIntyre, arise out of communities, and are understood to begin with the articulation of beliefs and practices by persons of authority or in authoritative texts. Such articulations lead to the development of a procedure for enquiry, whereby the world is understood through the prism of beliefs and values of the tradition in question and this thereby becomes a mode of rationality.[67] Inevitably, the community will at some point encounter the limitations of their own mode of rationality when their prism is unable to deal with what the community encounters.[68]

Such a situation leads to an epistemological crisis wherein the community realizes that its tradition and mode of rationality is incapable of dealing with the problems or new insights that are being faced and, as a consequence, new beliefs and systems must be developed through the process of 'imaginative conceptual innovation.' This process involves the creation of new and more adequate modes of rationality that can then be compared to the older, less adequate ones, all with a view to explaining reality in ever more comprehensive and accurate ways.[69] Traditions are therefore self, and communally, correcting and, according to MacIntyre, over time this process leads to genuine knowledge about reality.[70]

---

extensively on Ian Markham's excellent summary of this part of MacIntyre's theory as well as Porter's interpretation. The footnotes below indicate where the relevant points appear in each author's commentaries, as well as in MacIntyre's original text where appropriate.

65. Markham, "Faith and Reason," 259.
66. Ibid., 260.
67. Ibid.
68. Ibid. See MacIntyre, *Whose Justice? Which Rationality*, 355.
69. Markham, "Faith and Reason," 260. See MacIntyre, *Whose Justice? Which Rationality*, 362.
70. See Porter's discussion of this point in *NR*, 63.

A Response to the Challenge: Emmanuel Levinas

A further response to the challenge of finding a middle way between foundationalism and epistemological relativism, complementary and yet distinct from MacIntyre, can be found by looking to Levinas's nuanced understanding of the *Saying* and the *Said* in *Otherwise than Being*.[71] In his distinguishing between the Saying and the Said, I would argue that Levinas seeks to cross the same divide that MacIntyre deals with above. That is, how can one acknowledge the limitations of our understanding of something (in this case, nature) and yet still claim to have some legitimate access to it?

In the Saying and the Said, Levinas provides a methodology that can respond to the tension between foundationalism and epistemological relativism. As we have seen, he understands the *Saying* as the primary communicative dimension of meaning in which one is addressed by the infinity of the Other which cannot be encapsulated in any form of philosophical theory. This communicative dimension of meaning is distinct from what is *Said* about it: the response of consciousness which attempts to make meaning out of the Saying and, in a formal sense, does this through the means of particular philosophical theories. On their own, the Saying and the Said can be linked with the concerns of epistemological relativism and foundationalism (respectively). The Saying can be linked with the concerns of epistemological relativism because it highlights the limitations of philosophical theories and language as containers for meaning, and the ongoing need for the philosophical skepticism which breaks them open. The Said can be linked with the concerns of foundationalism because it acknowledges the need for philosophical articulation. The unique insight of Levinas here is that the Saying and the Said cannot be separated: the Saying is oriented towards the Said and, given that the Said cannot encapsulate the fullness of the reality of the Saying, it is consistently undone, revised and re-written (so to speak) in view of the Saying. This, for Levinas, revealed the importance of philosophical skepticism, whilst at the same time acknowledging the necessary and legitimate role of the philosophical theories which skepticism seeks to question.

From a methodological perspective, the dynamic tension that exists between the Saying as something which we do not have a pure philosophical access to and the Said as that which we articulate in response to this (even with the knowledge that it is tentative and may be undone) can become a paradigm for our approach to knowledge, in a similar way to MacIntyre's approach above. On this view, there is an awareness of the limitations of

---

71. In the following I build on what was developed in chap. 1.

any particular epistemology (the Said) and an openness to the ongoing revision, or breaking open of this, in light of new insights and experience (the Saying), a position which effectively finds a middle ground between foundationalism and epistemological relativism. To strengthen this approach further, we could add to Levinas's understanding an insight from MacIntyre's approach about the ongoing development of tradition which would suggest that, in the breaking open and revising of the Said, it is consistently more adequate, whilst never able to 'totalize' the mystery of the Saying which it seeks to express.

The Possibility of a Robust Realism and Porter's Response to the Challenge

Whichever of these perspectives that we take, they lead us to conclude that we *can* come to a robust realism—an accurate knowledge which, without claiming that it is all-encompassing, does provide us with some genuine insight, in this case, into the natural world.[72] However, Porter wants to acknowledge a further question which relates to what stake the theologian has in defending such an approach. As we will see, the answer she develops in dialogue with the scholastics corresponds to some of what we noted earlier about the theological reasons for utilizing a natural law approach.

For Porter, the reason for grounding a theory of natural law in a robust and realistic knowledge of nature lies in the doctrine of Creation, especially as it was understood by the scholastic lawyers and theologians of the later Middle Ages. As she notes, these scholastics affirmed and developed their understanding of the doctrine of creation in response to the Cathar movement.[73] Against the Cathars, who believed that the world was "more or less corrupt, imperfect or downright evil" and therefore not the creation of a good God, the scholastics affirmed the goodness of creation and "the unity and supremacy of God as Creator, the goodness of the visible and material world, and the unity of Scripture as God's self-revelation."[74] As an immediate response, this was directed against the tendency for the Cathars to reject the material world and to dismiss significant portions of Scripture (including

---

72. Note carefully that I follow Porter's understanding of the word *realism* here. In Porter's own words, an approach such as MacIntyre's (and I would add Levinas') "offers an example of a philosopher who rejects Enlightenment foundationalism, while at the same time affirming a robust form of realism according to which we are able to attain genuine knowledge and to express that knowledge in true and (I would add) meaningful speech." *NR*, 64; parenthesis in original.

73. Ibid., 65.

74. Ibid., 65–66.

the Old Testament and some parts of the New Testament).[75] Furthermore, it had significance above and beyond this for two major reasons. First, Porter argues that the scholastics employed their concept of natural law to argue that Creation, and especially the nature of the human person, was fundamentally good.[76] Second, she argues that their methodology in engaging with natural law has profound implications for our understanding of God's revelation "and by implication, God's creative, providential, and redemptive activity."[77] From this perspective, genuine insight into nature yields correlatively genuine insight into the goodness of God's creation *and* into God's will.[78] We now turn, therefore, to Porter's understanding of *nature*.

INTELLIGIBILITY: PORTER'S UNDERSTANDING OF NATURE

Nature as Creaturely Intelligibility

For Porter, who here follows the later scholastics such as Albert and Aquinas, 'nature' is understood "primarily in terms of the natures of specific kinds of creatures, regarded as the intelligible principles of their existence and their causal powers."[79] What underlies this perspective is the idea that this nature is intelligible and can therefore be understood according to its own internal principles of operation.[80] The scholastics (and Porter following them) see God's creative abilities as expressed in the inherent wisdom of the created order, rather than as miraculous intervention.[81] Porter also places considerable weight on the continuities between other creatures and the human person without losing sight of our distinctive capacity for reason:

> Every creature manifests certain orderly patterns of action, simply as such—to be, to maintain its existence—and in addition, every living creature manifests further, more complex patterns,

---

75. Ibid., 65. Porter explores these points in more detail in *NDL*, 52, 74–80.

76. *NR*, 66.

77. Ibid., 66–67 Cf. the argument that was formulated in above as to why a natural law approach is appropriate for the task at hand.

78. This point should be nuanced with the observations we made earlier regarding the legitimate caution of the naturalistic fallacy thesis.

79. Ibid., 69.

80. Ibid.

81. This is not to say that the scholastics, or Porter, see no role for special intervention. Rather, they could be described as cautious in using miraculous intervention as an explanation for natural phenomena too readily. See ibid.

for example, orderly growth and reproduction. Because we are both creatures and animals, we too manifest these orderly patterns of action. In this way, the intelligible structures of natural processes provide the basis for the properly rational activities of the human creature—and these rational activities, in turn, are given coherence and direction by the natural processes out of which they stem. "Nature is reason" in the sense that reason is itself a natural capacity, and in its functioning it is informed or mirrored by the intelligible order manifest in our own humanity, and in the world within which our lives are embedded.[82]

What we can notice here is that Porter understands reason as framed by the intelligibility of nature itself.[83] Whilst reason is understood as a natural human capacity, it cannot be separated from the intelligibilities that underlie it on a prerational level.[84] More specifically, since intelligibility implies purposiveness and this purposiveness is understood according to the nature of a given creature as a whole, prerational nature for the human creature provides starting points and aims for the operations of reason.[85] In this sense, reason is always underdetermined, or directed, by the prerational nature which underlies it and, since this prerational nature is also intelligible, reason draws on it and completes it in what Porter calls a "distinctively human fashion."[86]

Methodological Implications

This last point, and Porter's language regarding reason's operation in a "distinctively human fashion," needs to be underscored. This is because of the tendency we noted earlier in some recent natural law theories which tend to approach the human person in a physicalist way that ignores the complexities that arise when we operate out of a more comprehensive understanding

---

82. Ibid., 71. By way of pointing forward to a discussion that will take place later in the book, in Thomistic language what Porter is referring to here are the natural, sensing, and rational *appetites*. We need only name these now, and will return to a closer consideration of the appetites in chap. 3.

83. Ibid.

84. There is a point of congruency here between Porter's approach and Rahner's understanding of the human person's prerational nature as "constitutive" of what it means to be human. See Rahner, "Natural Science and Reasonable Faith," 29. Quoted in Pope, *Human Evolution and Christian Ethics*, 35.

85. NR, 72.

86. Ibid., 72. We will return to this point and develop it in detail in chap. 5.

of the human person. From Porter's perspective, such a view is unsustainable and unconvincing because:

> even our most basic inclinations are inextricably bound up with the exigencies of our life as rational and social creatures, and we cannot adequately interpret them unless we see them within the context of human life considered as a whole.[87]

For example, if we consider the human person's natural inclination towards reproduction, this means that Porter's approach does not begin with an understanding of the reproductive act, or the supposed purpose of a particular organ, and proceed from this point to a norm about sexual relations. Rather, she begins with an understanding of the place that sexual relations have in the context of a human life considered as a whole and then seeks to develop moral conclusions from this point.[88] As such, the approach is teleological, because it relies on an account of "what human life considered as a whole should look like and what purposes the different inclinations and functions of human life serve within that context."[89]

We should also avoid the temptation to assume that Porter wants to impose such an account on the human person. Indeed, such an approach would make her theory a "totalization," and thus incompatible with the philosophy of Levinas. Rather, instead of imposing a view of the human person on any given interpretation of her natural inclinations and their appropriate expression, Porter seeks to create dialogue between different sources of truth which provides an interplay between observations of natural inclinations, understandings of human life as a whole, more speculative philosophical and theological considerations as well as reflection on human experience.[90] As Porter notes, this follows the example of the scholastics who built up their concept of natural law:

> through an ongoing process of reflection; basic human inclinations, needs, and desires, were placed within wider contexts set by theological and philosophical considerations, while at the same time they also provided an experiential foundation for developing and modifying those considerations.[91]

---

87. Ibid., 75.
88. Ibid., 77.
89. Ibid.
90. Ibid., 78–79.

91. Ibid. This corresponds to MacIntyre's "tradition constituted and tradition constitutive enquiry" and the argument developed above regarding the Levinasian dynamic between the Saying and the Said.

The resulting theoretical account of what it means to be human is thus open to change in light of new insights, which provides a condition of possibility for integrating the insights of Levinas into her theory of natural law, a point to which we will return later on.

NATURAL INTELLIGIBILITY AND TELEOLOGY IN PORTER'S THEORY

Can Teleology be Convincing Today?

In view of the scholastic understanding of nature as an expression of God's creative wisdom, especially in terms of the intelligible natures of specific creatures, one can see the theological argument behind the teleological approach which Porter takes. To summarize this perspective, Porter quotes the following from Aquinas:

> God is said to direct the creature towards its end, by bestowing on it a particular nature with distinctive causal principles, in virtue of which it will naturally act in such a way as to attain its end—which is nothing other than the perfect realization of its form, that is to say, the fullest possible expression of the distinctive kind of creature that it is.[92]

Given the methodology Porter is developing, which requires that sources of insight into reality are mutually co-correcting, her argument must engage not only with theology but with the natural sciences as well. The question she must face, therefore, is: to what extent does a teleological approach align with what we can know about nature today?

For some natural scientists, such an alignment is untenable. For example, an understanding of the theory of evolution which suggests that a species as a category of creatures has no real existence apart from being a tool for identifying the creatures from which they evolved would rule out an appeal to teleology. This is because, on this view, the category of species is a classification which *we* give to random groupings of creatures that cannot accurately be grouped in this way from the perspective of nature alone.[93] Porter points out, however, that this is not the only understanding

---

92. *ST*, I-II 93.5 Quoted in *NR*, 88. On Porter's use of the language of "perfection," see chap. 3.

93. *NR*, 89. Porter points out that Richard Dawkins argues for this perspective, see Dawkins, "Accumulating Small Change." See also Dawkins, *The Ancestor's Tale*, esp. 1–12.

of 'species' acceptable from a scientific point of view.[94] Indeed, it is possible to argue that the uniqueness of the creatures that we group into the category of 'species' and the corresponding intelligibilities proper to each species, are justification for their categorization in the first place.[95] For example, the categorization of birds as a species of winged vertebrates allows us to acknowledge the particular modes of operation that are intelligible for a bird and not, for example, a fish. We can also acknowledge that the well-being of a bird will be inextricably tied up with the kind of creature it is and so, to continue with our example, confidently state that it is natural and therefore helpful for the well-being of a bird to live, develop and reproduce above water and not below. For these reasons, Porter is committed to holding "some account of development according to which the ways creatures engage their environment, and the lines of development they exhibit, are integrally connected to the kinds of creatures they are."[96]

For Porter, this is best expressed by an Aristotelian understanding of the formal cause. This concept provides a way in which to understand the different components of living creatures as intelligible in their relationship to a species specific pattern of functions and activities. All of these components are oriented towards the more general teleological aims which are common to all creatures, such as survival and reproduction.[97] If this is the case, it means the following:

> The proper form of a given kind of living creature can only be adequately understood by reference to some idea of a paradigmatic instance of the form, that is to say, a healthy and mature individual of the kind in question. It is only by reference to this paradigm that we are able to identify immature, sick, or defective individuals of this kind as such[98]

As Porter points out, it is common for us to make such distinctions. We can distinguish "a scrawny puppy from a robust puppy, a sick horse from a healthy horse," and so on.[99] Such distinctions rely on a teleological concept of what it means to live well, or to flourish, as a particular creature, and we need not doubt that such concepts are accurate reflections of reality, notwithstanding a willingness to improve them if better information comes along.

94. *NR*, 89.
95. Ibid., 93–94.
96. Ibid., 96.
97. Ibid., 100–101.
98. Ibid., 101.
99. Ibid., 102.

Teleology and Creaturely Flourishing

The argument developed above leads Porter to state a presupposition which will underlie the rest of her theory of the natural law. That is, she will argue that we can develop a similar concept of what it means to flourish as a human person and, correlatively, what it would mean to live in a way which provides the conditions within which such flourishing can occur.[100] Porter acknowledges that such a concept will inevitably be more complex, given that human persons are relatively non-specialized and are highly adaptive, which is evidenced in the variety of forms that human life can take in which flourishing can occur.[101] However, she also notes that these forms are not without their limits, and that there are some forms of life which constrain rather than promote human flourishing.[102] What is perhaps more important for Porter, though, is that "there are recurring components of human existence which will form the basis for happiness and well-being for almost all persons."[103] With this in mind, we will now consider Porter's concept of human nature and we will begin to see how the Levinasian insight can be integrated into her theory.

HUMAN NATURE, TELEOLOGY, AND FLOURISHING IN PORTER'S THEORY

Preliminary Cautions and Considerations

To what extent can we claim to be able to develop a convincing and robust concept of human nature? In answering this question, we find ourselves confronted with the same problems that we noted earlier regarding our access to knowledge about reality, which are compounded by Levinas's strong warnings against 'totalization.'[104] Porter shows an awareness of this concern and seeks to provide a methodology for developing a concept of human nature which, whilst robust, is consistently open to revision in light of ever greater insight and can honor the uniqueness of the human person whilst preserving aspects of stability and continuity.[105] As we have seen a number

---

100. Ibid.

101. Ibid., 103. Cf. Gascoigne, *Freedom and Purpose*, 58.

102. *NR*, 103.

103. Ibid. See also Pope, *Human Evolution and Christian Ethics*, 129–57, esp. 129. We will return to consider the concept of happiness in detail in chap. 3.

104. See chap. 1.

105. In this, she follows a more general understanding of natural teleology which she develops in *NR*, 89–103.

of times now, her methodology provides her with the tools with which she can honor such concerns.[106] Nevertheless, whilst aware of the danger of reductionism in developing an understanding of the human person, Porter asserts that

> it is difficult to make a plausible case that there is no sense in which we can be said to share in a common nature, or that this nature cannot in any way be understood in terms of its continuities with the natural world more generally understood. We know a great deal about what we might call the natural history of the human animal, the environmental conditions it needs to live and flourish, and its characteristic patterns of behaviour and way of life.[107]

What is more, she argues that such information needs to be organized into a coherent concept which gives insight into the kind of creatures we are, with some reference to an account of what it means to be a mature, fully developed, and flourishing human person.[108] Porter notes that such an approach can lead to some concerns regarding whether or not the more vulnerable members of the human community—the handicapped, the very young, or the very old, for example—possess these characteristics and hence whether or not they would still count as human persons.[109] Whilst acknowledging the concern, Porter argues that developing a concept of the paradigm for a flourishing human person does not in any way mean that handicapped, immature or senile persons should not be included in the category of human persons itself, any more than "an immature chick or a sick hen is not a bird."[110] She thus regards it as a fundamental error to move from the development of a general paradigm of what it means to flourish as a human person to the conclusion that the paradigm itself should be used as

---

106. See *NR*, 104. This point should be underlined. Porter seeks to provide the methodology for developing such a concept and begins to develop it in a number of areas. She does not, however, claim that this task is done in its entirety in *Nature as Reason*.

107. Ibid., 107. This should be understood in terms of MacIntyre's understanding of "tradition constituted and tradition constitutive enquiry," see above.

108. Ibid.

109. Ibid. For further discussion of the meaning and criteria for counting as a human person, see Rudman, *Concepts of Person and Christian Ethics*, 26–40. Rudman's discussion of Peter Singer and Michael Tooley's moral philosophies is a case in point regarding the dangers of limiting concepts of person. See Rudman, *Concepts of Person*, 42–59.

110. *NR*, 108. Pope makes a similar point in regards to developing an account of human flourishing, cf. Pope, *Human Evolution and Christian Ethics*, 147–48.

a tool to determine who should be included within the category of human person.[111] Nor would Porter see such a paradigm as achieving the kind of specificity which would negate the uniqueness that is essential to the human person, of the kind that Levinas made us aware in chapter 1. In other words, it should not be seen as a box into which the human person must fit if he is to be considered as flourishing, but rather a framework for understanding the common features of human flourishing which, as a framework, is intended to provide structure and guidance for moral reasoning and responding to the ethical demand in human relationships, but may be subject to adjustment and even change. We will continue to explore the implications of this point throughout the following chapters.

The Possibility of a Paradigm for What it Means to Flourish

Porter begins to develop the methodology for coming to a paradigmatic concept of what it means to live as a human person by arguing that our paradigmatic concepts of all types of creatures, including ourselves, necessarily incorporate what we can know about patterns of behaviour which lend themselves towards the possibility of a life of well-being.[112] This should be expected because, after all, creatures are defined as creatures because they engage in activity and are not merely static. This means that an adequate paradigm should incorporate an account of what counts as maturity or well-being for a given creature, including ourselves, which will be "couched in terms of the optimal way of life and patterns of behavior observed in creatures which are flourishing in accordance with their specific ideal of existence."[113] Furthermore, with reference to such an account, we can begin to analyze individual creatures through a) their position on a developmental scale which begins with immaturity and moves to maturity and b) whether

---

111. *NR*, 108. As an analogy to what Porter is arguing here, this would be akin to suggesting that it would be undesirable for a medical professional to work from a paradigm of what it means for the human person to be healthy because they may no longer see sick individuals as persons. Furthermore, here Porter returns to her use of MacIntyre we explored above in order to show how such a concept would be developed. What is instructive about this approach is that it does not expect to begin with a fully developed concept of what it means to be a human person, because this will necessarily be the end, rather than the beginning, of the process. See ibid., 111. Finally, it does not build on the naïve assumption that we can have direct access to human nature (or the nature of any other kind of creature) outside of our own sociocultural context, but rather points to our ability to come closer to the truth of things through the ongoing task of enquiry. See ibid., 113.

112. Ibid., 114.

113. Ibid.

or not they lack certain features which are common to their kind and more or less required for a life of flourishing.[114] The practical value of such an approach rests in its allowing us to recognize what an individual requires for a life of flourishing and, in turn, what can be done to ensure that these conditions are met if we encounter an individual for whom the conditions required for flourishing are lacking. Indeed, when it is put in this way, we can see that we operate out of such an understanding (at least implicitly) all of the time. After all, it would be impossible to assess the validity of therapeutic interventions for creatures (human or otherwise) who are suffering in one way or another without some measure of the ideal goal towards which they are directed.

This also leads us back into Porter's justification for utilizing a teleological approach in her theory of natural law. That is, on this understanding of the nature of a creature, we necessarily have recourse to a paradigm of flourishing by means of which an individual's level of maturity and deficiencies can be identified, understood and, in some circumstances, responded to.[115] Hence, we can now answer the question we began this section with, that is, to what extent is it possible to develop some account in terms of the human person? In response to this question, Porter argues that "we can confidently claim to know a great deal about what it means to be human, and by implication, what a good life for the human person would look like."[116] However, she also cautions that:

> our knowledge of ourselves will be more complex, and for that reason more subject to provisionality and error, than our knowledge of other kinds of creatures—because we are hardly disinterested observers of ourselves, and even more because we are considerably more complex than even the most advanced subrational animals. Our ideas about what counts as human flourishing, in particular, will be more complex than parallel views regarding other kinds of animals, if only because there appear to be a wide variety of ways in which human persons can flourish and no immediately obvious criteria by which to judge among them.[117]

---

114. Ibid.
115. Ibid., 115.
116. Ibid., 115–16.
117. Ibid., 117.

In Dialogue with Aristotle: Formal and Final Causes and Their Relationship to Natural Intelligibility and Human Flourishing

To develop a paradigm for human flourishing, Porter returns to the Aristotelian concept of the formal cause which was introduced above. As noted there, this refers to the different intelligible components of living creatures and their relationship to a species-specific pattern of functions and activities, all of which are oriented towards the more general aims which are common to all creatures, such as survival and reproduction, as well as more specific aims which are unique to the creature in question. She then links this with the Aristotelian understanding of final cause, understood "as the ideal for the full development and functioning of a specific kind of creature," arguing that these are, in reality, one and the same thing.[118] The implications of this claim need to be explored further, because it is crucial for understanding Porter correctly. What she is arguing here is that the final cause of a creature, understood as the state of flourishing for that creature, reveals itself in the formal cause of the creature, understood as the intelligible relationship between the individual components of a creature and the specific patterns of action and behaviour which enable flourishing, because these aspects of the creature are *naturally oriented* towards its flourishing, that is, its final cause. This means that a) when a creature is functioning according to the natural intelligibility appropriate to its kind it will naturally be in the state of flourishing, and b) our concept of what it means for that creature to flourish can draw on our understanding of its formal cause and that, if this understanding aligns with reality, it should correspond to the creature's final cause understood as the teleological goal towards which it is oriented.

It must also be stated that we have an incredible diversity of material to consider in order to develop our understanding of the human person's formal cause and we must therefore develop an organizational principle with which we can engage and organize this material in an intelligible way. Porter turns to Aquinas for this principle and follows his lead in developing an account of human nature which is based on our natural inclinations, beginning with the most general, which we share with other animals, and moving to our more unique and specific capacities.[119] We now turn to an exploration of these points.

---

118. Ibid., 118. As Monte Ransome Johnson notes, Aristotle argues that "the end is determined 'with reference to the kind of excellence native to it.'" Johnson, *Aristotle on Teleology*, 85. Johnson includes further discussion of final causality at 182–87.

119. *NR*, 119.

Developing a Paradigm for What it Means to Flourish as a Human Person

For Aquinas, and for the vast majority of natural law theorists who follow him, the most basic and general feature which is shared amongst all creatures and is at the very foundation of natural law, is the fact that creatures exist and desire their ongoing existence.[120] What is more, according to Aquinas, creatures do not just desire their own individual existence, but are oriented towards the "full and integrally complete development" of the cosmos in its entirety.[121]

For the human person, this desire for existence is expressed in a general form which we share with higher animals in that we choose to live in areas which allow us to live in relative safety and provide the means by which we can easily seek out food. To add to this point, as well as being congruent with the point made above about concern for existence beyond the individual, we are oriented towards a form of reproduction which includes both the sexual activity necessary to reproduce and the social activity necessary to provide the conditions within which our young are able to develop and eventually flourish themselves.[122] Porter uses this analysis of the orientation towards existence and the expression of this that we share with other animals as the framework within which the specifically human activities and functions which seek to specify what the human orientation towards existence looks like can be rendered intelligible.[123] When it comes to our specific way of enacting this orientation, Porter argues that humans are inclined towards forming long-lasting bonds; sexual behaviour which recognizes these bonds and is (more or less) regulated as such; caring for children over an extended period of time; and, on a higher level still, the hierarchical organization of communities and the maintaining of social order through sanctions and rewards. What is more, the particular shape of the orientation towards these systems in different contexts is enacted through an appeal to knowledge about what it means to flourish, which arises from the activities of speculative reason. This last point is worth emphasizing, because it reveals the role that reason plays in determining what it means for the human person to flourish. Whilst flourishing is grounded in our prerational nature, it is specified through the operations of reason and so we can expect that such a process will give rise to a diversity of conceptions

---

120. Ibid.
121. Ibid., 120.
122. Ibid., 121.
123. Ibid., 122.

about what it means to flourish. These will need to be engaged with critically, a point to which we will return in chapter 3 and which we will develop in detail in chapter 4.

For now, we return to the foundations of Porter's theory which, arising out of her understanding of the human person, she names as an ethical naturalism. She understands ethical naturalism as the human experience of morality which, she argues:

> is an expression of the distinctive inclinations and activities proper to the human animal, especially (but not only) the distinctive forms of human social behavior. As such, morality should be understood as a natural phenomenon, "natural" in contrast to "transcendentally grounded" or "implicitly divine." At the same time, human morality in all its diverse forms reflects the goodness of the human creature, and as such it is an expression of God's will that creatures should exist and flourish—whatever we are to say more specifically about the substance of particular moralities.[124]

Morality, on this view, is the intelligible human way of engaging with the deeply social reality which is an integral part of our humanness and is concerned with what is good precisely because what is good is tied up with the flourishing proper to the human creature.[125] As we will see in chapter 3, Porter will take this point and go on to argue that the intelligible human expressions of this reality can be found in the virtues. Before we move to that part of Porter's theory we need to do two things. The first is to remind ourselves that for Porter, following the scholastics, the moral dimension of the human life cannot be separated from the prerational inclinations which underlie it. Indeed, it *should not* be separated from these, because they are reflections of God's creative wisdom and, as such, express something of God's will which, as we have noted above, corresponds with what is truly good for human nature.[126] The second is to ask how Levinas's specific insight into the prerational nature of the human person can be integrated into Porter's theory as an essential aspect of what it means to be human on a level prior to our rational operations. It is to this task that we now turn.

---

124. Ibid., 126.

125. Cf. Pope's similar argument about the naturalness of morality, Pope, *The Evolution of Altruism*, 85–87.

126. Cf. *NR*, 135.

INITIAL LINKS BETWEEN PORTER AND LEVINAS

Revisiting Core Arguments of Both Authors

It is at this point that we can introduce the insight of Levinas into the discussion of Porter's theory of natural law for the first time. As we have seen, Porter understands the human person as intelligibly and naturally oriented towards flourishing, and she sees this exemplified on the prerational and, as we will see later, rational levels. Porter understands this intelligible orientation as a reflection of God's creative wisdom which is, as such, freighted with moral significance. Following Aquinas, she takes these points and argues that we can begin to analyze the morality (or not) of human behavior broadly inasmuch as it relates to the prerational orientations which it seeks to express and its contribution to, or diminishment of, the human person's overall flourishing. The paradigmatic instances of these will become our focus in the next chapter.

In exploring the phenomenology of Emmanuel Levinas in chapter 1, we found that he grounds his observations of the experience of human subjectivity in the insight that the human subject always finds herself, or becomes aware of herself as a subject, in a state of profound relationality in which the experience of the value of the Other, understood as any other human person, is inescapable. In one of his many great reversals, Levinas used this insight to turn the "I am" of the Cartesian *cognito* into a "here I am" which acknowledges that the rational and subjective dimensions of the human person arise only in an inescapable state of relationality. We also saw that Andrew Tallon argues that Levinas points towards the human person as created with an affectability which is prior to and unintended by the subject, but is nevertheless the essential characteristic of his being.

We noted that Tallon refers to the experience of this phenomenon as a 'preintentional affective attunement' which, he argues, demonstrates that we are prerationally oriented in such a way that we are profoundly and inescapably affected by the Other. For Tallon, this means that the interpersonal encounter is an 'amplification event' in which we experience our prerational orientation as an outwardly oriented and intensive recognition of the value of the Other.[127] This is always prior to our subjectivity but conditions and shapes the very nature of that subjectivity and, correlatively, it is prior to our rationality but conditions and shapes the very nature of that rationality.

---

127. Tallon, "Levinas's Ethical Horizon," 56.

Links between Porter and Levinas

It is here that we can begin to develop a link between the Levinasian insight and Porter's theory of natural law. First, a methodological comment is necessary, for phenomenology and natural law theory may at first seem too distinct as fields of enquiry for any meeting points to be meaningful. Nonetheless, I would suggest that this is a relatively simple hurdle to overcome through looking closely at the distinct—yet related—focuses of the two methodologies. First, phenomenology essentially seeks to understand human experience and, in Levinasian terms, looks to understanding what the human experiences of consciousness and responsibility tell us about how we as persons are constituted. Natural law, in the framework that Porter is using, relates more to concepts of what it means to be human, which rely heavily on the human sciences and on paradigms of human flourishing. Its focus is less on how we experience ourselves and more on what we understand about ourselves.

The two methods are distinct, but not mutually exclusive. Andrew Tallon's work is illustrative of this sense. Tallon outlines the *experience* that Levinas points to, and then seeks to understand the embodiment that *makes that experience possible*, through looking closely at affective neuroscience. The point is an anthropological one. Human experience is mysterious, but its condition of possibility is human embodiment, which can be understood in a meaningful way as we have seen above and, as we have also seen, when understood can provide important insights into human flourishing and ethics. Where Levinas makes an observation about how we experience ourselves and how responsibility is at the heart of this, Porter can look to the natural constitution of the person, how it makes possible such experience, and therefore how such experience and nature can become morally normative. It is on this foundation that the links between the two thinkers below are made.

In the first instance, these links ground themselves in the fact that Porter takes our prerational nature seriously and argues that something of the morally relevant flourishing towards which we are oriented is revealed in the nature of the orientation itself, as expressed in her argument about the close relationship between the human person's formal and final cause. If we integrate this starting point with the Levinasian insight, we can begin to see that an adequate understanding of human flourishing must be developed out of recognition of the human person's prerational orientation towards affectability in the face of others of our own kind. This is because, as Porter argues, the operations of rationality are always underdetermined by the prerational nature out of which the ability to reason arises. From this perspective, a concept of human nature which ignores the profoundly relational—and ethical—character of our existence becomes a damaging 'totalization' because it does not correspond with reality and therefore cannot be understood as an adequate paradigm for human flourishing, which would mean that any moral conclusions that are developed in dialogue with it will be deficient.[128]

Further to this point, both Levinas and Porter suggest that ethics is something that is *unchosen by* but *constitutive of* the human person, albeit through using different methodologies noted above. Levinas does this by way of his argument that ethics is first philosophy and that we are always-already in a state of responsibility and able to perceive value. Porter does this by way of her argument that morality is our natural capacity to act and to reflect on action in such a way as to orient our lives towards the flourishing. When these perspectives are combined the result is an exciting grounding point for the discipline of ethics itself. That is, the moral life is natural precisely because human persons are prerationally and intelligibly oriented towards recognition of *value*, especially the value of other persons. Such an orientation necessarily leads to the discipline of ethical reflection because the orientation itself underdetermines the operations of reason and therefore has an influence on how it operates from the very beginning.[129] On this view, ethics cannot be understood as an appendage to more 'fundamental' philosophical or theological thought precisely because we are naturally ethical creatures at a level prior to our ability to choose to be anything else. This means that the process of ethics "begins not as a cognitive one, nor as the result of a free decision to become ethical" but is rather "an affective process prior to thinking, reasoning and deciding."[130]

---

128. In the next chapter we will explore what an adequate paradigm would look like.

129. A point to which we will return in chap. 5.

130. Tallon, "Levinas's Ethical Horizon," 60. What can be added to this link to consolidate it further are Thomas Ryan's observations regarding Aquinas's approach to what he refers to as "primordial moral awareness." This concept is understood as the human person's foundational grasp of certain moral principles. Ryan's argument begins with Aquinas's question as to whether knowledge of the natural law can be separated from the human heart, to which Aquinas answers "no," see *ST*, I.94.6. Building from this, Ryan explores how Aquinas articulates the specific form of foundational knowledge of the natural law, and reveals that this is expressed in the treatise *De Malo* as *ratio practica seu affectiva*, which is best translated as a form of affective, personally felt awareness that is constitutive of the nature of the human person. See Ryan, "Conscience as Primordial Moral Awareness," 91. I am grateful to Dr Ryan for pointing out this link in his comments on the manuscript.

CONCLUSION

In this chapter, we have turned from an exploration of the phenomenology of Emmanuel Levinas to the process of discovering some of the ethical implications of this, for which we have engaged with Jean Porter's theory of natural law. At the beginning of the chapter, we explored contemporary concerns about the theory of natural law, critiqued the physicalist and New Natural Law approaches, and argued that, despite the problems with these, it was still desirable to engage with a natural law approach. We then turned to a detailed consideration of the naturalistic fallacy and developed a critical response to this. The chapter moved on to explore the grounding of Porter's methodology in a critical understanding of nature, after which we turned to a detailed consideration of how we can develop what Porter refers to as a robust realism for this understanding. From this point, we moved to a consideration of intelligibility, teleology and flourishing, and argued that a critical understanding of these can assist in developing a paradigm for what it means to flourish as a human person. Our journey through the chapter concluded with an initial dialogue between Levinas and Porter in which we noted the importance of both of the prerational dimension of the human person and their observations that ethics is a natural phenomenon.

The chapter has shown that Porter's consideration of nature as nature, whilst revealing that nature is morally significant, is not immediately normative in the sense that the paradigm remains broad and requires recourse to further knowledge about what it means to flourish as a human person. As such, a consideration of our prerational nature alone is not enough for the discernment of moral norms, because we have no way of evaluating the diverse and often contradictory ways through which human persons are able to express the prerational nature that grounds them.[131] If we were to stop at this point, Porter argues that we might be able to formulate a paradigm for flourishing that leads to some very general principles which express how we ought to manifest our natural patterns of behavior:

> but if these are to be at all plausible as expressions of universal tendencies, they will necessarily be too broad to serve as moral principles, without further—necessarily particular and contentious—specification.[132]

It will therefore be the task of chapter 3 to explore the next dimension of Porter's theory which aims to provide such a specification.

---

131. *NR*, 126.
132. Ibid.

3

Prerational Nature, Happiness, Virtue, and Jean Porter's Approach

INTRODUCTION

THIS CHAPTER CONTINUES WITH the detailed exploration of Porter's theory of natural law and moves from her consideration of the moral significance of prerational nature to the integration of virtue ethics into her theory. When considered in relationship to the book's overall argument, it continues to develop an understanding of Porter's theory in order to create further links with Levinas throughout. Furthermore, in its discussion of Porter's approach to virtue ethics, the chapter provides the foundation for the integration of the virtue of solidarity which occurs in chapter 6. Finally, through its explanation of Porter's understanding of justice as the virtue which ensures that each is given its due, the chapter reveals the need for further specification of what exactly is *due* to the human person; this requires an appeal to a developed anthropology. This stimulates a move towards chapter 4 in which the work between Porter and Levinas is combined with an appeal to an anthropological vision informed by the Catholic tradition.

The chapter begins with a consideration of Porter's understanding of natural well-being and the distinction between this and the morally specific concept of happiness. Noting that Porter, following Aquinas, understands happiness as achieved through the virtues, the chapter then moves to consider the contemporary shift towards virtue ethics in moral philosophy and theology, and situates Porter's response within this discussion. The chapter explains the foundations of Porter's virtue ethics approach, departing from her briefly to consider the Thomistic understanding of vice and its relationship to the theological concept of sin, and the implications of this for the argument developing in the book. After this point, the chapter considers the virtues of temperance, fortitude and justice as they are understood in Porter's theory, and makes a number of links with Levinas throughout. Noting that Porter's understanding of the virtue of justice requires recourse to a conceptual understanding of the human person, the chapter concludes by pointing towards the appeal to an anthropological vision informed by the Catholic tradition which becomes the focus of chapter 4.

WELL-BEING, FLOURISHING, AND HAPPINESS

The Terminology of Well-being, Flourishing, and Happiness

In chapter 2, we saw that Porter understands the human person as sharing in common concerns with all other creatures (the acknowledgment of the good of existence and the desire to continue existing) and that these are specified for us in much the same way as they are for other animals in our natural orientation towards the reproduction of our own kind. As a methodology, then, Porter's theory begins with the basic commonalities of creaturely existence and continues to specify these in accordance with the kind of creature in question. This means that further specification can be given to the concept of a human person along these lines as a mammal and a primate and, correlatively, that the appropriate form of flourishing for the human creature will correspond, at least on a general level, with the form of flourishing that we share with other creatures which fall into these categories.[1] However, Porter rightly notes that the human person flourishes in a way that differs from these other forms of creaturely existence because of our capacity to reason which, as we have also noted, allows us to express our prerational nature in a great diversity of ways and in a variety of contexts. The following from Porter provides clarification in this regard:

> the ideal of flourishing implicit in an adequate concept of human nature cannot serve as the basis for a natural law account of morality without the introduction of further principles to provide specification. At the same time, if the considerations advanced in the last chapter are persuasive, we will be suspicious of any attempt to "specify" the concept of human flourishing in such a way as, in effect, to render morally irrelevant our shared

1. *NR*, 141.

nature as living creatures of a specific kind. The task at hand, therefore, is to specify the general idea of human flourishing in such a way as to give it moral content, while still holding on to the main lines of the idea in some recognizable way.[2]

This means that Porter's theory needs to develop further principles of specification in order to provide a concept of what it means to be human. Furthermore, these principles must be sufficiently robust to enable an evaluation of relative goodness of different ways of expressing our prerational human nature.[3] In order to facilitate this move, Porter requires a terminological shift to facilitate discussion about natural well-being (which she sees as equated with the term 'flourishing') in contrast with the further specification of such natural well-being that can provide moral content as indicated above.[4] As such, she refers "to the condition indicated by a general normative ideal of human flourishing as well-being" and "the distinctively moral ideal specifying and qualifying it as happiness."[5]

Porter notes that the introduction of the term 'happiness' into her approach, whilst consistent with a Thomistic approach to natural law, raises a number of difficulties. We turn now to consider some of these.

Understanding Happiness from a Thomistic Perspective

Happiness, as understood in Porter's theory, draws heavily on Aquinas' understanding of the concept. In this section, we will turn to commentators on Aquinas to develop an understanding of his concept of happiness, before returning to Porter's theory to show how she aligns with Aquinas on this point.

Happiness is at the heart of Aquinas' ethics. As Stephen Pope notes, the section of the *Summa theologica* which is focused on ethics "begins not with the question, "What moral law must I obey?" but rather with the question, "What is true happiness?"[6] This aligns closely with his teleological approach to all of creation which would suggest that an understanding of anything

---

2. Ibid., 142. Note that where Porter refers to the "last chapter" she is referring to chap. 2 of *Nature and Reason*, which also corresponds with chap. 2 of the current work.

3. However, as we might expect, Porter is suspicious of attempts to specify human nature so much as to make our prerational nature irrelevant for moral discourse. See ibid.

4. On Porter's suggestion that flourishing is frequently equated with what she refers to as well-being, see ibid., 145.

5. Ibid., 143.

6. Pope, "Overview," 32.

must be informed by "comprehending its end or purpose."[7] For Aquinas, this end is conceived as 'happiness.' In order to understand his use of the word, it is necessary to note that the *Summa theologica*, as well as Aquinas' other works, rest on theological presuppositions rather than philosophical ones. Accordingly, Aquinas understood the end and purpose of all creation as union with God and, correlatively, the complete and perfect happiness of the human person as fulfilled only in the union with God which occurs in the eschaton.[8] This creates a difficulty in terms of how Aquinas' account of happiness can be used in the sense that Porter is suggesting—if human happiness is a state that can only be achieved in the afterlife, what help is the concept in providing specification for the flourishing that occurs in this life?[9]

The answer to this question can be found by developing Aquinas' teleology further as being not only concerned with a creature's end, but also with the way in which it gets there. As such, a living creature's journey towards its ultimate end is fulfilled by way of its natural orientation towards flourishing according to its specific kind, in the sense that we described in chapter 2.[10] For the human person, this occurs not only on the natural level but also involves the capacity for intentional and rational action. As such, there is a sense in which the human subject actively participates in her orientation towards, or away from, happiness.[11] In other words, the human person is connected to God in this life through activity.[12] When it comes to the link between happiness as an eschatological state and the relevance of this for specifying what it means to flourish as a human person, Aquinas suggests that the active participation in an orientation towards happiness in this life can give the human person a genuine experience of happiness, albeit an incomplete one.[13] As such, he creates a distinction between *beatitudo*

---

7. Ibid.

8. Kent, "Habits and Virtues," 124; Pope, "Overview," 33; Trabbic, "The Human Body and Human Happiness in Aquinas's Summa Theologiae," 554; Wang, "Aquinas on Human Happiness and the Natural Desire for God," 322; Wieland, "Happiness (Ia IIae, Qq. 1–5)," 57, 62, 67.

9. Aquinas himself poses, and deals with, this question in *ST*, I-II 5.3. The answer he develops in this and other articles which relates to complete and incomplete happiness is explored below.

10. On this connection between happiness and creaturely activity, see Wieland, "Happiness," 62.

11. *ST*, I-II 3.2 (ad 4). See Wieland, "Happiness," 62.

12. Wieland, "Happiness," 62.

13. Wang, "Aquinas on Human Happiness," 323, 327. See *ST*, I-II 4–5 which creates the distinction between complete and incomplete happiness. Wang specifies further on his page 327: "Happiness, in other words, is not just something which happens *to* us.

imperfecta (the incomplete happiness of the kind just noted) and *beatitudo perfecta* (the complete or perfect happiness which exists only in union with God).[14]

When understood as an incomplete happiness, or an active participation in the journey towards complete happiness, we should emphasize that this is not incomplete in the sense that it is the reflection of some flaw in the human condition. Rather, it is a part and parcel of our constitution as temporal and developmental beings. The following from Georg Wieland is helpful in this regard:

> Humans are connected with God through activity. . . but under the conditions of the present life, this connection is neither permanent nor simple, because the connection is repeatedly interrupted and must always be newly begun. Therefore the term "incomplete" happiness is befitting.[15]

There is thus a sense in which the human person can have a true but incomplete experience of happiness even before she reaches her final fulfilment.[16] This implies a hierarchy of goods, which includes the good of imperfect happiness that can be experienced in this life through human action and the good of ultimate happiness towards which the former is oriented. As Bonnie Kent has pointed out, taking seriously one of these does not necessarily exclude the other:

> Having as one's ultimate end the complete happiness possible only in the presence of God does not prevent one from regarding the happiness of this life as an intrinsic good. A good can be loved both for its own sake and for the sake of God, as an end in itself and yet as subordinate to a higher end (Ia IIae, q. 70, a. 1, ad. 2). Book I of the *Nicomachean Ethics* explains how ends are

---

Part of our fulfillment is to be actively involved in that fulfillment. But in this present life human activity can never be unified or continual. We have to act in time, in the present, moment by moment, and therefore our activity is necessarily fragmented."

14. Wang, "Aquinas on Human Happiness," 323. This highlights the importance of understanding Aquinas's ethics in theological terms, which demonstrates one of the possible weaknesses of Porter's theory as noted at the beginning of chapter 2.

15. Wieland, "Happiness," 62. Here Wieland aligns with what Aquinas argues against the objection that happiness cannot be related to human action because the "happy person remains happy." In response, Aquinas demonstrates the link between human action and happiness and also emphasizes the transient nature of human life as does Wieland in this quote. See *ST*, I-II 3.2 (ad 4).

16. Wang, "Aquinas on Human Happiness," 323. As Aquinas points out, in *ST*, I-II 5.3: "a certain participation of happiness can be had in this life: but perfect and true happiness cannot be had in this life."

architectonically ordered, with some as ends in their own right and yet subordinate to further ends. To deny that some good is the *ultimate* end is not necessarily to assert that it has, like a tetanus shot, merely instrumental value.[17]

As such, Aquinas is able to reconcile the worldly aim of living a happy life with the ultimate end of happiness in union with God.[18]

Given that he aligns the incomplete happiness of the former with human action, however, Aquinas needs to account for the kinds of activity in which human happiness consists.[19] It is this that leads Aquinas from his consideration of happiness to a consideration of moral action in the *Summa* and he argues there that the condition of possibility for incomplete happiness is to be found in the character dispositions known as virtues.[20]

Locating Porter's Understanding of Happiness within the Thomistic Perspective

In view of what has been developed above, it is possible to understand more clearly what Porter means when she turns to the Thomistic understanding of happiness in her theory. First, we should note that Porter shows an awareness of both complete and incomplete happiness in her writing on the topic.[21] She is, however, explicit about her approach being focused on Aquinas' understanding of incomplete happiness, which she variously refers to as 'incomplete,' 'imperfect,' 'natural' or 'connatural' happiness, and this aligns with her focus on the moral life as it is expressed in terrestrial existence, as distinct from the theological concerns of union with God in the afterlife.[22] Furthermore, her understanding of incomplete happiness corresponds with Bonnie Kent's analysis of Aquinas above which demonstrated the plausibility of a focus on incomplete happiness without this negating the importance of complete happiness.[23] Finally, Porter follows Aquinas in her insistence that incomplete happiness "consists in a life of virtuous activity, through

---

17. Kent, "Habits and Virtues," 125.
18. Goodman, "Happiness," 464.
19. Wieland, "Happiness," 62.
20. As Aquinas notes, incomplete "happiness is the reward of works of virtue." ST, I-II 5.7. See also Wieland, "Happiness," 63. Cf. Trabbic, "The Human Body and Human Happiness," 557.
21. See for example NR, 144; Porter, *Ministers of the Law*, 152.
22. See for example NR, 144; Porter, *Ministers of the Law*, 97, 151, 154.
23. See Porter's discussion of this in terms of understanding the different senses of happiness as different levels or stages. NR, 158.

which the individual achieves the fullest possible development and expression of her powers as a rational agent."[24]

As such, it is the possibility of incomplete happiness that provides Porter with the means by which to propose the kind of specification that the morally relevant, but morally indeterminate, concept of natural well-being requires.[25] Furthermore, this understanding of happiness carries with it a link to the virtues as those character dispositions which specify what it means for the human person to be oriented towards incomplete happiness, and thus to be participating fruitfully in their journey towards ultimate happiness. It is out of this Thomistic framework that Porter's understanding of happiness should be understood. With regards to specific terminology, given that from the outset of her discussion of happiness Porter explicitly notes her focus on incomplete happiness, she proceeds to use the shorthand 'happiness' to refer to this throughout her books. Whilst this usage can result in confusion if one begins to read her discussion of incomplete happiness after the distinction has been made, it does facilitate the flow of the text. Given that I will be quoting from Porter below I will follow her in this usage. In what follows, all references to 'happiness' should be understood as 'incomplete happiness' in the way that has been described above.

Well-being to Happiness via the Virtues

We have seen that Porter argues for the need to qualify her account of human well-being further in order for it to demonstrate the "most appropriate way in which men and women can attain and enjoy the activities constitutive of well-being."[26] Furthermore, we have seen that both she and Aquinas understand happiness as consisting in the life of virtue. These two points,

---

24. Porter, *Ministers of the Law*, 97; cf. 151, 154. See also *NR*, 161. Note also *ST*, I-II 5.7, which was explored above.

25. In this way, her approach focuses on what Aquinas refers to as the *acquired* virtues, that is the virtues that correspond with the moral life and are oriented toward imperfect happiness by means of human activity. These are distinct from what he refers to as the *infused* virtues, which are graciously given by God to the baptized and are oriented directly toward spiritual union with God. Bonnie Kent provides helpful clarification on this point, "While naturally acquired moral virtues make people well suited to the human affairs and earthly happiness that concern all—because we are all human—infused moral virtues make people well suited to the life Christians must live because they are Christians: persons belonging to the household of God, with love of God as the highest good, faith in God's word, and hope for the happiness of the afterlife." Kent, "Habits and Virtues," 122. While not a focus here, this point is discussed in terms of a possibility for future research in the book's conclusion.

26. *NR*, 143.

when held together, provide an important link between well-being and happiness. This is illustrated in the following discussion in which Porter begins to refer to the virtues as 'perfections':

> The virtues are not merely instrumental to the attainment of connatural happiness, therefore; rather, the practice of the virtues is constitutive of the life of happiness in its natural, properly human form. This is so, precisely because the virtues are perfections. That is to say, taken singly they represent the fullest possible development and exercise of the discrete faculties of the human agent, and operating in tandem they comprise the perfection of the rational agent, that is to say, its happiness. At the same time, however, Aquinas does not sever all components of a naturally good human life. Rather, the virtues are dispositions through which the relevant desires and capacities of the human agents, as these are naturally directed towards the pursuit and enjoyment of the many components of organized well-being, are oriented towards rational and appropriate operations. It is easy to focus on Aquinas's emphasis on the ways in which the virtues bring rationality to our diverse desires. It is important to remember, in addition, that in order to count as perfections of the relevant capacities, the virtues must also preserve and even strengthen the agent's orientation towards natural goods, without which human life could not be sustained or developed.[27]

As such, the concept of happiness does precisely what Porter suggests is needed to complement the understanding of natural well-being and its relevance to moral reflection thus far. It takes seriously the natural orientation of the human person towards flourishing and the natural goods required for that flourishing, and yet can provide further specification in evaluating the diversity of ways in which the human person can flourish through recourse to an account of the virtues. We will turn to a detailed consideration of this point below.

Furthermore, a focus on happiness and the virtues can account for some of the complexities of human life that an account of well-being alone

---

27. Porter, *Ministers of the Law*, 154. The use of the word "perfection" here should be understood in the Thomistic sense as that which makes the human person "right," "complete," or, in language more akin to what has been used above, allows her to experience happiness. Keenan provides a helpful clarification of this Thomistic understanding of perfection: "'Perfect' should here be understood in two senses; the virtues are perfections of the person who has them, insofar as they are the full development of the individual's capacities for knowledge and action, and at the same time they lead to actions that are perfect, that is to say, good in every relevant respect." Keenan, "The Virtue of Prudence (IIa IIae, Qq. 23–46)," 262.

cannot. For example, there are readily available examples of persons who may not be considered as flourishing in a natural sense, and yet they clearly embody the life of virtue and, correlatively, happiness.[28] One only needs to think of the sick person who remains courageous and temperate despite her illness, or the parent who courageously neglects his own well-being to protect his children. On Porter's view, these persons may still be considered as virtuous (and therefore happy) even despite the fact that, either because of circumstance or choice, they are not in a state of natural well-being. Correlatively, it is not difficult to think of persons who live a life of natural well-being, but do so in an immoral way. Nevertheless, the distinction between well-being and happiness should not be extended too far. Whilst it is true that some aspects of natural well-being are not required (or can be sacrificed) to live in a virtuous way, at least a foundational level of natural well-being is required for a person to be able to cultivate the virtues that constitute the life of happiness.[29]

Given the introduction of virtue, it will be helpful to consider contemporary thought in the field of virtue ethics for more insight in terms of what this understanding of happiness involves, and also to show how Porter's theory aligns with this.

VIRTUE ETHICS

Virtue Ethics in Contemporary Moral Discourse

The integration of a reflection on virtue into Porter's theory aligns her approach to natural law with *virtue ethics*, one of the three major contemporary approaches to ethics in contemporary moral philosophy.[30] In this section we will explore virtue ethics, broadly considered, and some of the reasons for its popularity in contemporary discourse. After this general consideration, we will move towards locating Porter's theory within contemporary discussions surrounding virtue ethics, before exploring Porter's specifically Thomistic approach to the virtues and showing the relationship between these and the consideration of nature as nature that we have been developing thus far.

---

28. As Porter notes, "[O]n some views true happiness is not only distinct from but wholly independent of well-being, in such a way that it makes sense to say of someone that she is happy even though she is sick, isolated, and deprived of the capacities or opportunities for effective action." *NR*, 144.

29. Trabbic, "The Human Body and Human Happiness," 558.

30. The other two being deontology and consequentialism. See Hursthouse, "Virtue Ethics," 2421.

A number of authors locate the 'return' of virtue ethics to contemporary discourse in Elizabeth Anscombe's 1958 article "Modern Moral Philosophy," in which she argued that modern ethical theories should move away from considerations of right and wrong acts (which had been the preoccupation of the deontological and consequentialist approaches) and towards an evaluative consideration of the character traits of agents.[31] Such an approach provides a valuable alternative to the other prevalent ethical theories because, as William Spohn notes, it can provide "a more comprehensive picture of moral experience and stands closer to the issues of ordinary life."[32] Virtue ethics has also become popular in the contemporary context for a number of more general reasons. In the first instance, virtue ethics has attracted attention from both the continental and analytic schools of philosophy and, as such, provides an important bridge between these traditions.[33] In the second instance, virtue ethics has been able to respond to postmodernism's critiques of the 'meta-narratives' of the Enlightenment, while at the same time avoiding the nihilistic tendencies of the same.[34] In the third instance, which is particularly important in view of our exploration of Levinas and his warnings about "totalization," virtue ethics has become attractive because of its reticence to provide highly specific judgments about particular actions without "an ongoing sensitive engagement with the ethical dimensions of our daily lives."[35] On this view, attention to the uniqueness of who and what is encountered in daily life and the context in which they are encountered is essential for a virtuous disposition. As such, virtue ethics is characterized by an in-depth reflection on what it means to be *attentive* to the ethical dimensions of "daily life" in order to be able to apply more

---

31. Anscombe, "Modern Moral Philosophy." See Battaly, "Introduction: Virtue and Vice," 1; Hursthouse, "Virtue Ethics," 2421; Rachels, *The Elements of Moral Philosophy*, 175. Porter also names Philippa Foot and Iris Murdoch as key influences in the return of virtue ethics, and suggests that the work of Alasdair MacIntyre served to draw widespread attraction to the approach. Porter, "Virtue Ethics," 107.

32. Spohn, "The Return of Virtue Ethics," 60. See also Keenan, "Proposing Cardinal Virtues," 710.

33. Becker, "Virtue Ethics, Applied Ethics and Rationality," 268.

34. Ibid., 271. Becker argues that virtue ethics has been able to achieve this through acknowledging both the commonality of the virtues, and the relevance of "situation-specific" information that determines how they are expressed both in the context of cultures and individual moral lives. Virtue ethics' focus on *character* as distinct from *action* also provides a corrective to the fragmentation of human life because it understands moral action not in terms of individual acts, but primarily in terms of the narrative of moral disposition which takes form over the course of a lifetime. See ibid., 272–74.

35. Ibid., 270.

abstract principles of morality.³⁶ The specific virtue to which this kind of reflection refers is *prudence*, and we will consider Porter's understanding of prudence and its relevance to the book's argument in detail in chapter 5.

Whilst this aspect of virtue ethics can be considered one of its strengths, it has also been argued that it is one of its major weaknesses. Most often, this has been expressed as concern for a lack of prescription and prohibition that is found in virtue ethics and, so the argument goes, a lack of adequate guidance in moral situations which results from this.³⁷ The former problem has been successfully refuted by Rosalind Hursthouse in her argument about virtue-rules, which she understands as certain prescriptions or prohibitions which are implied in the language of the virtues themselves. From this standpoint, the very naming of a particular character disposition as a virtue (e.g. justice) carries with it both a prescription (do what is just) and a prohibition (do not do what is unjust).³⁸ The focus of arguments against virtue ethics is currently, therefore, concerned with the latter argument—whether or not the virtues can provide moral guidance that is sufficiently detailed to be adequate—which has been framed by asking whether or not virtue ethics needs to be supplemented with a principles or rules based approach.³⁹ We have indicated part of an answer to this concern above in our consideration of the openness of virtue ethics to unique moral information and will return to this problem in chapter 5 when we consider the virtue of prudence and the limitations of moral knowledge in view of the argument developed throughout the book.⁴⁰

The "Return" of Virtue Ethics: Basic Features of the Approach

The virtue ethics movement has been widely understood as a 'return,' rather than something new, because a reflection on morally good character traits has foundations in both the Eastern tradition (especially in the work of Confucius) and in the reflections on virtue found in the Western tradition in the works of Plato and Aristotle.⁴¹ Building on the reflections on the vir-

---

36. Hursthouse, "Virtue Ethics," 2422.

37. Ibid. Cf. Rachels, *The Elements of Moral Philosophy*, 187–88.

38. Hursthouse, "Virtue Ethics," 2423.

39. Ibid. Rachels takes such an approach, see Rachels, *The Elements of Moral Philosophy*, 186–69. See also Steutel and Carr, "Virtue Ethics and the Virtue Approach to Moral Education," 9.

40. For a philosophical response to this issue, see McAleer, "Four Solutions to the Alleged Incompleteness of Virtue Ethics."

41. Hursthouse, "Virtue Ethics," 2421.

tues from these authors, contemporary virtue ethics understands a virtue as a stable and good character disposition which expresses itself more or less consistently in the way that an agent is motivated and/or acts in a diversity of circumstances.[42]

Before moving to consider Porter's specific approach to virtue ethics, it is worth mentioning Spohn's summary of the characteristics of a virtue ethics approach, and then Stuart Rachels' criteria for an adequate theory of virtue ethics, both of which will allow us to situate Porter's approach more clearly in relationship with contemporary virtue ethics.

Spohn's summary of common features in virtue ethics is as follows:

1. Moral evaluation focuses primarily on an agent's character, rather than on specific actions.

2. Good character produces practical moral judgments based on beliefs, experience, and sensitivity more than on (or instead of) rules and principles.

3. A moral psychology gives an account of how virtues and vices develop.

4. A theory of human fulfillment describes the goal towards which virtues lead and/or of which the virtues are components.

5. Increasingly, attention is paid to the cultural shaping of virtues and what relation, if any, exists between specific historical manifestations of virtues and more universal traits.[43]

Rachels' criteria for an adequate approach to virtue ethics is explained here:

> A theory of virtue should have several components: (a) an explanation of what a virtue is, (b) a list specifying which character traits are virtues, (c) an explanation of what these virtues consist in, and (d) an explanation of why these qualities are good ones for a person to have.[44]

In the following section, we will locate Porter's theory within Spohn's characteristics and Rachels' criteria.

---

42. See Battaly, "Introduction: Virtue and Vice," 3; Rachels, *The Elements of Moral Philosophy*, 176.

43. Spohn, "The Return of Virtue Ethics," 61. Spohn's later work uses this same list. See Spohn, *Go and Do Likewise*, 28.

44. Rachels, *The Elements of Moral Philosophy*, 175.

Situating Porter's Approach within Contemporary Virtue Ethics

In terms of Spohn's first characteristic, that a virtue ethics approach focuses on an agent's character, as we will see below, Porter's approach is primarily concerned with the kind of consistent character traits that enable a person to embody the happy life. This also links closely with Spohn's second characteristic, that practical moral judgments are produced out of good character, as distinct from moral judgments which are based on rules and principles. This point is further exemplified in chapter 5, in which we will consider the link between practical reason, prudence and the first principles of natural law, and also the role that prudence plays in determining the mean of the virtues in concrete situations. Porter's approach does not include any detailed consideration of the developmental moral psychology of how virtues and vices develop (Spohn's third characteristic), although her understanding of virtues as being expressed in paradigms of action which allow individual persons to grasp the point of the disposition and apply it in the context of their own life does have something of a developmental flavor.[45] We will explore this point further below. Furthermore, her approach provides a detailed consideration of how virtues arise out of and are linked to the prerational inclinations of the human person. We will consider this part of Porter's theory in various sections below as well.

Spohn's fourth characteristic refers to a theory of human fulfillment which reveals the goal towards which the virtues are oriented or of which they are components. Such a teleological approach is a core part of Porter's theory, and we have seen this in the links between well-being and happiness noted earlier, which will also be revisited below. This understanding of human fulfillment is further developed in chapter 4 wherein the argument will include a more detailed vision of human happiness to enhance its paradigm for the virtue of justice. Finally, we will see later in this chapter that Porter recognizes the universal qualities of the virtues, whilst acknowledging the need to turn to historically and culturally situated accounts of human happiness in order to specify them further, thus fulfilling Spohn's fifth characteristic which looks towards an acknowledgment of the universal and historical aspects of virtue ethics.

In terms of Rachels' criteria, we have seen that Porter's approach to virtue ethics incorporates the definition of virtue included above, and that she also specifies this in her own approach below. This fulfills Rachels' criterion (a), that a theory of virtue should have an explanation of what a virtue

---

45. This also corresponds well with Spohn's later work in which he explores in more detail the area of moral development as it relates to the virtues and relates it to cultural paradigms. See Spohn, *Go and Do Likewise*, 31–32.

is. In fulfilment of his criterion (b), that a theory of virtue should include a list specifying which character traits are virtues, and his criterion (c), that a theory of virtue should include an explanation of what these virtues consist in, we will see in several parts of this chapter and in chapter 5 that Porter focuses her attention on the virtues of temperance, fortitude, justice and prudence, whilst retaining an openness in her scholarship towards considering other character traits as virtues.[46] Furthermore, by including the virtue of solidarity in this list and demonstrating its significance in chapter 6, the book's argument will further fulfil this criterion. In each of these sections, our detailed engagement with the virtues will serve to explain what each consists in. Finally, in consideration of Rachels' criterion (d), in each of the abovementioned sections, we will note carefully the links that Porter makes between the virtues in question and the paradigm for the well-being and flourishing of the human person that will continue to develop over this and the next two chapters, thus demonstrating why these particular traits of character are good for the human person.

In view of this, it is clear that Porter's approach aligns with the 'return' of virtue ethics. In what follows, we will explore it in more detail.

THE FOUNDATIONS FOR A THOMISTIC ACCOUNT OF THE VIRTUES: PORTER AND OTHERS

Virtue, Well-being, and Happiness Revisited

As indicated above, Porter links happiness with the human person's prerational nature, understood as natural flourishing or well-being, and begins to develop an argument for the virtues as the character dispositions which both secure well-being and direct the expression of it in the most appropriate ways. In this way, the virtues act as the bridge between well-being and happiness because they can simultaneously protect and encourage the basic well-being proper to the human creature whilst moving this towards the kind of expression of human nature which corresponds with human happiness.

The virtues are thus essentially related to the prerational inclinations of the human creature which are oriented towards natural well-being. As such, when our understanding of prerational nature becomes more accurate in the way that was discussed in chapter 2, so too will our understanding of the virtuous dispositions which align the expression of this with happiness. Correlatively, the virtues provide a framework for understanding behaviors

---

46. See for example Porter, "Chastity as a Virtue."

which can analyze whether or not they are the most appropriate expression of well-being or, alternatively, whether in some instances natural well-being is unnecessary or can be set aside for the sake of happiness. These points set the foundation for Porter's Thomistic understanding of virtue and enable us now to move into this in more detail.

Porter's Understanding of Virtue in Detail

Following Aquinas, and in agreement with the contemporary approach to the virtues that we have noted above, Porter understands the moral virtues as *habitus*, stable dispositions of character which correspond with human happiness.[47] More specifically still, her entry on virtue ethics in the *Cambridge Companion to Christian Ethics* defines a virtue in the following way:

> A virtue is a trait of character or intellect which is in some way praiseworthy, admirable or desirable. When we refer to somebody's virtues, what we usually have in mind are relatively stable and effective dispositions to act in particular ways, as opposed to inclinations which are easily lost, or which do not consistently lead to corresponding kinds of action.[48]

Further to this, Porter argues that the virtues are normally expressed through paradigmatic kinds of actions, as distinct from pure, abstract concepts.[49] On this view, a paradigm expresses the virtue in its fullest sense. As an example, for the virtue of temperance, the paradigmatic expression may be found in the person who is presented with a large banquet of food and chooses only to consume what is necessary for his own well-being. When such a virtuous disposition is enacted within the context of an individual's life, it will have something of an agent-relative character, given that a fully grown adult will require more food to nourish her natural well-being than would a child.[50] The point of such a paradigmatic expression of a virtue,

---

47. *NR*, 163. Bonnie Kent makes the point in a similar way in her commentary on Aquinas's understanding of habits and virtues, in which she defines a habit (and a virtue following this) as "a durable characteristic of the agent inclining to certain kinds of actions and emotional reactions, not the actions and reactions themselves." Kent, "Habits and Virtues," 116–17. On the close link between Aquinas's definition of habit and virtue see p. 119. Cf. also Pope, "Overview," 34. See Spohn's first and second characteristics of a virtue ethics approach noted above.

48. Porter, "Virtue Ethics," 96. See also *ST*, I-II 49.1–2. Kent, "Habits and Virtues," 117. See Rachels's criterion (a) for a virtue ethics approach noted above.

49. *NR*, 181. On this point Porter again follows Aquinas for whom all virtues were linked with paradigmatic kinds of actions. See Porter, "Virtue Ethics," 182.

50. Porter, "Virtue Ethics," 184–93.

therefore, is pedagogical, rather than prescriptive, inasmuch as it is concerned with the imparting of the kind of practical and moral knowledge which aids an agent in expressing his prerational inclinations in the most appropriate way.[51] As such, the paradigmatic expressions of virtue can be understood as related to the clichés that we associate with particular dispositions of character. As Porter notes:

> Clichés of temperance, bravery, and the like are clichés for good reason—they convey patterns of behavior which would exemplify the virtues for most persons under most circumstances, because they reflect needs and situations common to us all.[52]

What is more, the fact that such paradigms are so commonly held as clichés of a given virtue means that they are embodiments of the community's process of developing and ordaining particular patterns of behavior which correspond to what is truly good for the human person.[53] That is, the ongoing process of reflection on what counts as a truly human life has led to the development of paradigms which "reflect collective judgments about

---

51. Ibid., 196. Porter develops a similar argument in terms of the virtue of chastity, which she understands as a subset of the virtue of temperance, which is specifically concerned with the appropriate expression of the human creature's appetite for sexual interaction with other persons. See Porter, "Chastity as a Virtue." This also aligns with the argument that Spohn proposes with regards to the development of virtue through engagement with particular paradigms of action: "Virtues are internally shaped by cultural stories that indicate how to be fair, honest or chaste." Spohn, *Go and Do Likewise*, 32.

52. *NR*, 198. Here Porter provides examples of these clichés inasmuch as they refer to both vices and virtues: "Only a greedy little boy would eat three Big Macs in one sitting; a brave little girl will not allow herself to be pushed around by the class harridan; and so forth."

53. Which, if we follow the argument of chap. 2, occurs through the means of what MacIntyre calls "tradition constituted and tradition constitutive enquiry" or what I have suggested with Levinas is the ongoing revision of the Said in light of the Saying. As such, according to the argument we developed above, the paradigm should be taken seriously as an authentic (albeit incomplete) insight into what counts as human flourishing. Cf. Pope's point (which provides another link between Porter's argument regarding the link between nature as nature and virtue) that the "*potential* for virtue is provided by genotypes and biological constitutions and it is developed by choices made in proper social and cultural environments. It is *actualized* by the process of moral development in which the agent is gradually enabled to assume responsibility for cultivating his or her own moral freedom. This sense of freedom is neither expanded nor even maintained by isolated subjects. It is extended and strengthened, or retarded and weakened, by habits, friends, work, and other social and cultural circumstances." Pope, *Human Evolution and Christian Ethics*, 184, cf. 162. This also links with Spohn's fifth characteristic of virtue ethics approaches noted above, that they pay close attention to the cultural mediation of the virtues.

the kinds of reactions and behavior that would be broadly reasonable for most persons in most circumstances."[54] Of course, the uniqueness and complexity of an individual's life and the context in which it unfolds will often mean that the virtues will need to be expressed in ways that differ from the paradigms themselves. For example, we may not find ourselves presented with a banquet of food as in the paradigm above, but it is likely (especially in the Western world) that we will often find ourselves with the opportunity to consume more food and drink than is needed to secure well-being. Indeed, in some cases, this is apparent to the extent that well-being can actually be undermined through excessive consumption.[55] For this reason, paradigms of virtue should be understood as both literal expressions of what it means to embody a particular virtue and examples which allow a person to grasp their underlying point, understood as why this or that particular action is an expression of this or that virtue and how (or whether) such an expression would translate into different circumstances.[56] As such, a person who has grasped the point of a paradigm will be able to adapt it and apply it in the context of her own life situation.[57]

This movement towards grasping the meaning of paradigms of virtue and then seeking to express them within the context of the complexity of a unique human life, which includes relating them to other virtues, necessarily moves into a more detailed exploration of how they are situated within a whole web of interpersonal relationships, as well as speculative beliefs about what counts as the good.[58] We will return to consider this point in more detail below. Now, however, we turn to those character dispositions which do not correspond with human happiness: namely, the vices.

---

54. Cf. NR, 199. In an article on moral beauty, Thomas Ryan makes a similar point as he attempts to account for the overwhelming interest, admiration, and assent to particular ways of acting that is found when people encounter others who are broadly considered as moral heroes. As an example, Ryan recounts a story of a Czech prisoner who has been sentenced to death and reaches out to his executor in an act of "soft subversion," which expresses both forgiveness toward the executioner and solidarity with fellow prisoners at the same time. See Ryan, "By Way of Moral Beauty," 24.

55. On the link between temperance and proper bodily function, see Cates, "The Virtue of Temperance (IIa IIae, Qq. 141–170)," 325.

56. On the educational role of the virtues, see for example Carr and Steutel, "The Virtue Approach to Moral Education."

57. NR, 199.

58. See Cates, "The Virtue of Temperance," 327. Cf. Spohn's second characteristic.

Vice and Sin in Thomistic Virtue Ethics and Their Relationship with Porter's Theory

In light of the argument we have been developing above regarding the virtues and their role in securing happiness, it is necessary to ask how we can classify and understand that which undermines human happiness. Given that the Thomistic approach to the virtues is primarily theological, it should not surprise us that this dimension of Aquinas' approach includes some discourse on the problem of sin. It may be surprising to note that Porter's own Thomistic approach does not contain any significant commentary on sin and how this concept fits into her theory of natural law, although this does align with her use of Aquinas in a more philosophical than theological sense. It will, however, be helpful for us to depart from Porter on this point and include some discussion of Aquinas' understanding of sin and how it fits in to his virtue ethics approach and, whilst Porter does not include this specifically in her own theory, we will see that it remains congruent with her argument and provides further opportunity for reflection when we come to consider each of the specific virtues. It will also provide the beginnings of an appeal to an anthropological vision informed by the Catholic tradition which will be developed further in chapter 4, as well as an integration of Levinas's observation that human beings so often do not respond in ways that respect the Other. This section will be relatively brief, and is intended to outline the relationship between virtue, vice, sin and the understanding of natural law that we have been developing thus far.[59] This will give us the tools with which to note the specific implications of the approach in relationship to each of the virtues that we will explore below.

The Thomistic approach to sin aligns with the traditional Catholic understanding of sin as that which damages, or destroys, one's self or one's relationship with God and/or one's neighbor.[60] The concept of sin in Aquinas can only be fully understood, however, by locating it within his understanding of natural law and the virtues which we have been considering

---

59. In what follows, I consider sin largely in terms of sinful dispositions, with some discussion on sinful actions. All of this should be balanced with an awareness of the subjective factors that contribute to human agency and diminish, or enhance, the ability that a human person has to take responsibility for his actions. In Aquinas's moral psychology, this important consideration is reflected in his discussion of the will, in which he argues that those actions that are not actively willed by the human person, but happen because of unconscious reasons, properly fall into the category of *natural* rather than *moral* action. This point will be noted below in our consideration of the will. For a concise and clear exploration of current thinking in moral theology on subjective responsibility, see Gascoigne, *Freedom and Purpose*, 68–92, 99–102.

60. See Connors and McCormick, *Character, Choices and Community*, 203.

thus far. As we have seen, the human person is naturally oriented towards his own well-being and, through the specification that is provided by the virtues, towards his happiness. As we have also seen, this happiness is akin to an active participation in the complete happiness that can be found in God. It is not complete happiness, which is achieved only in eternal life, but a kind of incomplete happiness akin to the fullest possible flourishing that a human creature can achieve in her earthly life. What is significant about this account is the close link between human happiness and well-being which, whilst remaining distinct, are inherently related. We have also seen that both Aquinas and Porter understand happiness as being constituted in the life of virtue, and that the character dispositions which undermine the virtues (and therefore happiness) are referred to as vices.

Aquinas follows Aristotle in this naming of the dispositions which incline us towards acting against the virtues as *vices*.[61] As we will see below, Aquinas understands different virtues as enabling a person to achieve the most appropriate expression of a particular human inclination. Correspondingly, they allow a person to avoid the vicious dispositions which would incline her towards expressing natural inclinations in ways which do not correspond with her own happiness, or the good more comprehensively considered to include the happiness of others as well.[62] For example, the virtue of temperance acts to moderate the expression of (among others) the human desire for food, in such a way that a person eats neither too much nor too little. On this view, the virtue avoids the vices of both gluttony (a consistent inclination to consume too much) and deficiency (a consistent inclination to consume too little).[63] Building on this argument, the reason for a vice being defined as such corresponds with its undermining of what is good for the human person which, in this case, also corresponds with her natural well-being.

It is here that Aquinas moves the Aristotelian approach towards a Christian theological one by linking this understanding of *vice* with *sin*.[64] This link is perhaps most clearly illustrated in the following oft-quoted line from the *Summa Contra Gentiles*, "we do not wrong God unless we wrong our own good."[65] From this standpoint, sin corresponds with vice precisely

61. Note that the category *vice* can also be understood through the lens of Levinas's philosophy. I develop this point in detail in chap. 6.

62. Pope, "Overview," 34. See also Harrington and Keenan, *Jesus and Virtue Ethics*, 100.

63. We will return to this virtue more specifically below.

64. On the close links between *vice* and *sin* in Aquinas, see Sweeny, "Vice and Sin (Ia IIae, Qq. 71–89)," 152.

65. The original reads *Non enim Deus a nobis offenditur nisi ex eo quot contra nostrum bonum agimus*. See SCG, 3, 122.

because, in undermining her natural expression of the good through the virtues, the human person undermines her orientation towards God in happiness. Stephen Pope provides clarification on this point:

> Sin in the formal sense is essentially a corruption or privation of what belongs to a person naturally. It always involves a kind of imbalance, inordinateness, or deviation from what is good for the person.[66]

As such, our understanding of sin must be informed by our understanding of what count as the virtuous dispositions which correspond with what is truly good for the human person. This is a point to which we will return below when exploring how it relates to each specific virtue. When it comes to the virtue of justice, we will explore it by way of its relationship to a robust anthropology which seeks to understand what is truly good for the human person in dialogue with revelation.

It is possible to introduce an analogy here (Aquinas' own) which will help in clarifying these points further. In view of what we have been developing above, we can see that Aquinas' understanding of the virtuous life is akin to his understanding of the properly human life and, in this sense, is analogous to being physically healthy. When one is physically healthy, all of one's bodily functions work together for the good of one's self as a whole. When one is hampered by physical illness, there is a disruption in normal bodily function and, as a result, one's physical health is diminished (more or less, depending on the severity of the illness). According to Aquinas, the latter can be understood as analogous to sin: it disrupts and damages a human person's ability to live in the states of well-being and happiness.[67] We can also extend the analogy and argue, as Aquinas does, that sins are more or less serious depending on the extent to which they distort the goods required for the happy life.[68]

It is here that we can provide the link back into Porter's theory: given that Porter's concern is to provide a moral theory which can express what is truly good for the human person through an understanding of virtues which embody the happy life, those dispositions which undermine these

---

66. Pope, "Overview," 34. See also Rhonheimer, "Sins against Justice (IIa IIae, Qq. 59–78)," 287, also 292. Cf. also Gascoigne, *Freedom and Purpose*, 96–97.

67. Sweeny, "Vice and Sin," 151.

68. According to Aquinas, then, "in matters of action reason directs all things in view of the end, and thus the higher the end which attaches to sins in human acts, the graver the sin," I-II 73.3. Here Aquinas continues with the analogy of bodily sickness sin: the more serious the cause of the sickness, the more serious its effects. Analogously, the higher the end that sin distorts, the more harm it will do. See also Sweeny, "Vice and Sin," 160.

goods would clearly be considered vicious on her view and, therefore, theologically, sinful. What is more, Aquinas' understanding of sin and its relationship with specific acts is congruent with Porter's own methodology, especially as it is presented in her account of the virtues and their relationship with specific acts. That is, the primary concern for both authors is the disposition towards acting in a certain way, and not with the acts themselves.[69] This is not to say that the acts are unimportant, there may indeed be some actions (such as murder) which are inherently contradictory to the virtues. The point is that that the morality of the action flows out of particular dispositions and not the other way around. Nevertheless, there is also a sense in which action can deepen or weaken particular dispositions, and this is a point to which we will return in our consideration of each of the specific virtues below.

At this point we have developed an understanding of sin at a formal level and, as noted above, this will be expressed more specifically when we come to consider each of the cardinal virtues. Before moving to these, however, we turn to some further explanation of the Thomistic anthropology which underlies Porter's thought and is a necessary foundation for an adequate understanding of the specific virtues we will be exploring.

Prerational Inclinations and Their Relationship to the Appetites, the Passions, and the Cardinal Virtues

Thus far in this chapter, we have been exploring how virtue fits into Porter's theory and its relationship with human well-being and flourishing, grounded on our exploration of prerational nature in chapter 2, and how these concepts can be complemented with the Thomistic understandings of vice and sin. At this point, it is possible for us to develop further the link between the prerational orientation of the human person towards what counts as well-being and the specific virtues that express this in happiness.[70] This specification can occur when we acknowledge that, on Porter's view, each of our natural inclinations is linked to a particular virtue which, in turn, enables the expression of the natural inclination to occur in an appropriate

---

69. On this methodological point, Pope notes that specific precepts and acts are dealt with late in the *Summa*, which, he argues, indicates that their inclusion has the purpose of encouraging growth in virtuous dispositions (and away from vicious ones) rather than vice versa. Pope, "Overview," 37. For further explanation of this point, see Connors and McCormick, *Character, Choices and Community*, 216–17.

70. Note the link here with Rachels's criterion (d) for a virtue ethics approach noted above, that it will include "an explanation of why these qualities are good ones for a person to have."

way.⁷¹ This is part of the reason for Porter's focus on the so-called 'cardinal' virtues of temperance, fortitude, justice and prudence, because these "represent traits of character which contribute in straightforward and fundamentally important ways to human well-being, whether at the individual or collective level, or (usually) both."⁷² She continues the argument as follows:

> Moreover, they seem to be almost universally recognized and admired in some form, and this is of course not unrelated to the fact that they contribute to human well-being in such basic ways. Almost everyone can see that restraint, courage, fairness, and good judgment have some point, given the exigencies and common aspirations which structure human life, and it is this grasp of the point, the telos of these qualities, which makes it possible to recognize them, even when they take unfamiliar forms. The language of the virtues provides the closest thing we have to a universal moral language.⁷³

What is more, the cardinal virtues as paradigms for appropriate action refer to the distinct dimensions of the human person that we have been exploring thus far. That is, they can provide guidance on how our prerational orientation towards survival and relationship can be expressed most adequately and, as we will see in chapter 5, the distinct role of reason in this process. To understand this point in more detail, it is necessary to employ the Thomistic terminology of *passions*, *will* and later, *intellect*. On Aquinas' view, both the passions and will can be understood as appetites of the human creature which, following our analysis in chapter 2, are intelligibly oriented towards the human creature's well-being.⁷⁴ Porter specifies further, "an appetite is an inclination toward some end which is exigent, or at least

---

71. *NR*, 176. Porter follows Aquinas here, see *ST*, II-II 108.2. See Rachels's criterion a) for a virtue ethics approach noted above.

72. *NR*, 181. This is the beginning of Porter's fulfillment of Rachels's criterion b) noted above, that an adequate virtue ethics "provides a list specifying which character traits are virtues."

73. *NR*, 181. As Porter notes, not all authors agree that the traditional cardinal virtues are fundamental. For example, James Keenan argues that the virtues of justice, fidelity, self-care, and prudence would be more appropriate as cardinal virtues. See Keenan, "Proposing Cardinal Virtues." While acknowledging the validity of Keenan's argument, I propose that my exploration of Porter's theory here and below reveals that the virtues of temperance and fortitude (which Keenan's revised version of the cardinal virtues replaces with fidelity and self-care) are still valid as cardinal virtues, especially given their role in perfecting the expression of the human person's prerational appetites. See also Spohn's fifth characteristic of a virtue ethics approach, as noted above.

74. *NR*, 256. On the consistent link between passions and appetites in Aquinas, see also White, "The Passions of the Soul (Ia IIae, Qq.49–70)," 103. Pope also links Thomas's use of the word *passions* with his use of the word *emotions*. See Pope, "Overview," 33.

appropriate to the existence and flourishing of a specific kind of creature."[75] In the case of the passions, this refers to the human person's prerational inclination to desire that which is required for survival and reproduction and, in the case of the will, this refers to the person's orientation towards the good as such, which is apprehended by reason.[76] We will return to the will below. For now, we focus on the passions.

Porter follows Aquinas in understanding the passions as our capacities to experience desire for those goods which ensure that the basic necessities of natural well-being are met (food and drink, for example) and our ability to counter resistance in the pursuit of what is good.[77] As Kevin White notes, the word 'passion,' in this Thomistic sense refers to the experience of being pulled, or even yanked, towards some object of desire and, as other authors have noted, this is closely related to our contemporary understanding of affectability or emotion.[78] Such an aspect of our humanity, White argues, is morally significant precisely because it serves to direct the attention of the human person, a point which we will develop further in this chapter and in chapter 5.[79] As we have indicated above, Aquinas identified two unique types of passions, following two types of appetites that characterize the human person. The first of these can be broadly understood as the 'concupiscible appetite' which draws the human person towards those goods that are basic to human survival: food, drink, and sex.[80] The second of these can be understood as the 'irascible appetite,' a term which Aquinas uses to refer to the confrontational power that arises in the human person when goods become difficult to attain.[81] There is thus a link between the concupiscible and irascible appetites, which White explains in the following way:

---

75. *NR*, 256.

76. Ibid., 254.

77. See ibid., 192.

78. White, "The Passions," 103. See for example Ryan, "Positive and Negative Emotions in Aquinas," 144.

79. White, "The Passions," 103, 111.

80. Cates, "The Virtue of Temperance," 321. Furthermore, the emotional pull toward these goods is expressed through the dispositions of love, desire, or delight and is undermined through the correlative dispositions of hatred, aversion, and sadness. See *ST*, I-II 26–39.

81. As above, the irascible appetite is expressed through courage and hope in the positive, and is undermined by fear and despair in the negative. Interestingly, Aquinas's discussion of the irascible appetite includes a consideration of anger, which is somewhat ambivalent and, without conceding such a thing as "righteous anger," does acknowledge that anger can have both good and evil objects. See *ST*, I-II 40–48. On anger, see 46–48.

> The concupiscible appetite seems to operate as continually as perception, the irascible only in special circumstances. Arousal of the latter signals interruption in the smooth concupiscible flow of love toward the delightful and of hatred away from the painful: suddenly desire and aversion are no longer enough to ensure this flow; an obstacle has appeared; the soul responds by tensing for struggle. In meeting its new, elevated object, the soul seems to become more alert and potentially stronger.[82]

Understood in this way, the appetites (and therefore passions with them) refer to those dimensions of the human person which are prerationally oriented towards well-being and can therefore be specified in happiness. As such, they "are part of our creaturely nature and therefore good in themselves; the key moral challenge they present lies in their proper ordering rather than in their repression."[83] To move to an understanding of what it means to order these inclinations properly, we turn now to the virtues which are associated with them. As we have noted above, each is linked with a specific cardinal virtue. In the case of the concupiscible appetite and our inclination towards the goods required to exist and continue existing, the virtue is temperance and, in the case of the irascible appetite and the desire to counter resistance when pursuing goods, the virtue is fortitude.[84] We will explore each of these in turn and, in so doing, further our understanding of the relationship between prerational nature, the virtues and happiness.

THE VIRTUES OF THE PASSIONS: TEMPERANCE AND FORTITUDE

The Virtue of Temperance

In order to explore the virtue of temperance and its relationship with the human person's natural orientation towards survival and reproduction, it is worth drawing on a concrete example. This is a helpful approach because, as Keenan has pointed out, virtues should always relate to concrete living and, as we have seen above, Porter argues that all virtues are expressed in paradigmatic kinds of actions.[85] Whilst we have noted above that temper-

---

82. White, "The Passions," 109. Cf. Cates, "The Virtue of Temperance," 322; Pope, "Overview," 33.

83. Pope, "Overview," 33.

84. To follow on from the footnote above, which suggests that *passions* are equivalent to *emotions* in more contemporary terminology, the concupiscible appetite would be understood as a positive emotion and the irascible appetite a negative one.

85. Keenan, "Proposing Cardinal Virtues," 709.

ance can refer to the goods of food, drink, and sex, for the sake of specificity we will take as our example, as Porter does, the natural human inclination towards nourishment through food.[86] Clearly, this inclination is oriented towards our overall well-being, given that its enactment provides us with the raw materials, as it were, which are necessary to exist and to continue existing as a human person.[87] However, the inclination itself does not specify what we *should* eat and it does not engage in the moderation of meal size and frequency, or the appropriate place that the inclination has when it is considered within the life of the human person as a whole. As such, it orients us towards what is good, but it does not provide a framework which is capable of moderating the expression of this orientation, or situating it within human life considered as a whole.[88]

It is here that the operation of the virtues of the passions as the appropriate specification of prerational inclinations fit. In the case at hand, the prerational orientation towards the good of food would be directed towards the virtue of temperance which, in this case, enables one to moderate his consumption of food. *Moderation* is a key term here, because the virtue points not only to the *restriction* of the amount of food or drink one consumes but also to the necessity to consume some food and drink in the first place. In this sense, the mean of the virtue avoids both the vices of deficiency in regards to food (which would refer to uncapped aversion) and, of course, gluttony (which would refer to uncapped desire).[89]

Porter explains the point we have been developing thus far in this way:

> Because our inclinations regarding food and drink are so vital to our life and well-being, and yet are so unreliable as guides toward our overall interest, we need dispositions of restraint with respect to them—or better still, we need to discipline and shape them in such a way that they serve as more reliable guides to what is truly good for us. By the same token, we only need a little experience and reflection to see that these qualities of temperance are desirable for ourselves and admirable in others.[90]

As we have seen above, such dispositions are expressed through paradigmatic kinds of actions (as distinct from pure, abstract concepts, or

---

86. For Porter's own articulation of this example see *NR*, 180. As such, the focus will remain set on the expression of this appetite as desire and its opposite aversion.

87. It also thereby corresponds to the basic level of natural law that humans share with all other creatures.

88. Cates, "The Virtue of Temperance," 321.

89. Ibid., 321, 328–29.

90. Ibid., 180.

abstract rules) which allow the human person to grasp the point of virtuous disposition a paradigm represents and enact it within the context of his own life. In terms of temperance, as we also noted above, such a paradigm could be found in the person who is presented with a banquet of food but chooses to consume only what is necessary for his own well-being. What we can add here is that the virtue of temperance possesses something of an agent relative character. That is, the amount of food or drink that secures well-being and provides the foundation for the happiness of the human person depends on a number of factors. To state the obvious, the 6 foot 3-inch adult will require more food and drink to achieve well-being than will the 3 foot 6-inch child. Nevertheless, the mean of the virtue will be expressed within the context of a unique human life which must account for a great deal more than simple well-being. Temperance may be able to tell us something of what happiness looks like for the human person in the way in which she goes about her survival, but it does not necessarily tell us how she should direct other dimensions of her prerational nature. For that, we need an appeal to further virtues. We continue, therefore, to the virtue of fortitude. As we will see, our discussion of fortitude introduces further complexities into our analysis of the virtues which were not immediately apparent in our consideration of temperance.

The Virtue of Fortitude

Porter notes that the virtue of fortitude or (as it is also known) courage, presents a particular problem in our understanding of virtue considering it was most frequently understood in classical texts as associated with courage on the battlefield, and in Christian works as relating to courage in the face of martyrdom. Clearly, these involve two rather different activities with two very different objects.[91] And yet, and as Aquinas pointed out, each understanding of the virtue has some commonalities, "as both reflect a willingness to endure death for the sake of some greater good."[92] In view of this, Porter argues that, although the virtue itself is primarily understood in its most extreme sense as courage in the face of death, it can also be plausibly understood as referring to the courage that is shown in other contexts. Indeed, such courage at its most basic level is essential for the moral life, as R. E. Houser notes:

---

91. Ibid., 183.
92. Ibid., 183.Cf. Houser, "The Virtue of Courage (IIa IIae, Qq. 123–140)," 309.

> Without some level of confidence in preparing to act, some ability to accomplish the task at hand, some ability to endure obstacles, and some constancy in pursuing the end, no act could ever be accomplished.[93]

As such, the virtue of fortitude refers to what it means for a person to act in an appropriate way in the face of some perceived obstacle, and therefore links with the irascible appetite that we noted above. In the same way that temperance finds the mean between gluttony and deficiency, fortitude's appropriate expression avoids the vices of *cowardice*, understood as a lack of courage in the face of any perceived hardship, and *foolhardiness*, understood as the lack of an adequate awareness of one's limitations, exemplified in the person who consistently places himself in extreme situations with the potential for great harm for the sake of little good.[94]

Whilst this provides us with a degree of moral guidance, as we can see in the following example, the virtue itself lacks a certain degree of normative weight without recourse to some broader account as to what it means to be human and, as a consequence, what counts as an act of fortitude:

> Imagine the situation of someone who spends much of his adult life as a professional soldier, with much experience of battle and many occasions for displaying physical courage. Now suppose that this man undergoes a kind of moral or religious conversion, which leads him to adopt a strict pacifism. This conversion will lead him to renounce much of what he previously prized and did under the rubric of courageous behavior—aggressively attacking the enemy, withstanding hostile fire on the battlefield, and the like. Yet he may well find himself called upon to exercise other forms of courage, perhaps as difficult in their way—patience in the face of ignominy, willing submission to arrest and detention (supposing, say, he refuses to follow orders to fight), even submission to death (supposing he is court-martialed and shot). These qualities of patience, forbearance, and the willing submission to death are defensibly forms of courage, or closely allied to it—they find their field of operation in situations of risk

---

93. Houser, "The Virtue of Courage," 308. On this point, Porter includes the example of someone who risks a large sum of money for some greater good. See *NR*, 184. Cf. Pope, "Overview," 43. Here Pope distinguishes between courage as a general virtue, understood as that which "gives the emotional stability required for the exercise of each and every virtue" and as a special virtue, which "enables the agent to endure or resist challenges to steadfastness of mind, especially in situations involving moral danger." While this specification is not made explicit in Porter's own commentary on fortitude, it is congruent with her development of the virtue.

94. Kane, "Fortitude, Virtue Of," 822.

and potential or actual loss, and they are characterized by a willingness to risk or forgo lesser goods for more important goods. Yet these are not just examples of turning the same quality of aggressive physical courage to different ends, as if the soldier were to switch sides in the middle of a war; they represent distinctive ways of acting and comporting oneself in response to the actions of others, informed by very different views about the overall value of physical aggressiveness, and therefore its appropriateness, or not, as an expression of courage.[95]

This point introduces an interesting complexity into our discussion of virtue. As we saw, it was rather simple to posit a particular paradigm for the virtuous expression of the prerational inclination towards food, drink, and sexual relations, the primary means of survival for the human person. Our consideration of fortitude has highlighted the fact, however, that certain paradigms of virtue will be necessarily related to broader considerations about, in this case, the relative value of something like physical aggression or involvement in war as an expression of courage. More broadly still, such values are typically understood in the midst of a consideration of the appropriate shape of human life considered in its entirety. These considerations are what Porter refers to as 'speculative' considerations.[96]

To begin such considerations, we would do well to remember that—as Levinas so powerfully pointed out—we are not individual persons attempting to survive in isolation, but rather *communal* persons attempting to survive *together*. This means that any appropriate expression of any particular virtue must also acknowledge that human persons are not simply self-referential creatures, and that part of our prerational nature orients us towards a concern for the Others with whom we share our lives.

By way of example, the expression of temperance that we noted above must be further specified if we are to understand it as truly virtuous. It may be that enjoying a light meal is an expression of temperance on an individual level, but can it be considered virtuous if the meal is eaten at the expense of another's survival? Furthermore, in the same sense, whilst one might exemplify courage on the battlefield as in the example above, could

---

95. *NR*, 227–28.

96. A note of caution is in order in terms of Porter's use of this word, because she does not mean speculative in the sense that they are *merely speculative*, which is the way in which the word is frequently used today. Rather, she is pointing toward the operations of speculative—or theoretical—reason. This dimension of reason is chiefly concerned with epistemology: knowing something, as distinct from practical reason, which is oriented toward doing something. See Keenan, "The Virtue of Prudence," 265. Here Keenan draws on Westberg, *Right Practical Reason*, 4. We return to develop this point in more detail in chap. 5.

this be considered virtuous if the battle was waged on immoral grounds? Certainly, Aquinas would not have seen either of these as truly virtuous actions. In fact, strictly speaking, Aquinas would see such dispositions as *habits* and not as virtues.[97] This is because they lack the perfections of justice and prudence. At this point, we can turn to consider the virtue of justice. We will consider prudence in chapter 5 after first having established in chapter 4 a suitable multi-dimensional understanding of the human person as a criterion to which prudence can be applied.

THE VIRTUE OF JUSTICE

Preliminary Discussion and Links with Levinas

The need for a virtue such as justice acknowledges that virtues such as temperance and fortitude, whilst necessarily self-referential, are enacted in the midst of a web of interpersonal relationships with other persons who are valuable and who must therefore be considered in the complex task of expressing human nature in the most appropriate way.[98] At this point of the book, this should not surprise us. As we have seen, the virtues can be understood as aligning the human person's expression of her prerational, natural intelligibilities with happiness. As we have also seen, the insights of Levinas which we explored in chapter 1 suggest that on a prerational level, human persons are constituted in such a way that they can recognize the value of other persons and are motivated to respond. It is therefore natural for us to want to be in relationship, and natural for us to value relationship. If all of these insights are true, then we can expect that over the course of human history communities would have developed specific paradigms of action which acknowledge the value of other persons and seek to take them into account in the task of moral decision making. We can find such a paradigm in the virtue of justice.

Porter notes that Aquinas understood justice as a particular virtue which, as such, "is grounded in a particular human capacity and functions within a delimited sphere of operations, just as the other virtues do."[99] Following Aquinas, Porter grounds her understanding of the virtue of justice

---

97. Kent, "Habits and Virtues," 123.

98. On the level of complexity that is added to reflections on virtue ethics when justice is engaged, see Porter, "The Virtue of Justice (IIa IIae, Qq. 58–122)," 272, 274. See also Gallagher, "The Will and Its Acts (Ia IIae, Qq. 6–17)," 75.

99. Porter also notes that this understanding is grounded in the long standing tradition of considering justice as one of the four cardinal virtues. See *NR*, 203. See *ST* II-II 58.5–7.

in the classical jurist's definition of the term which was expressed in the Code of Justinian. On this view, justice is "the constant and perpetual will to render to each one that which is his due."[100] It is distinct from the virtues of fortitude and temperance, which are virtues of the passions, because it is a virtue of the will and, as we have noted above, the will is oriented not to the fulfillment of this or that good, as are passions, but rather to the good in itself.[101] Its field of operation is also distinct from these virtues because it is concerned with external actions "through which we maintain (or violate) right relations with other persons."[102] This means that the expression of the virtue does not have an agent-relative character, as did temperance and fortitude, but rather that its expression is determined by criteria that exist independently of the individual.[103] Before exploring this point in more detail, it is worth spending some more time unpacking what Aquinas, and Porter following him, understand the will to be so as to assist in our understanding of justice and its relationship to the other virtues.

The Will and Self-Love

An understanding of the will lies at the heart of Aquinas' ethics.[104] Indeed, he would argue that, in the absence of the operations of the will, the actions of the human person lack a corresponding moral quality, falling instead into the category of natural activity.[105] As David Gallagher notes, Aquinas' understanding of the will corresponds broadly to what he refers to as *free-will*. To understand it in a more comprehensive sense, however, one must locate it within the Thomistic understanding of appetites. Recall that above we considered the concupiscible and irascible appetites—the passions—which incline a person towards certain goods that are required for a living creature to exist and reproduce. More specifically still, Aquinas would call these 'sensing appetites' which, as we indicated in chapter 2, are the kinds of natural inclinations that the human person shares with other sentient

---

100. *NR*, 203. See also Porter, "The Virtue of Justice," 272. Cf. *ST* II-II 58.1.

101. *NR*, 203. See also Porter, "The Virtue of Justice," 272, 276–77. The existence of such an orientation is acknowledged by Stephen Pope: "We have a natural inclination not only to this or that class of goods, say, for food or drink or sex, but also, and more importantly, to what in general or what is comprehensively good." Pope, *Human Evolution and Christian Ethics*, 179. See also Porter, "The Virtue of Justice," 272.

102. *NR*, 203. See ST I-II 60.2,3; II-II 58.8.

103. Porter, "The Virtue of Justice," 273.

104. As Gallagher notes, Thomas devotes "an extended discussion to the will and willed action (Ia IIae, qq. 6–17)." Gallagher, "The Will and Its Acts," 69.

105. Gallagher, "The Will and Its Acts," 69.

creatures.[106] The will, on the other hand, is a 'rational appetite,' a type of appetite that is found only in creatures with the use of reason.[107] As with the sense appetites, the rational appetite involves a natural orientation towards what is good for the human person. The difference is, as Gallagher notes, that what is "good can be apprehended at the level of intellect—grasped under some universal formality of goodness—and so the agent can tend toward the good by means of an appetite distinct from sensitive appetite."[108]

As such, Aquinas introduces the will as an appetite which refers not only to the human creature's orientation towards this or that aspect of her existence (the concupiscible appetite's orientation towards survival and reproduction, for example), but rather is oriented towards what counts as good for her comprehensively considered, which includes her rational capacities.[109] This latter point is particularly important because, as we will see, Porter understands properly human natural inclinations as inherently linked with their mediation through reason, and here we can see that the Thomistic view understands the will as that aspect of the human person which performs this mediation.[110]

Following Aquinas, Porter argues that this understanding of the will manifests itself primarily in the love of self, which Aquinas understood as second only to love of God. It is worth noting that neither Porter nor Aquinas see a contradiction between the life of happiness, the life of virtue and the love of self, because to love one's self is to desire to be happy, and true happiness *is* the virtuous life.[111] Nonetheless, if our understanding of happiness is to correspond with what we know about the human person as oriented towards an acknowledgement of the value of others, the will cannot remain self-referential. On its own, self-love is not sufficient: it needs to become outwardly focused. As a perfection of the will, the virtue of justice

---

106. Ibid., 70.

107. Ibid.

108. Ibid., 71. This links with Porter's suggestion that the virtues need to appeal to speculative considerations, given that these link with the functions of the speculative—or theoretical—intellect.

109. Ibid., 71–72. In Porter's words, the will is "spontaneously oriented towards the agent's overall good." *NR*, 205.

110. We will return to this point in chap. 5 when we will consider the will's role as mediating between prerational nature and reason in more detail.

111. *NR*, 205–6. More specifically, as Ryan notes, Aquinas argues that "a) healthy self-love is an essential component of Christian living, b) we must have love for our body as a gift from God, c) concern for one's own good is integral to moral virtue or self-transcendence." Ryan, "Healthy Shame? An Interchange between Elspeth Probyn and Thomas Aquinas," 9. See *ST*, II-II 25.4; 25.5; 26.6.

aims to orient it away from itself and towards a more comprehensive disposition towards the good, which includes the good of others.¹¹²

For Porter, this reorientation of the will is a further alignment of the human person with happiness, because it moves towards this overall goal of human existence. It is worth quoting Porter at length here, because her commentary can lead us to a point at which we can strengthen the bond between her approach and the Levinasian insight still further:

> We might say with Aquinas that each person naturally and necessarily seeks his own happiness, while adding that one's happiness is not all that the agent seeks. After all, on Aquinas's view the will is oriented toward the good as such, not toward this or that particular good, and for that very reason it can only operate on the basis of intellectual judgments that this or that object or state of affairs is good. We are certainly capable of conceiving of good things or situations which are greater than ourselves. So it would seem that nothing prohibits us from loving and pursuing these greater goods, in addition to or even to the detriment of our own individual good. Seen in this way, justice would add something to the natural orientation of the will which not only develops and completes it, but supersedes it.¹¹³

It is at this point that Porter departs slightly from Aquinas although, as we will see, she remains true to his overall methodology. Aquinas suggests that the link between self-love and justice exists because, for a person to attain happiness, she must be in a state of right relations with those around her and her community at large.¹¹⁴ However, Porter believes that there is a better way of linking self-love and justice, and she develops this in view of Aquinas' argument that "right self-love can only stem from a correct appraisal of one's nature."¹¹⁵ At this point, Porter's theory reveals a capacity to integrate the insights that we have developed in chapter 1, namely, that we are naturally oriented towards participating in, and valuing, relationship with other persons. We are consistently reminded that we are profoundly

---

112. *NR*, 207.

113. Ibid., 208–9. Given the relationship between the will, self-love, and the virtue of justice, Porter warns against separating the virtue of justice from those of the passions, and instead argues that it should be understood as a virtue that exists in constructive dialogue with the virtues of the passions, guiding and directing these in ways that are appropriate within the web of interpersonal relationships of which the human person is a part. See ibid., 204.

114. Ibid., 209–10. Cf. Gallagher, "The Will and Its Acts," 72. See for example *ST*, I-II 92.1 *ad* 3; II-II 47.10.

115. *NR*, 210. See *ST*, II-II 25.7

relational creatures and any adequate account of self-love, according to Porter, must take into account this fact of human nature:

> With respect to the issue at hand, this will include recognizing the fact that we are naturally social animals, and our characteristic way of life involves participating, from birth to death, in a complex network of social relationships. As Aristotle long ago remarked, we are social animals, and today we are frequently reminded of the relational character of human existence. While this claim has been interpreted in dubious ways, there is a sense in which it is certainly true—the sense, that is to say, in which it points to a fundamental feature of our distinctive way of life as animals of a certain kind, namely, highly social primates. Hence, reflection on our relational character will bring us, once again, to look at the way in which "nature as nature," stemming from prerational aspects of our nature, informs "nature as reason," that is to say, the moral exigencies of a distinctively human natural law.[116]

In the first instance, Porter cautions that this general observation should not be understood as something which applies to humans alone. After all, we share some of our social characteristics with other animals, especially the higher primates.[117] Porter warns, however, against overstating this correlation. Instead, she argues that the human way of engaging in social interaction *is* the characteristic which distinguishes a specifically human way of achieving well-being:

> On the most fundamental level, no one could come into existence and develop into a flourishing maturity without the care and guidance of others, and not just one's immediate family, either. In innumerable ways through our lives we rely on others for basic sustenance, security, and protection and support in

---

116. *NR*, 210. Note that Pope makes a similar point about self-love: "one can understand that self-love is neither good nor bad, neither a virtue nor a vice, but simply an expression of human nature, and therefore capable of displaying either adherence to, or departure from, right reason. Self-love is virtuous when it properly relates one to the good, vicious when it distorts this relation." Pope, *The Evolution of Altruism*, 81. See also Ryan, "Aquinas on Compassion,"161.

117. See *NR*, 210–11. Porter further cautions that this insight should not be understood as the beginnings of some form of social determinism. As she has stated elsewhere, natural inclinations *underdetermine* moral conclusions, but they still allow for a diversity of expressions of these. An example of this can be found in close, interpersonal relationships that are clearly a manifestation of a deep human drive to connect, but that also play out in a plethora of ways according to the individuals who participate in the relationship, their cultural and historical context, and so on. See ibid., 211.

> times of need. Moreover, apart from some communal context we would not be able to exist and to flourish in accordance with our most distinctive capacities for rationality as expressed in speech and deliberation. By the same token, most or all of the activities, commitments, and goals which give meaning and structure to our lives presuppose some kind of communal practice.[118]

This argument is not to be understood as some form of social determinism which would suggest that we are simply programmed to treat one another justly. Even a simple observation of interaction between humans would reveal that this is not the case. It does, however, further the argument that we developed in chapter 1, that human persons are oriented towards acknowledging the value of others, and acknowledging the value of the community at large. It also reveals the extent to which the true good of the human person is aligned with the good of others.[119] For Porter, this is true at a fundamentally *natural* level: "no one could come into existence and flourishing maturity without the care and guidance of others."[120] For Levinas, this is true at the level of consciousness, for there would be no "I" without the experience of the Other. Both authors develop these arguments with different methodologies, as noted above. The congruency of their insights, however, is clear.

Setting the Scene for the Virtue of Justice

We cautioned in chapter 1 that the observation of our profoundly relational nature alone does not mean that it will be enacted appropriately or, we can now say, *justly*, and that caution remains. As Porter has made clear in her account of other natural inclinations, there is a diversity of ways of expressing them, and not all of them are equal, which means that it would be possible for someone to live within and benefit from a life in relationship without ever doing so justly.[121] By way of example, we can return to the person of temperance who, whilst only eating and drinking what is required for his own

---

118. Ibid., 213. Pope develops a similar argument in his own consideration of the relationship between self-love, neighbor-love, and love of God: "When ordered properly, love for God, self, and neighbor is not fundamentally in competition. Conflict can and does exist, obviously, but here it takes place within the larger scheme of cooperation and caring for the common good." Pope, *Human Evolution and Christian Ethics*, 239. See also Pope, *The Evolution of Altruism*, 59, cf. 79.

119. See Aquinas's understanding of mutual indwelling—something Porter does not include—*ST*, I-II 28.2

120. *NR*, 212.

121. Ibid., 214.

well-being, may do so with the full knowledge that the required production and preparation of his food and drink is built on an unjust system of slave farming, and takes place to the detriment of the environment—an action which could hardly be considered just.

We must therefore return to the definition of justice as the "constant and perpetual will to render to each individual his or her due" and develop this further.[122] In doing so, it will help to ground ourselves in Porter's understanding of virtues. As we have seen, Porter sees the virtues as communally created and ordained dispositions of character which embody the prerational inclinations of the human person in happiness. Furthermore, they are expressed in paradigmatic actions that act as pedagogical tools which aid individuals in their moral navigation through life. In view of this, we can ask what exactly a paradigm of justice might look like, and how it would be complemented with the enhanced awareness of the value of other persons that we have developed in chapter 1.

Porter herself does not seek to develop a detailed account of this paradigm. We can, however, take some guiding principles from the way in which she understands justice itself, and from the way in which she has developed her theory thus far. Porter believes that the definition of justice she has been building on (to render to each his or her due) is the most plausible definition of this virtue, despite its generality.[123] She gives three reasons for this. First, it acknowledges that justice is concerned with the claims of others given that it corresponds with neither withholding what is due nor causing harm and, as a virtue of the will, is not dependent on an individual's passions.[124] This means that it is binding for all individuals, and is not agent-relative in the same way that the virtues of the passions are.[125] Second, as a virtue of the will, and with its focus on 'the due,' justice points us towards a speculative understanding of what precisely is due to other human persons.[126] This is because, as we have noted, the will which justice perfects is a rational appetite, a "distinctively human capacity to desire whatever the intellect judges to be good" and, as such, "always presupposes an intellectual judgment that a given object of choice is in some way good."[127] Hence, justice appeals to a

---

122. Ibid., 215.

123. Ibid., 217.

124. Porter, "The Virtue of Justice," 273; NR, 217. Cf. Martin Rhonheimer's understanding of justice: "[J]ustice has to do with the relationship to one's fellow human beings: to them as persons, to their lives, their physical integrity, and the material and spiritual goods to which they are entitled." Rhonheimer, "Sins against Justice," 287.

125. See Porter, "The Virtue of Justice," 272, cf. 274.

126. Speculative, as understood in terms of the clarification given above.

127. Porter, "The Virtue of Justice," 275. See ST, I-II 9.1; 19.3

"reflective sense of what it means to live in a community, what one's place in that community is, and what kinds of claims others can make on oneself."[128]

Elsewhere, Porter describes this as a form of 'settled policy' on what counts as good for the human person, something which draws on not only the insights of individuals, but primarily the insights of communities.[129] This means that it can be understood as developed through the means of Porter's understanding of tradition which, as we have seen, follows the thought of Alasdair MacIntyre. This gives us reason for appealing more explicitly to an anthropological vision informed by the Catholic tradition and the understanding of what is 'due' to other persons that has been developed therein. Finally, Porter argues that justice presupposes that our understanding of what is due to other persons will also influence our understanding of the self, given that we have seen the close correlation between the development of the self and the self's relationship with others. This will provide us with further opportunity to develop the Levinasian insight in relationship with Porter's theory and especially in relationship with the virtue of justice.

As such, our consideration of the virtue of justice requires us to engage with the speculative account of the human person and what is due to him, which can be found in the Catholic tradition. We turn to this task in the next chapter.

CONCLUSION

In this chapter, we have continued our detailed consideration of Porter's theory of natural law and, in so doing, have moved from her understanding of prerational nature and towards the integration of virtue ethics into her approach. We began our exploration of this dimension of Porter's theory by explaining her use of the term *happiness* as the necessary specification of the way in which the intelligibilities of prerational nature (which are expressed by the terms natural well-being and flourishing) can be expressed, the need for which we noted at the end of chapter 2. The integration of virtue into Porter's theory led us to consider contemporary discussions surrounding virtue ethics, and to analyze how Porter's theory relates to these. In terms of the book considered as a whole, this provided a way of linking the robust discussion between Levinas and Porter and, correlatively, opens up the possibility for considering the virtue of solidarity in light of the virtue of prudence, a topic to which we will return in Chapters Five and Six.

128. NR, 217. Cf. Porter, "The Virtue of Justice," 277.
129. Porter, "The Virtue of Justice," 275.

After this part of the chapter, we analyzed the foundations of Porter's approach to virtue ethics by revisiting the relationship between natural well-being, happiness and the virtues, before briefly turning away from Porter to consider the opposite of virtue—vice—and its relationship to the theological concept of sin. We then explored the virtues of temperance and fortitude. The chapter then turned to the virtue of the will—justice—and explained how, as a virtue of the will, the virtuous disposition of justice orients a human person's concern for the good away from a sole focus on themselves and towards a focus on the good more comprehensively considered. On this latter point, we saw that Porter suggests the need to appeal to speculative considerations of what counts as the good of the human person in order to discover, more specifically, what is 'due' to him or her. This observation led the chapter to propose a shift to a focus on an anthropological vision informed by the Catholic tradition. This will be the focus of chapter 4.

4

An Anthropological Vision Informed by the Catholic Tradition

INTRODUCTION

THIS CHAPTER MARKS A further methodological shift within the book's argument towards an exploration of official Vatican teachings and also the personalist moral theology of Louis Janssens, specifically his understanding of 'the human person integrally and adequately considered.' When considered in relationship to the argument being developed as a whole, the chapter builds from Porter's suggestion that the virtue of justice needs to operate in dialogue with a developed anthropology which can help to specify what precisely is 'due' to the human person. The specific anthropological vision it develops is informed by the Catholic tradition, as was indicated in the introduction. The chapter is largely integrative in its focus and frequently links its anthropological vision to what has been developed in Chapters One, Two and Three, whilst opening up the possibility for the introduction of the virtue of solidarity in chapter 6. Finally, it provides the necessary material to show why an appeal to this anthropological vision leads to the conclusions suggested by the work as a whole and, as such, is frequently cross-referenced in Chapters Five and Six.

The chapter begins by developing what it refers to as a 'paradigm for justice within a Roman Catholic framework,' which arises out of Porter's argument that the virtues appeal to particular paradigms for action in their description. Inasmuch as it refers to the virtue of justice, this paradigm takes the form of a developed anthropology which can specify what is due to the human person. In this case, the paradigm is informed by the Catholic tradition. The chapter therefore develops core components of this paradigm which include the Catholic understanding of human dignity as well as Pope Paul VI's concept of transcendent humanism. Later, the chapter refines these core components still further by introducing Louis Janssens's understanding of 'the human person integrally and adequately considered' and explores each of Janssens's eight dimensions of the human person, and then develops this further by adding to it the concepts of vulnerability (which links with the discussion of Levinas in chapter 1) and sin (which builds from the discussion which began in chapter 3).[1] The chapter concludes by revisiting the core points of the anthropological vision developed throughout, re-emphasizing its role in relationship to the virtue of justice, and pointing forwards to Chapters Five and Six.

A PARADIGM OF JUSTICE WITHIN A ROMAN CATHOLIC FRAMEWORK

Foundations

The magisterium of the Roman Catholic Church's definition of justice is grounded in the same definition that Porter builds on in her theory: justice "consists in the constant and firm will to give their due to God and neighbor."[2] The word *justice* comes from the Latin word *ius*, which is translated as "right," which implies that justice is concerned with certain rights.[3] According to the official teaching of the Church, these rights, when they

---

1. Note that the section on sin focuses largely on personal sin, but that this should not be understood as the book's neglect of the important dimension of social/structural sin. This latter dimension of sin is dealt with in more detail in chap. 6.

2. *CSDC*, no. 201: "*Justice is a value that accompanies the exercise of the corresponding cardinal moral virtue*. According to its most classic formulation, it "consists in the constant and firm will to give their due to God and neighbor." From a subjective point of view, justice is translated into behaviour that is *based on the will to recognize the other as a person*, while, from an objective point of view, it constitutes *the decisive criteria of morality in the intersubjective and social sphere*." Here the *Compendium* draws on (respectively), ST I-II, q. 6; *CCC*, 1807; *PT*, no. 55. The 1971 document from the World Synod of Bishops, *Justice in the World*, notes the powerful connection between justice and the gospel message: "Action on behalf of justice and participation in the transformation of the world fully appear to us as a constitutive dimension of the preaching of the Gospel, or, in other words, of the Church's mission for the redemption of the human race and its liberation from every oppressive situation." *JW*, No. 6.

3. McBrien, *Catholicism*, 943.

refer to the human person, are grounded in the dignity and nature of the human person (which we will consider in detail below) and make a particular moral claim on other persons as well as on society.[4] In this sense, rights are the foundation of the duties which flow from them.[5] Following from this, justice is "concerned with *rights* and with *duties* which correspond to those rights."[6]

To align this more closely with the language Porter has introduced us to, rights are bound up with human happiness in the sense that a person has a right to happiness, and the conditions which are required to achieve that state place a moral claim on other persons and society in general. This link between persons and rights is by no means a new development. It is widely recognized—in both ancient and more modern studies of the human person—that there is a close relationship between the title 'person' and certain rights.[7] This link, however, still remains at a very general level. As Stanley Rudman's *Concepts of Person and Christian Ethics* demonstrates, there is no one agreed upon definition or understanding of the human person and, as Charles Curran has pointed out, whatever definition and understanding of the person we begin with will influence, ground and direct what we understand as due to him or her.[8]

To develop a paradigm of justice in view of the initial sketch we made in the last chapter, we must therefore refine our speculative understanding of the human person, because only when we have a more detailed understanding of the person can we begin to discuss what is due to her in an intelligible way. As we have seen, we always engage with such activities in the midst of a specific tradition. According to Porter, this is not a weakness in our approach to the development of an ethical framework. It is rather an acknowledgment of the specifically human way in which communities come to an awareness of truth, as demonstrated by Alasdair MacIntyre's "tradition constituted and constitutive enquiry." Furthermore, it gives us reason to take seriously the tradition of which this work is a part, namely the Roman

---

4. This point is summarized in *CDSC*, 152–55. Here the compendium draws on a diversity of ecclesial documents, with a special focus on Pope John Paul II's *Centesimus Annus*, 47. It also draws on *DH*, 1; *GS*, 26, 27, and 41; *VS*, 80; *EV*, 7–28.

5. See *GS*, 26. Cf. *CDSC*, 156.

6. McBrien, *Catholicism*, 943.

7. Rudman, *Concepts of Person*, 53. This relationship between the title "person" and certain rights seems to have arisen in Roman culture where the title implied certain civil rights. See Rudman, *Concepts of Person*, 16. Cf. Hittinger, "The Coherence of the Four Basic Principles of Catholic Social Doctrine: An Interpretation," 795.

8. See Rudman's *Concepts of Person*, which is a systematic exploration of different understandings of the human person and the ethical implications that follow from these. See also Curran, *Catholic Social Teaching*, 127.

Catholic tradition, and the specific insights into the human person that this tradition has developed. From a theological perspective this is a positive development because it draws an indelible line connecting our concept of the human person and the truth claims of revelation, and therefore situates the book's development of ideas clearly within the discipline of Roman Catholic ethics.[9] So what is the Catholic understanding of the human person?

Core Components of the Paradigm

There are three essential aspects which underlie the Catholic understanding of the human person and therefore underlie all Catholic ethics: 1. Human Dignity, 2. The Person as Social Creature and 3. Transcendent Humanism.[10] I wish to develop these aspects in the following two ways: First, I will begin with the Catholic understanding of human dignity because this is indeed the foundation for the Catholic understanding of the human person, and I do not believe that we can come to an understanding of what is due to each person within the tradition without using this as our starting point. Second, I wish to focus on the idea of transcendent humanism which I will argue, from a methodological perspective, incorporates the idea of the human person as social creature. This is because a transcendent humanism can account for all dimensions of the 'human person adequately considered,' a body of thought that I will introduce below which *includes* the observation that the human person is a social creature. In the following paragraphs, therefore, I will explore the official Catholic teaching on human dignity and how this is related to justice, and then the concept of a transcendent humanism, especially as this is expressed in the body of personalist thought, largely attributable to Louis Janssens, known as the 'human person integrally and adequately considered.'[11] As we will see, this exploration will provide us

---

9. This point should be tempered with the observation that the understanding of the human person developed in the Catholic tradition is *grounded* in revelation, and not directly revealed, as *Gaudium et spes* makes clear: "[T]he constitution must be interpreted according to the general norms of theological interpretation. Interpreters must bear in mind—especially in part two—the changeable circumstances which the subject matter, by its very nature, involves." GS, footnote 1.

10. Fleming, "Understanding Trade," 2.

11. It should be noted that this phrase was originally used in one of the official commentaries on *Gaudium et spes*, which sought to clarify article 51's statement that "the moral aspect of any procedure . . . must be determined by objective standards which are based on the nature of the person and his acts." For clarification, the commentary noted that this expression means that "human activity must be judged insofar as it refers to the human person integrally and adequately considered." See *Schema constitutionis pastoralis*, 37–38. Translated and explained in McCormick, *The Critical Calling*, 14. I explain the concept as it was developed by Janssens below.

with a rich understanding of the human person which, whilst not immediately prescriptive, does provide us with *enough* morally relevant content for understanding what is due to all human persons, and therefore for the development of the speculative component of our paradigm of justice.

Human Dignity

Human dignity is foundational for the Catholic understanding of the human person and, in what follows, I will explore both the source and scope of that dignity. To do so, I will engage primarily with two documents from the ecclesial magisterium: Vatican II's *Gaudium et spes* and Saint John Paul II's *Evangelium vitae*.[12] I have chosen *Evangelium vitae* because, whilst it is widely known for its condemnation of abortion and euthanasia, at a foundational level it is also a "precise and vigorous reaffirmation" of the Catholic understanding of human dignity.[13] As such, even though the gaze of the encyclical is firmly set on specific issues, these issues are dealt with out of the encyclical's understanding of human dignity and are also situated within a wider context of threats to human dignity such as poverty, malnutrition, an unjust distribution of goods, the arms trade, war, abuse of the environment, the drugs trade and certain kinds of sexual activity.[14] As a synthesis of the Catholic understanding of human dignity, the encyclical is highly relevant for the task at hand—as Richard McCormick rightly pointed out soon after it was published, "there is nothing new or unexpected in this encyclical."[15] The close links between *Evangelium Vitae* and *Gaudium et spes* will be noted in the footnotes throughout this section.

Evangelium Vitae begins its discourse on human dignity by affirming the distinctiveness of human life in contrast with the lives of other creatures, and John Paul II uses this foundation to suggest that the unique good of the life of the human person from a Catholic perspective is tied to the intimate

---

12. On the foundational role that human dignity plays in *Gaudium et spes*, see Kelly, *New Directions in Moral Theology*, 28.

13. *EV*, no. 5.

14. See ibid., no. 10. Cf. no. 87. See also Dadosky, "The Church and the Other," 313. It is also worth noting that the methodology the encyclical employs grants its understanding of human dignity significant doctrinal weight. John Paul II understands his condemnations of abortion, euthanasia, and murder as affirmations of what has always been church teaching and he bases these on the natural law, Scripture, tradition, and the teachings of the ordinary and universal Magisterium. See for example *EV*, no. 57. This issue is dealt with in detail in Sullivan, "The Doctrinal Weight of Evangelium Vitae."

15. McCormick, "The Gospel of Life," 10.

relationship between the human person and her creator.[16] This is not to suggest that there is no continuity between the human person and the rest of creation, a position which would immediately invalidate the link between the Catholic understanding of human dignity and the emphasis that Porter's theory places on the links we share with other creatures in our prerational nature, but rather that the human person is unique in a way that transcends other creatures.[17] Nowhere is this more evident than the affirmation of Genesis 1 that the human person is created in God's image and likeness (Gen 1:26–7), a point which is strongly stated in both *Evangelium vitae* and *Gaudium et spes*.[18] *Evangelium vitae* interprets this affirmation as referring to the relationship between God and the human person: the fact that the human person is called into life means that he is immediately involved in a radical relationship with the Creator and it is the sacredness implied by this relationship that is the location of an individual's inviolable dignity.[19] Significantly, from the point of view of this work, the grounding of human dignity is essentially relational: the human person is defined and dignified because of his relationship with God. In this way, the person is understood not as an object which God owns, but rather a subject created in the image of God with whom God enters into relationship.[20]

This relationship is defined by both its origin and its destination, which means that it is essentially teleological, a point which aligns well with Porter's Thomistic approach. As we noted in chapter 3, Porter refers to happiness as the goal towards which human life is oriented and understands this in an eschatological sense as the perfect happiness that is achieved in union with God, and in a temporal sense as the human person's participation in

16. *EV*, no. 34. John Paul II finds scriptural support for this claim in Gen 1:26–27 and Ps 8:6.

17. *EV*, no. 34. This point should be emphasized, because it is clear that Pope John Paul II saw no incongruence between the Catholic understanding of the human person and the theory of evolution. See Pope John Paul II, "Address to the Pontifical Academy of Sciences—October 1996." The International Theological Commission develops the theological case for this position in more detail, see CS, especially nos. 62–70.

18. See *EV*, no. 34; *GS*, no. 12. Cf. Gen 1:26.

19. *EV*, no. 40. Cf. *GS*, no. 12.

20. See Keenan, *A History of Catholic Moral Theology*, 86. Keenan locates a development in the Catholic tradition's understanding of human dignity and the sanctity of life in the teaching of John Paul II. Whereas in *Humanae Vitae* (1968), for example, the argument for the sacredness of human life relies on God's ownership of life and God's willing it to be sacred and dignified, the teaching of John Paul II aligned the sacredness of human life more clearly with *Gaudium et spes*' use of Genesis 1:26–27. According to Keenan, the argument changed to one which focused on the human person being made in God's image: "as God's person is inviolable, so is God's image." See Keenan, *A History of Catholic Moral Theology*, 85.

happiness by means of the acquired virtues. *Evangelium Vitae* also encapsulates both dimensions of this teleology for the human person—for John Paul II it refers to the goal of "fellowship with God in knowledge and love,"[21] understood as eternal life and the journey towards this that begins with earthly life which, in turn, is given breadth and depth by its orientation towards an eternal good.[22] To link this back with our commentary on human dignity, this means that true fellowship with God, the source of human dignity, has both immanent and transcendent dimensions, which implies that the dignity it secures is understood as both temporal (it applies at any given moment of time) and eternal (it applies across the earthly lifespan of a human person and into their eschatological future).[23]

It is on this foundation that *Evangelium vitae* develops its practical conclusions about what is due to the human person, primarily in terms of the human person's right to life, the basic good without which no temporal human flourishing is possible. The encyclical's focus on abortion and euthanasia must therefore be understood in the context of its understanding of human dignity. It would be a mistake to conclude, however, that the only implications of this understanding of human dignity involve the beginning and end of life.[24] Both *Evangelium Vitae* and *Gaudium et spes* make it clear that the dignity of the human person must be understood across a lifetime and that our understanding of dignity must therefore be grounded in a full understanding of what counts as human flourishing.[25] This requires that we develop the Catholic understanding of the human person further through its emphasis on 'transcendent humanism,' which will draw us into closer dialogue with *Gaudium et spes* and also with the rich body of reflection on social life known as Catholic Social Teaching.

Transcendent Humanism

'Transcendent humanism' is the name given by Pope Paul VI in his encyclical *Populorum Progressio* to those complementary aspects of the human person which must all be accounted for if human dignity is to be acknowledged,

---

21 *EV*, no. 38.

22. Ibid. We will develop this point below in our consideration of *transcendent humanism* and *the human person integrally and adequately considered*.

23. Richard McCormick shares this interpretation of *Evangelium vitae*, albeit in less detail. See McCormick, "The Gospel of Life," 11.

24. On the problem of reducing the rich concept of "human dignity" to the "dignity of life," see Kirchhoffer, "Benedict XVI, Human Dignity, and Absolute Moral Norms."

25. This is especially true in *Gaudium et spes*, as we will see below.

and which begin to paint a picture of the Catholic tradition's rich understanding of the human person.[26] Paul VI's understanding of transcendent humanism relies on the idea that the human person's purpose is to achieve self-fulfillment through moving "from less than human conditions to truly human ones."[27] To do so, a person needs to be alive and have the basic material goods required to survive as a living creature (food, water, shelter, etc.), which we must account for in order to respond adequately to human dignity.[28] Nonetheless, Paul VI subordinates material goods above and beyond the basic goods of survival to transcendent goods, suggesting that the move from a less than human condition to an authentically human condition involves moving from basic survival to a desire for peace, the common good and—above all—faith.[29] The concept of 'transcendent humanism' therefore incorporates what it means to be fully human, including growth towards fellowship with God in knowledge and love.

Transcendent Humanism and the Human Person Integrally and Adequately Considered

As I have indicated above, I will develop an argument here to show that the concept of 'transcendent humanism' can be further specified through a consideration of Janssens's development of an understanding of 'the human person integrally and adequately considered' and the further development of this concept by a number of other moral theologians. This link begins with the obvious personalist focus that we have been exploring in ecclesial teaching thus far: justice is grounded in human dignity, and our response to human dignity is, as Charles Curran noted, influenced, grounded and directed by our understanding of the human person which means that we must understand what we mean by the human person before we can hope to respond adequately. Paul VI's transcendent humanism is a further affirmation of this: the move from less than human conditions to fully human conditions must take into account all aspects of the human person, including their orientation towards God. Whilst never explicitly referring to Paul VI's transcendent humanism, Janssens noticed the groundwork for a similar personalist approach in *Gaudium et spes*, especially in its focus on

---

26. *PP*, 20. On the development and context of this concept, see Sniegocki, *Catholic Social Teaching*, 126.

27. *PP*, no. 20. As such, it shares with Porter a teleological approach, which is oriented toward human flourishing.

28. Ibid., no. 20. Cf. Pope, *Human Evolution and Christian Ethics*, 290.

29. *PP*, no. 21. Cf. Deck, "Commentary on *Populorum Progressio*," 299–300.

the human person in Part I, and the way the understanding of the person developed in this part of the document was applied to specific issues in part II.³⁰

In his most thorough commentary on the personalist focus in this document, Janssens argues that *Gaudium et spes* grounds its ethical framework in a personalist model which synthesizes what we have been exploring above.³¹ That is, as Roger Burggraeve notes, "it is only when we approach the human person integrally or holistically that he or she is given their due."³² Janssens grounds his commentary on the Catholic understanding of the human person by pointing towards one of the first drafts of *Gaudium et spes* Part II, which argued that spouses must determine the moral character of their sexual activity, especially its procreational aspect, according to "objective criteria based upon the dignity of the human person."³³ In the final document, this text reads as follows: "the moral aspect of any procedure... must be determined by objective standards which are based upon the nature of the human person and his acts."³⁴ Janssens turns to the official commentary on *Gaudium et spes* and notes the following in relation to this part of the document:

> In the official commentary it is explained: 1, that in this expression a general principle is formulated, one which is applicable not only to marriage and sexuality but also to the entire domain of human activity (*agitur de principio generali*), and 2, that it is affirmed through the choice of this expression that "human

---

30. Janssens, "Artificial Insemination," 3. On the links between the methodology of *Gaudium et spes* and *Populorum Progressio* see also Aubert, *Catholic Social Teaching*, 233. Regarding the specific article by Janssens, it is important to note that whilst the focus of the article's title is on a particular moral issue, he devotes the first half of it to developing the personalist criterion he finds in *Gaudium et spes*. A number of authors have based their commentaries on *the human person adequately considered* on this article because of the way in which it succinctly articulates the personalist methodology contained in *Gaudium et spes*. See for example Gula, *Reason Informed by Faith*, 66–73; McCormick, *The Critical Calling*, 14–16; Salzman and Lawler, *The Sexual Person*, 103–4. In a tribute to Janssens's contribution to moral theology, Roger Burggraeve points out that this article is the best synthesis of Janssens's understanding of the human person integrally and adequately considered. See Burggraeve, "The Holistic Personalism of Professor Magister Louis Janssens," 31. Keenan also acknowledges the importance of the article in his overview of Janssens's moral theology. See Keenan, *A History of Catholic Moral Theology*, 144, n. 25.

31. Janssens, "Artificial Insemination." We will explore the specifics of this commentary below.

32. Burggraeve, "Holistic Personalism," 31.

33. Janssens, "Artificial Insemination," 4.

34. GS, 51. Cf. Janssens, "Artificial Insemination," 4.

activity must be judged insofar as it refers to the human person integrally and adequately considered" (*actus diiudicandos esse. . . quatenus illi ad personam humanam integre et adequate considerandam pertinent*) In other words, in order to determine whether or not an act is worthy of man or morally good, one must apply the criterion of "the human person adequately considered," i.e., in all his essential aspects or constitutive elements.[35]

Janssens then goes on to ask what these essential aspects or constitutive elements are, and turns to the understanding of the human person promulgated in *Gaudium et spes* to identify them and explore them more closely. We will list the aspects that Janssens found in *Gaudium et spes* and then explore them in detail in a moment. Before doing so, it is worth repeating a caution that Janssens gives at the beginning of his own exploration of the human person adequately considered. That is, even though we can separate and identify different aspects of the human person, ultimately these belong to one and the same person and so are not distinct, but rather synthetic and necessarily related.[36] The purpose of separating them is therefore methodological and intended to provide clarity, rather than to dissect the human person into her component parts, as it were.[37] It is also worthwhile reiterating Levinas's strong warnings against 'totalization': the human person adequately considered is a tool for understanding persons only, and a tool that is being used in this book as part of an ethical framework which is seeking to understand the person in order to better know what is due to her. As such, it gives us a useful insight into the mystery of the human person, but it does not exhaust this mystery or encapsulate it in its entirety.

A Paradigm for Justice: The Human Person Integrally and Adequately Considered

Todd Salzman and Michael Lawler provide the following helpful summary of the dimensions of 'the human person adequately considered' that Janssens developed from the theological anthropology of *Gaudium et spes*:

> The human person is (1) a subject, (2) in corporeality, (3) in relation to the material world, (4) in relation to others, (5) in relation to social groups, (6) in relation to God, (7) a developmental

---

35. Janssens, "Artificial Insemination," 4. The reference for the original Vatican commentary is *Schema constitutionis pastoralis de ecclesia in mundo huius temporis*, 37-38 Cf. Kelly, *New Directions in Moral Theology*, 29-30.

36. Janssens, "Artificial Insemination," 4.

37. Ibid. Cf. Christie, *Adequately Considered*, 27.

An Anthropological Vision Informed by the Catholic Tradition   147

historical being, and (8) fundamentally equal to all other human persons and yet uniquely original.[38]

We will now explore each of these eight dimensions in turn, grounding our exploration in the work of Janssens and also appealing to the work of others who have developed his original framework.

The Human Person is a Subject

The first dimension of the human person adequately considered acknowledges that the human person is an active subject, as distinct from a passive object.[39] Janssens argues that *Gaudium et spes* highlights four dimensions of human subjectivity: first, that humans are normally conscious creatures; second, that human persons are called to act according to their consciences; third, that they are oriented towards acting in freedom; and, finally, that persons are called to act responsibly.[40] All of this, as Janssens notes, is what makes *moral* action possible in the first place.[41] Richard Gula furthers these observations in his commentary on the human person adequately considered as follows:

> To speak of the human person as a *subject* is to say that the person is in charge of his or her own life. That is, the person is a moral agent with a certain degree of autonomy and self-determination empowered to act according to his or her conscience, in freedom, and with knowledge.[42]

Janssens, Gula and Kevin Kelly all draw a link between this aspect of the human person and the moral implication "that no one may ever use a human person as an object or as a means to an end the way we do other things of the world."[43] For Janssens, this points towards an unconditional moral demand which prohibits exploitation.[44] Crucially, for our development

38. Salzman and Lawler, *The Sexual Person*, 103.

39. Janssens, "Artificial Insemination," 5.

40. Ibid., 5. Cf. GS, 15, 16, 17, 31, and 55, respectively. Janssens includes a footnote at this point to note that the use of the phrase "normally called to consciousness" acknowledges the presence of pathological conditions in some persons, which do not allow for the development of consciousness and that this does not, in any way, act as a qualifier for the dignity of these persons.

41. Janssens, "Artificial Insemination," 5. Cf. Gula, *Reason Informed by Faith*, 68–69.

42. Gula, *Reason Informed by Faith*, 68.

43. Ibid. Cf. Janssens, "Artificial Insemination," 5; Kelly, *New Directions in Moral Theology*, 31. See also GS, 27.

44. Janssens, "Artificial Insemination," 5.

of a paradigm of justice, this dimension of the human person adequately considered encourages moral responses which allow human subjectivity to flourish in such a way that persons are able to act freely on the basis of a conscience which is given the opportunity for adequate formation.[45] Such an approach to morality must therefore be *empowering* and encourage an appropriate degree of autonomy, as distinct from an approach which simply imposes moral responses from above, as it were. In developing these points, Kelly notes that they imply a form of moral action which invites the active participation of all and, as a consequence, prohibits all forms of totalitarianism and also "provides a critical point of reference for assessing what level of social intervention is humanly acceptable in different situations."[46]

The importance of this dimension of the human person has been expressed in the body of thought known as Catholic Social Teaching (CST), especially in the principles of participation and subsidiarity. These principles are closely related and we will consider each in turn. We begin with participation, which refers to:

> *a series of activities by means of which the citizen, either as an individual or in association with others, whether directly or through representation, contributes to the cultural, economic, political and social life of the civil community to which he belongs. Participation is a duty to be fulfilled consciously by all, with responsibility and with a view to the common good.*[47]

As such, the principle recognizes the subjectivity of the human person and acknowledges the need to respond to this by means of allowing and encouraging the active participation of all persons in all aspects of community life. Such an emphasis on participation also requires that individuals be informed as clearly and accurately as possible in situations wherein they are making decisions which will have an influence on their own, or the community's, good. Two examples are instructive here. In the first, Kelly points out that responding adequately to this dimension of the human person in a situation of medical treatment highlights the importance of informed consent.[48] In the second, the *Compendium of the Social Doctrine of the Church* argues that true democracy fosters participation by ensuring that human

---

45. Gula, *Reason Informed by Faith*, 69.
46. Kelly, *New Directions in Moral Theology*, 31.
47. CSDC, no. 189; italics in original. Here the *Compendium* is drawing from GS, 75 and CCC, 1913–1917.
48. Kelly, *New Directions in Moral Theology*, 31.

subjects at all levels of society are "informed, listened to and involved in the exercise of carried-out functions."[49]

Moving from participation takes us beyond the consideration of individual subjectivity and towards the kind of social subsidiarity that responds to Kelly's warning regarding totalitarianism and his affirmation of the need to carefully assess the appropriate levels of social intervention. As such, it aligns with both the subjectivity of the human person and the dimension which refers to the human person's participation in social groups and institutions which we consider below. Subsidiarity refers to a principle of social order which holds that social entities should be able to "perform the functions that fall to them without being required to hand them over unjustly to other social entities of a higher level, by which they would end up being absorbed and substituted, in the end seeing themselves denied their dignity and essential place."[50]

As a consequence, the principle of subsidiarity responds to the subjective dimensions of the human person through a model of social participation which prevents totalitarianism. At the same time, it does not follow that there are no circumstances in which a higher-order social entity can intervene for the good of a lower-order entity or for the community as a whole. The emphasis in such an instance should be on *subsidium*—on helping lower-order entities to participate more fully in the social order.[51]

In view of this, the first dimension of the human person integrally and adequately considered can account for the Levinasian warning against "totalization," especially when this is understood as the reduction of any human person to a passive object over which another can have control. Recall that, for Levinas, as we noted in chapter 1, the reduction of the human Other to anything less than an infinity is a violence because it is the type of action that belongs to the sphere of labor—the activity of the grasping hand which seeks to take what is outside of itself and bring it "home" in order to build up the 'I.' As such, it does not belong to the relationship between an "I" and the Other. It is not difficult to see why Levinas saw this as a violence: thinking about the Other in a way which reduces her to a passive object will inevitably lead to the kinds of actions which embody this thought which, in the social sphere, have their most radical manifestation in the forms of totalitarianism which Kelly rightly points out are incongruent with this dimension of the human person. To hold up the person as subject is to reject totalization.

49. *CSDC*, no. 190. Cf. *CA*, no. 46.
50. *CSDC*, 186.
51. See ibid.

The Human Person is a Subject in Corporeality

The second dimension of the human person adequately considered acknowledges the bodiliness of the human person as an integral part of who he is. In a move to avoid any possible dualism between body and spirit, Janssens argues that although we are both spirits *and* bodies, these dimensions of ourselves make up the one being, which means that what "concerns the human body. . . also affects the person himself."[52] Linking with the importance of the nature of the human person that we have been building from throughout the book, Kelly notes that the inseparability of the body and soul were an integral part of Aquinas' moral theology.[53] In view of this, he laments the "anti-corporeal dualism" that has frequently crept into Christian moral discourse to such an extent that it has clouded our sense of human freedom:

> We have tended to look for some hidden aspect of ourselves where we are completely undetermined and to locate human freedom at that point. In reality our freedom is embodied freedom. In other words, it is precisely through our bodies that we are able to be free. What we sometimes refer to as our 'limitations' are in fact simply the current boundaries of our present abilities. They are the package of gifts we have to live our lives with.[54]

If it is true that our embodiment is the "package of gifts we have to live our lives with" then it follows that care of our bodies is critically important for a life well lived. There is thus crucial importance attached to the adequate care of bodily needs and, as a consequence, the health of the self and the health of others. To add to this, there is an acknowledgment of the limitations that exist in the capacities of our bodies, and Janssens finds support for this claim in *Gaudium et spes*.[55] He extrapolates the document's articulation of this point further here and notes, with a point of congruence with the natural law methodology that we have been developing thus far, that "we may not consider our bodily needs and tendencies merely as biological givens."[56] They are, rather, an intelligible aspect of our whole human person which is created in the image and likeness of God.

---

52. Janssens, "Artificial Insemination," 6.
53. Kelly, *New Directions in Moral Theology*, 32.
54. Ibid., 33.
55. Janssens, "Artificial Insemination," 6. Cf. GS, 27, which links human dignity with a number of destructive acts directed at the human body and names these violations of the integrity of the human person.
56. Janssens, "Artificial Insemination," 6. Cf. GS, 51. Cf. also Burggraeve, "Holistic Personalism," 34.

Gula builds on these points and argues that this dimension of the human person adequately considered challenges us to acknowledge that we express ourselves, as God's image, through our bodies. Whilst we have an interior subjective life, this is inevitably expressed in bodily and material ways. This means, for example, that "bodily expressions of love in a relationship ought to be proportionate to the nature of commitment between persons."[57] It also means that we should respond to the needs of our own bodies, and the bodies of others, in the same capacity as we would respond to human dignity for the rest of the human person.

The Human Person is Always in Relationship with the Material World

Janssens also notes that bodiliness is the mode by which the human person interacts with the material world and, like Heidegger, refers to the person as a "being-in-the-world."[58] The practical implication of this is that human persons need the things of this world and, because of this, transform the world through labor from a natural context into a cultural one.[59] As Gula rightly notes, however, this dimension of the human person is an ambivalent one. Our ability to transform the world is not a guarantee that we will do so in healthy and fruitful ways which "sustain human dignity and the common good."[60] To this warning, we can add Levinas's critique of Heidegger's being-in-the-world which suggested that the greatest problem with this understanding of the human person was that it allowed for the reduction of other persons to mere objects (elements) which could then be overcome and used as instrumental means for a less than human end.[61] The potential for an inadequate moral response when this dimension of the human person is highlighted above all others is thus a reminder that *all* dimensions must be held together—any selective use of this concept lends itself to a dangerous reductionism.

57. Gula, *Reason Informed by Faith*, 69. Christie develops Gula's point in a slightly more technical way by noting that, for Janssens, the operations of the intellect and will "function only through the situated bodily being." See Christie, *Adequately Considered*, 28.

58. Christie notes that Janssens himself denied direct parallels between his and Heidegger's work, but that their thought is at least philosophically congruent. See Christie, *Adequately Considered*, 18.

59. Janssens, "Artificial Insemination," 6. Regarding labor, cf. GS, 33–39. Regarding culture, cf. GS, 53–62. Janssens is quick to point out that this affirmation is not the granting of a license to overcome creation in a destructive way.

60. Gula, *Reason Informed by Faith*, 70.

61. See chap. 1. Also cf. dimension 1 (subjectivity), noted above.

Kelly understands this dimension of the human person in a slightly different way and, whilst acknowledging the link between this dimension and the way in which human persons interact with and transform the world in agreement with Janssens and Gula, places his emphasis on the continuity that exists between the human person and the rest of creation.[62] Acknowledging this continuity, Kelly argues, provides a reason for considering the intelligibilities of the natural world in order to better understand ourselves. In his own words: "our affinity with the rest of the material world has added enormously to our understanding of how we operate as human beings."[63] Such an affirmation is a point of congruence with Porter's natural law methodology which, as we have seen, grounds itself in an awareness of the continuities that exist between the human creature and the rest of the natural world.

When considered in relationship to the paradigm for justice that we are developing, these points require that the human person is understood in terms of her interconnectedness, continuity and interdependence with the rest of creation: the way one interacts with one part of creation will inevitably have some sort of effect on the whole of creation.[64] Within this affirmation lies the possibility for linking the argument being developed in this work into the current and legitimate turn towards an ecological ethics which acknowledges the responsibility that human persons have for the rest of creation. Regrettably, the confines of this work do not allow us to explore this point in detail here and, indeed, the anthropocentric nature of the argument will be noted as one of its limitations in the conclusion. Nonetheless, the fact that this possibility exists provides a crucial impetus for future development of the argument.

The Human Person is Always in Relationship with Others

The fourth dimension of the human person adequately considered will not surprise us, given our focus on Levinas in chapter 1. In Janssens's own words, the essentially relational nature of the human person means that "to be man is to be fellow man."[65] He goes on to argue that "this is so true that a child can only progress toward being a moral subject with and through others. Man becomes only by contact with those who have already become."[66]

62. Kelly, *New Directions in Moral Theology*, 37; 40.
63. Ibid., 40.
64. Cf. ibid., 38.
65. Janssens, "Artificial Insemination," 8.
66. Ibid. Cf. Christie, *Adequately Considered*, 43. As we saw earlier, Porter makes this same point in similar language. See *NR*, 218.

An Anthropological Vision Informed by the Catholic Tradition

From a theological point of view, *Gaudium et spes* links this dimension of the human person with the doctrine of Creation in the Image and Likeness of God, in view of the fact that the Biblical story on which this teaching is founded refers not to the creation of an individual, but rather the creation of male and female with one another.[67] What is especially interesting for the development of a paradigm of justice that aligns with Porter's theory of natural law is the link that *Gaudium et spes* draws between the relational aspect of the human person and the teleological language of "potential" which, in this instance, is akin to what we have been referring to as "happiness":

> Their (humankind's) companionship produces the primary form of interpersonal communion. For by his innermost nature man is a social being, and unless he relates himself to others he can neither live nor develop his potential.[68]

As such, the happiness of the human person is intimately bound up with the realization of her relational dimension and any moral framework which diminishes or ignores this does not account for the human person integrally and adequately considered. This provides us with a strong link between the insight into human nature we developed in dialogue with Levinas (that we are constituted in such a way that we are oriented towards valuing those with whom we are in relationship), Porter's Thomistic approach to natural law (that our natural inclinations reveal something of our intelligible nature and are oriented towards the flourishing proper to our kind which is specified in happiness), and the teaching of the magisterium (that we cannot, from a theological point of view, embody happiness in the absence of interpersonal communion).

When related to our paradigm of justice, this dimension of the human person requires that we acknowledge the essentially and indispensably relational nature of humanity and that we analyze carefully the expressions of this which allows for the happiness of all persons. Significantly, for our purposes, Gula links this dimension of the human person with justice, arguing that "through interdependence we discover that we bear mutual responsibilities."[69] As such, actions should be judged insofar as they "promote the kind of self-giving which sustains the well-being of life together."[70]

---

67. Janssens, "Artificial Insemination," 8. "God did not create man as a solitary. For from the beginning 'male and female he created them.'" GS, 12.

68. Ibid., no. 12; parenthesis added.

69. Gula, *Reason Informed by Faith*, 67. This is a good example of the link between the natural human capacity and the virtue that perfects it that we developed earlier, see chap. 3.

70. Ibid.

The Human Person is Always in Relationship with Social Groups and Institutions

Janssens observes that *Gaudium et spes*' understanding of the relational nature of the human person leads towards an understanding of the social groups that exist in order to structure social relationships and, if these systems are ethical, orient them towards the common good.[71] The human person's tendency towards living in such organized social groups is what comprises the fifth dimension of the human person adequately considered. Such an acknowledgment of social structures implies a respect for the customs and laws that exist in social groups, so long as these serve the common good.[72] In recognizing the integrity and importance of social groups as a whole, the personalism of *Gaudium et spes* is against any kind of individualistic ethic that would value the freedom of the individual over and above the needs of a social group.[73] There is thus a dynamic tension which exists between the value of human subjectivity and the acknowledgement that, for the purposes of the common good, a social structure may need to impose reasonable limits on human subjectivity for the good of the group as a whole.[74] As such, the Church's understanding of the human person avoids the extremes of both individualism and collectivism.

Janssens cautions, however, that social structures are a means to the end of the common good, and do not have a special dignity in and of themselves in any particular form. He reminds us that social structures are developed by human persons who are themselves limited, imperfect and changing and so, correspondingly, the structures themselves will be "limited, imperfect and changeable."[75] Both Janssens and Kelly affirm that they must be revised where appropriate "to accommodate them to changing circumstances, and to renew them by dynamic development, according to the growing possibilities of human dignity."[76]

---

71. Janssens, "Artificial Insemination," 9. Cf. Kelly, *New Directions in Moral Theology*, 37. See GS, nos. 23–32.

72. Janssens, "Artificial Insemination," 9. Cf. GS, no. 26, 74.

73. Janssens, "Artificial Insemination," 9. See GS, no. 30.

74. Kelly sees this as one aspect of the dialectic that exists in social groups and institutions whose ongoing development requires that they are characterized by both the harmony that keeps them together, and the tension that prevents them from becoming stagnant and forces them to develop. See Kelly, *New Directions in Moral Theology*, 45.

75. Janssens, "Artificial Insemination," 9. Cf. Gula, *Reason Informed by Faith*, 68.

76. Janssens, "Artificial Insemination," 9. Cf. Kelly, *New Directions in Moral Theology*, 47. GS, 26, 29, 30. By "growing possibilities of human dignity," Janssens refers to our ever-increasing understanding of the human person and, correspondingly, our ever-increasing awareness of what counts as human flourishing and therefore how to

What we can add to the observations of Janssens and Kelly here is the emphasis that the principle of subsidiarity, which we considered above, places on the importance of different levels of social participation, and the need to support and nourish all of these in a spirit of active participation oriented towards the common good. As we noted above, the implication of this principle is that the functions of lower-order social groups (local councils or governments, for example) should not be transferred unnecessarily to higher-order social groups (such as a federal government, for example). As a consequence, we can see that this principle acknowledges the good of social groups in the same way that Janssens and Kelly do, and also provides some practical guidance for how these groups can be supported in their participation in the movement towards the common good.

The Human Person is Oriented towards Relationship with God

Clearly, a Christian understanding of the human person would be incomplete without an acknowledgment of the possibility of relationship with God. Until this point, the paradigm of the human person we have been developing has been focused on the person only (it has been a humanism) but in this sixth dimension of the human person adequately considered, Janssens draws in the transcendent aspect of Pope Paul VI's 'transcendent humanism'.[77] As such, Janssens makes many of the same points about this transcendent dimension of the human person that we have described above: human persons are called to know, worship, and glorify God through all of their attitudes and activities, and Janssens finds abundant acknowledgment of this dimension of the human person throughout *Gaudium et spes*.[78]

Whilst, for Janssens, this is a move in the direction of the 'transcendent humanism' described by Paul VI, for Kelly it points towards a dimension of the human person more akin to the Levinasian understanding of desire. As we noted in chapter 1, Levinas understood the human person as oriented towards an awareness of the mystery that is encountered in the Other and characterized by a fundamental desire to seek out and reverence this mystery (as distinct from *need* which, at least as it pertains to the Other, would seek to grasp, overpower and reduce it to the Same). In a similar way, Kelly

---

nourish this for the human person adequately considered. See the commentary on the seventh dimension of the human person adequately considered below.

77. Indeed, this is what makes the personalism of *Gaudium et spes* and Janssens's development of this distinct from other forms of personalism that focus on the person alone. See Christie, *Adequately Considered*, 30.

78. Janssens, "Artificial Insemination," 9. See *GS*, 12, 34 & 34, 36, 48, respectively. Cf. Gula, *Reason Informed by Faith*, 68.

sees this dimension of the human person as "a way of expressing the openness of the human person to the experience of transcendence."[79] He goes on to argue that it "is that dimension of us that is able to register 'mystery' and not just 'puzzlement' in the face of those experiences in life which go beyond the limits of our human comprehension."[80]

Whilst the focus of both Levinas and Kelly herein is on the existential experience of human relationships, this need not be seen as excluding the possibility of a relationship with God akin to what Janssens refers to for this dimension of the human person. Indeed, one could link the three perspectives by positing an argument for the human capacity to experience transcendence (Kelly) being realized in the encounter with the face of the Other (Levinas) which is the condition of possibility for relationship with God (Janssens). Whilst the detailed development of such an approach would take us too far afield for the work at hand, it is worth noting that a similar argument can be found in the work of Michael Purcell on the relationship between Levinas and Christian theology, as well as independently by Karl Rahner.[81]

Inasmuch as it relates to the paradigm for justice that we are developing, this dimension implies that the openness to transcendence which characterizes human persons needs to be both acknowledged and allowed to flourish.

The Human Person is a Developmental and Historical Being

The seventh dimension of the human person adequately considered draws together some of the implications of the first dimension (the human person as a subject) and the fifth dimension (the human person in relationship with social groups) in terms of their manifestation within a developmental and historical context. Janssens's first observation here begins with developmental psychology's insight that each person's existence has a *developmental* history, and that this history can be traced through developmental stages.[82]

---

79. Kelly, *New Directions in Moral Theology*, 55.

80. Ibid.

81. See Purcell, *Mystery and Method: The Other in Rahner & Levinas*, especially the section of his book entitled "The Face of the Other and the Trace of God" on pages 287–92. Purcell's chapter also develops some links with the theology of Rahner on this point. Kevin Hart expresses the argument that Levinas and Purcell posit: "As we approach the other person, so we find ourselves in the trace of God." Hart, "Introduction: Levinas the Exorbitant," 2. In terms of Rahner himself, note his suggestion that "one can love God whom one does not see only *by* loving one's visible brother." Rahner, "Reflections on the Unity of the Love of Neighbor and the Love of God," 247.

82. Janssens engages with the work of Erik Erikson specifically on this point.

He takes this point and argues that, in order to understand each individual person adequately, we must have a sound understanding of his developmental stage as well as what counts as moral behavior for this stage. For example, we might praise an infant for following the commands of a parent simply for an ensuing reward, but we would expect that a morally mature adult would act out of a deeper sense of personal responsibility.[83] This has further implications on a more general level, especially for how one *responds* to each human person. A simple example will be instructive here: a curious child and a newly married couple who want to have children might both present with similar questions about how children are made but the answer given to this question will clearly need to be different to account for the developmental stage of these persons. To state the obvious, the necessary condition for an adequate response to this is that one is attentive to the developmental stage of those one encounters, and we will return to this point in the next chapter.

This individual, developmental history also manifests itself within the broader social structure of which a person is a part (see dimension five) and, as such, needs to be understood as a wider *cultural* history. It is this, Janssens argues, that is the essence of *Gaudium et spes*' plea for a new humanism which would manifest itself through authentic cultural development.[84] This cultural history incorporates all of the developments in understanding and ability that characterize cultural progress. Such developments can lead to a greater awareness of value, and therefore a more adequate moral response. Specifically, Janssens draws on the example of the sexual act which was once understood as a purely biological action which had procreation as its sole purpose, and is now understood as having a profoundly relational meaning as well which is reflected in *Gaudium et spes*.[85] These insights should also be balanced against the new possibilities for action which cultural progress

---

Janssens, "Artificial Insemination," 10. For an introduction to Erikson's thought, see Welchman, *Erik Erikson: His Life, Work, and Significance*.

83. Janssens's own example is that it is "essentially important to begin with the meaning of youth to morally judge behavior within that stage of life." Janssens, "Artificial Insemination," 10. Cf. Gula, *Reason Informed by Faith*, 70.

84. Janssens, "Artificial Insemination," 10.

85. Ibid. See *GS*, 49. Another instructive example is the developed awareness of the value of the subjectivity of the human person, and the condemnations of slavery that have come as a result of this. John Noonan provides an excellent overview of the development of magisterial teaching in this area specifically. See Noonan, *A Church That Can and Cannot Change*, especially 17–123. The first section of Noonan's book is appropriately entitled "The Unknown Sin," and clearly traces the development in awareness of value from early Christianity until the Second Vatican Council. Noonan's work is a valuable expression of what Janssens's is trying to express in terms of morally relevant cultural development. These points are also congruent with MacIntyre's tradition-constituted-enquiry, as explored in chap. 2.

allows for—activities which may or may not be expressed in ethical ways.[86] In view of this, Janssens argues:

> It is the specific task of ethics to inquire as to how the growing *possibilities* can be realized to serve the dignity of man and how the developing experience of *values* must enrich our activity.[87]

Ethics is therefore a dynamic activity, and one which must develop in line with our developing understanding of the human person integrally and adequately considered.[88]

Kelly builds from Janssens's explanation of the developmental dimension of the human person and sees this as an affirmation of the continuity of human life. As historical and developmental beings, he argues, our moral lives are made up not of a series of disconnected actions, but rather an ongoing development of character which takes place across a lifetime. This he explains with reference to the theory of fundamental option:

> Our so-called 'fundamental option' is not some out-of-history basic decision we make about our lives. It comes into being through the medium of the concrete choices we make in life. Once in being it is further consolidated by subsequent choices in the same direction, or it is weakened by choices inconsistent with it. It can even be radically changed through a choice which either is like the straw that broke the camel's back in terms of this weakening process or else is so deliberately and substantially contradictory to one's fundamental option that it constitutes a moment of 'conversion,' whether for good or for evil.[89]

Significantly, from the point of view of the book, Kelly argues that this understanding of the continuity and development of human life is aligned with a virtue ethics approach to moral theology.[90] As we noted in chapter 3, virtue ethics is appealing and unique because of its emphasis on the development of consistent character dispositions, as distinct from individual and separated acts. As Kelly notes, such an approach is congruent with this

---

86. See for example my exploration of the global trade movement, Fleming, "Understanding Trade."

87. Janssens, "Artificial Insemination," 10.

88. Ibid., 11. This relates to dimension three above. Cf. the points we made regarding Porter's theory's methodological openness to such ongoing revision in chap. 2, and the argument that our understanding of virtue will develop as our understanding of well-being improves in chap. 3.

89. Kelly, *New Directions in Moral Theology*, 51. We return to consider the theory of the fundamental option in more detail below.

90. Ibid.

dimension of the human person because of its acknowledgment of the fact that "the virtuous person is the outcome of a long history of acting in this way so that eventually acting virtuously becomes 'second nature' to such a person."[91]

As we have noted above, this dimension of the human person implies a need to acknowledge the particular developmental stage of individuals when making moral decisions. Further to this, it requires that our paradigm of justice can acknowledge the need for an historical/developmental consciousness which remains aware that moral action is something that has an influence not only now, in this unique moment in time, but also takes place in light of the past and with consequences for the future, both developmentally (for the individuals it effects) and historically (for the context in which it occurs).

Each Individual Human Person is Fundamentally Equal to All Other Human Persons While at the Same Time Uniquely Original

For the eighth and final dimension of the human person adequately considered, Janssens finds in *Gaudium et spes* an acknowledgment of a fundamental equality that exists between persons: we all participate in what it means to be a human person, albeit in a variety of capacities.[92] In this equality, we share with our fellow humans the ability to know, feel, desire and act, and we are also oriented towards an awareness of value, especially the value of other persons, as we acknowledged in chapter 1.[93] This fundamental equality, argues Janssens—following *Gaudium et spes*—is what makes the universalization of moral demands possible, and is the grounding for a common set of human rights which do not allow for discrimination based on culture, gender, race, color, socio-economic status, language, religion and so on.[94]

At the same time, an affirmation of fundamental equality is not equivalent to the suggestion that all human persons are exactly the same. As Janssens notes, within the framework of fundamental equality:

> each person is simultaneously an originality, a unique subject. Developmental psychology shows that each person has his own individual *temperament* (ways of acting and reacting),

91. Ibid.

92. Janssens, "Artificial Insemination," 12. Cf. Kelly, *New Directions in Moral Theology*, 53. See GS, 29.

93. Janssens, "Artificial Insemination," 12.

94. GS, 29. See also GS, 27. Cf. Janssens, "Artificial Insemination," 12. Obviously this equality is closely interrelated with fundamental human dignity.

his own talents or *capacities* (the instruments for acting), his own *drives* (the dynamic source of our behavior) and that each person, through interaction with his socio-cultural milieu, develops towards a unique, original *personality* with its individual character.[95]

From an ethical perspective, this means that all ethical decisions must be guided by what is universal, whilst at the same time allowing for the creative expression of the individual within this framework.[96] Additionally, as Janssens notes, allowing for this creative expression is what "forms the source of the richness and fruitfulness of community building in the society."[97]

JUSTICE AND THE PERSONALIST CRITERION

Revisiting Chapters Three and Four

In the last two chapters, we have been considering the virtues as the intelligible expression of our prerational nature which both secure our well-being and specify this in terms of its morally ideal expression in happiness. We noted that the virtues of temperance and fortitude, as expressions of the passions, are largely self-referential and that, in order to be truly virtuous, these need to be further specified with an acknowledgment of our profoundly relational nature. We noted, too, that Porter employs the virtue of justice, understood as that disposition which renders to each his due, to develop a paradigm for how the human person should act in relationship to others. Porter also noted that any paradigm of justice would need to be informed by a speculative account of what it means to be a human person or, in her own words, a "reflective sense of what it means to live in a community, what one's place in that community is, and what kinds of claims others can make on oneself."[98] Integrating all of these aspects, we turned to the Roman Catholic understanding of the human person, which is grounded in an inviolable dignity, the protection of which is at the essence of community life. This dignity is specified through the human person adequately considered. We have been doing this because, as Burggraeve noted, "it is only when we approach the human person integrally or holistically that he or she is given their due."[99]

95. Janssens, "Artificial Insemination," 12.
96. Cf. ibid.
97. Ibid.
98. *NR*, 217. Cf. chap. 3.
99. Burggraeve, "Holistic Personalism," 31.

The Personalist Criterion

What the preceding sections have been developing is what Janssens refers to as 'the personalist criterion.'[100] With such a criterion, it is possible to say that a paradigm of justice (and the actions which flow from this) is morally good and corresponds with the reality of the human person:

> if it in truth—according to reason enlightened by revelation—is beneficial to the human person adequately considered in *himself* (as a personal subject in corporeality, dimensions 1 & 2) and *in his relations* (in his openness to the world, to others, to social groups, and to God, dimensions 3, 4, 5 & 6).[101]

Integrated into this consideration is, as we noted above, an acknowledgment of the developmental stage of each person, as well as the wider historical/cultural context of which the paradigm of justice is a part. These observations challenge us to acknowledge the proximate nature of any such paradigm, and to be open to new understandings of value and also better techniques of response as these become available both for the individual and the wider culture of which she is a part.[102] In conjunction with all of these, the requirement to render to each their due also charges us with the task of acknowledging both *equality*—that there are some things common to us all, and *uniqueness*—that each person presents as someone unique, and must be responded to as such.[103]

The Personalist Criterion as Accountable to Levinas

This does not reduce our paradigm of justice to a simple subjectivism, but rather acknowledges that, whilst the human person shares at least seven characteristics with all other human persons, a core part of his humanness is tied up with his uniqueness, and that a truly moral response must acknowledge this. Such was one of the key insights of Levinas regarding the human person as an 'infinity' over which one can never posit a damaging 'totalization.' As we saw in chapter 1, Levinas was not opposed to 'totalizations' as such, he acknowledged their value especially inasmuch as they can

---

100. Janssens, "Artificial Insemination," 13.

101. Ibid. Note that I have substituted the word "dimensions" for "points" from the original text. This does not in any way alter the meaning of this quote, but it does align it more clearly with the language we have been using throughout.

102. Janssens, "Artificial Insemination," 13. Cf. dimension 7 above.

103. Or, as Janssens puts it, "we must, in our acts, respect the originality of all as much as possible." Ibid., 14.

help to organize society in such a way that the infinity of the human person is acknowledged and protected. Nonetheless, these 'totalizations' are not to be substituted for the infinity of the person, no matter how well developed and well intentioned they are. As we have seen, the eighth dimension of the human person can acknowledge this point, whilst still holding in tension those dimensions of personhood that all people share.

As such, the human person adequately considered provides us with a criterion which is objective (it "holds to objective criteria: the human person adequately considered in his essential aspects or constant dimensions"[104]) and yet remains open to the unique nature of all human persons. Such a criterion points us towards a paradigm of justice as a disposition of the will which is aligned with objective criteria in such a way that:

> we are genuinely prepared to place our activity as much as possible at the service of the promotion of the human person (self and others) adequately considered in himself as subject in corporeality and in his openness to the world, to others, to social groups and to God and to respect the originality of each person in our conduct as much as possible.[105]

Such an approach, in its acknowledgment of the need to allow for uniqueness and originality in the Other person, introduces an interesting challenge into the paradigm of justice and we can begin to frame this challenge in the following way, using the second dimension of the human person (that the person is a subject in corporeality) as an example.

The Personalist Criterion in Action: Corporeality

It is widely acknowledged that the bodily aspect of the human person, when combined with the understanding of human dignity developed above, admits certain rights for all persons. These include the right to adequate food and drink, the right to shelter, and the right to at least basic medical care.[106] That these goods are due to the human person is universal, by virtue of their being a response to an essential dimension of all human persons adequately considered. In our discussion of the virtue of temperance in chapter 3, however, we also noted that what constitutes an adequate amount of, say,

---

104. Ibid., 14–15.

105. Ibid., 15.

106. See for example, *GS*, 26; *PP*, 20; *CSDC*, no. 166; United Nations, "The Universal Declaration of Human Rights," United Nations http://www.un.org/en/documents/udhr/.No. 25.

food or drink, is largely an agent-relative definition (because an infant will require less food than an adult, a naturally tall person will require more drink for hydration than a naturally short person, and so on) which means that the virtue itself must be non-specific inasmuch as it prescribes actions in order to account for this point. That the human person needs nourishment through food and drink to achieve a state of well-being is universal but exactly how much food or drink is required to achieve this goal is not.

When it comes to our paradigm of justice, this means that our definition of what is due to each human person, whilst grounded in a universal human right and a universal human need that is oriented towards well-being, must also account for the unique way the right and need are made manifest in each individual. Justice as a paradigm can acknowledge that it is the right of all human persons to have nourishment through food and drink, but it cannot prescribe exactly *how much* food and drink is required for this. Of itself, this is not a startling insight, and it is unlikely that it would lead to dramatic changes in how, for example, a soup kitchen for the adult homeless is run (serving sizes could be standardized to nourish most, with the possibility of increasing or decreasing this if appropriate). Nonetheless, it takes on more complex implications when we consider the different needs that persons would present across a lifetime (a child will have different needs to an adult) and also different dietary requirements (for example, if we are attempting to respond to the need for nourishment for someone who has severe allergies to certain kinds of foods). At this point, the observation need not fundamentally alter our definition or paradigm of justice. Indeed, it shows its value, so long as it is combined with a careful attentiveness to each unique ethical situation, and we will return to this point in the next chapter.

VULNERABILITY

Thus far, we have been developing a paradigm for justice through a detailed exploration of the anthropological vision of the Roman Catholic tradition in terms of human dignity, transcendent humanism and the eight dimensions of 'the human person integrally and adequately considered' in an attempt to clarify what is 'due' to human persons, and what an adequate moral response to another human person needs to account for. I would argue, however, that there are two essential aspects of the human person which have not yet been accounted for and which accentuate the need for the kind of paradigm we have been developing—vulnerability and sin. I will explore each of these dimensions of the human person in turn and show how each is related to the argument that we have been developing in this chapter and throughout the book.

The Possibility of Vulnerability

What is particularly striking about the account of the human person developed in this chapter thus far is just how many possibilities for harm exist for the human person. Indeed, if one builds from the foundation of human dignity and acknowledges the eight dimensions of the 'human person integrally and adequately considered,' one can see at least eight general areas of possibility for great harm to be done and, to add to this, one can also acknowledge that harm can be done to one or a number of these dimensions without necessarily influencing the others. For example, a person's corporeal dimension might be well nourished, and her participation in moral and social life encouraged and valued, whilst at the same time her orientation towards the transcendent is abused through the means of damaging ideology or fundamentalism. On the other hand, a person's orientation towards the transcendent might be honored, nourished and encouraged to thrive whilst at the same time his corporeal dimension is abandoned or abused. Real-life examples of such harms are not difficult to imagine (or, worse still for many, to remember) and they point to another dimension of what it means to be human: to be *vulnerable*.[107]

That this vulnerability is an essential aspect of what it is to be a human person is at least implied by the anthropological vision we have been developing in this chapter—after all, there would be no reason to emphasize the need to protect human dignity and all that comes with it if that dignity was immune to threat and, as a consequence, never vulnerable to harm. Indeed, this vulnerability and the reality that different members of the human family are more vulnerable than others is explicitly recognized in CST in its emphasis on a 'preferential option for the poor,' and we will return to this in chapter 6. We turn back to Levinas now for an exploration of the vulnerability of the face of the Other for a way in which to explain how we experience this dimension of the human person.

Levinas and the Vulnerability of the Face

Levinas sees vulnerability as primarily constituted in the encounter between the "I" and the face and, as François Raffoul argues, Levinas's use of the

---

107. As Karl Rahner has pointed out, this experience of vulnerability and fragility is a constitutive element of the experience of being human. See Rahner, *Foundations of Christian Faith*, 91.

term 'face' is practically synonymous with the word 'vulnerability.'[108] As we noted in chapter 1, the Levinasian understanding of the term *face* refers to the encounter with the Other, understood as any other human person, and connotes the responsibility inherent in the relationship between the "I" and the Other. Yet despite this call to responsibility, we have also seen that the "I" may choose a method of response which contradicts the ethical call and reduces the Other to the Same, performing a violence in such a way that the Other is powerless to avoid it.[109]

Hence, whilst the fundamental call of the face to the "I" is to a response of non-violence, that call does not come with a means of persuading the "I" to obey.[110] In this sense, the face of the Other is, as Raffoul explains it, "radically stripped of protection, defenseless."[111] Burggraeve posits that it is almost as if the face tempts the "I" to towards violence in its sheer vulnerability and metaphorical nakedness.[112] Hence, as we have seen, the encounter with the Other is always ambivalent in its potential outcome: the "I" is free to respond in a helpful or harmful way, "the Other invests me with genuine freedom, and will be the beneficiary or victim of how I decide to exercise it."[113] The Other I encounter is the *vulnerable* Other.

Vulnerability, Power and Responsibility

That Levinas places an emphasis on *vulnerability* here as distinct from, say, weakness, makes this part of his theory particularly provocative. Vulnerability carries with it moral connotations, and these include the possibility of unjust violation.[114] That human subjectivity is constituted in the encounter with the vulnerable Other therefore implies that, as we have seen in chapter 1, this subjectivity carries with it the power for violence through 'totalization.' The Other is the vulnerable Other precisely because the "I" has the capacity to do violence to it. The "I" finds itself infused with this power to do harm even before it becomes conscious and capable of choosing the way in which this power is exercised.[115] Indeed, as Levinas has argued, it might be that the "I" comes into consciousness by way of the disturbing observation

---

108. Raffoul, *The Origins of Responsibility*, 184.
109. See chap. 1. See also Waldenfels, "Levinas and the Face of the Other," 71.
110. Davis, *Levinas*, 50.
111. Raffoul, *The Origins of Responsibility*, 187.
112. Burggraeve, "Violence and the Vulnerable Face of the Other," 30–31.
113. Davis, *Levinas*, 49.
114. Raffoul, *The Origins of Responsibility*, 188.
115. Burggraeve, *The Wisdom of Love*, 100.

that, in its blissful naivety and spontaneity, it is already prone to committing the violence of 'totalization.'

As we discussed in chapter 1, it is at this point of recognition that responsibility begins for Levinas. The encounter with the Other infuses the "I" with the power to do great harm and, correlatively, when this is recognized it carries with it the freedom to respond—to answer the vulnerable Other's ethical call. As Burggraeve and Peperzak noted in that discussion, the nature of this freedom is ambivalent: it can be used for further violence or to respond to the Other justly in a way which, according to the argument of the book, would be informed by the criterion for justice developed above.[116] Furthermore, as Gascoigne has pointed out, freedom and the capacity to answer or to respond are inherently linked to responsibility: where the "I" is free to respond, it can be held accountable for the nature of its response.[117] We will return to this point in the next section.

Vulnerability, Freedom and the Possibility of Sin

I would like to suggest that this way of thinking about vulnerability can complement the anthropological vision of this chapter. This is because it is helpful to remember that when we encounter another human person and seek to understand how to respond to her in a just way we do so precisely because we acknowledge that our encounter with her is an ambivalent one. That is, whilst we are naturally oriented in such a way as to recognize her value, the nature of our response to her is still uncertain and the possibility of our relating well to her is at the same time a possibility of causing her great harm and, if what is due to others involves responding well to (as distinct from harming) them, then this provides further impetus for the task at hand. Furthermore, in view of our exploration of the eight dimensions of the 'human person integrally and adequately considered,' we are able to acknowledge that the possibility of causing harm exists in a great diversity of ways and that this fact carries with it a need for careful attentiveness to the Other who is encountered in order to determine exactly what is due to *this* Other and in *this* situation. Whether it is bread, social interaction, education, or prayer is something that cannot be determined aside from contextual considerations. This point will be developed further in chapter 5.

Finally, the language of vulnerability is linked closely to the power of the "I" in the thought of Levinas, and therefore to its capacity for violence as well as the freedom to exercise this (or not) and the correlative

116. Ibid., 102; Peperzak, "Transcendence," 191.
117. Gascoigne, *Freedom and Purpose*, 62–63.

responsibility that is part of this. As such, we move now to a consideration of the fact that frequently the way in which persons respond to vulnerable Others undermines their happiness. In some instances, to be sure, this is because of the kind of "invincible ignorance" which may be a consequence of the seventh dimension of the human person we have noted above (that we are developmental creatures who are not omniscient and are thus able to make honest errors in judgment) or because of other impediments which render an acting agent incapable, or only partially capable, of making a free and well-informed response.[118] At the same time, the anthropological vision of the Catholic tradition we are building from has consistently acknowledged that the human person, whilst fundamentally oriented towards the good, at times freely chooses acts or dispositions which are harmful, and it has referred to these as sin.

SIN

In this section, I will develop the concept of sin as a dimension of what it means to be a human person as a final piece in the anthropological vision of this chapter. It is indeed surprising, and something of a shortcoming, that this was not included in Janssens's original account of the 'human person integrally and adequately considered,' given that sin is part of the theological anthropology of *Gaudium et spes*.[119] As we have seen in chapter 3, a substantial commentary on sin is also absent from Porter's theory. This absence, whilst perhaps conveying a more optimistic vision of the human person, neglects the experience of sin and the ongoing need for moral conversion. As Curran has noted, a lack of attention to sin in this regard causes more harm than good precisely because it underestimates the destructive consequences of this dimension of what it means to be human.[120] Rahner would also agree with this point in his argument that any consideration of Christianity which does not discuss sin is deficient.[121] I should point out that in this section I focus on sin as it exists on a personal level. This is not to negate, or deny the importance of, the reality of structural sin which has been analyzed by CST

---

118. Cf. *GS*, 16.

119. See below for *Gaudium et spes*' statements about sin.

120. Curran, *Loyal Dissent: Memoir of a Catholic Theologian*, 194. So committed is Curran to the importance of an awareness of sin that he has suggested the addition of a fifth mark to the traditional four marks of the church: "one, holy, Catholic, apostolic, and *sinful*." Curran, *Loyal Dissent*, 19. For a synthesis of Curran's views on this point, see also Curran, "Sin: Don't Lose All That Old-Time Catholic Guilt."

121. Rahner, *Foundations of Christian Faith*, 90. See also Tuohy, "Christian Anthropology," 99–100.

and its commentators. Indeed, I return to a consideration of this in chapter 6.

Sin refers to that dimension of the human person which acts—or is disposed to act—in a way which does not correspond with the good of self, others or God. What we have not yet noted is that the theological anthropology of the Catholic tradition understands this as part of what it means to be human, not essentially but existentially. For example, *Gaudium et spes* refers to the human person as "fallen into the bondage of sin"; "a weak and sinful being" characterized by internal divisions from which flow many of the problems of society; torn in a "dramatic struggle between good and evil"; plagued by limitation because of sin; and bent towards evil.[122] This is particularly evocative language in a document which is frequently noted for its optimism. For these reasons, our appeal to the anthropological vision of the Roman Catholic tradition would be incomplete without some discussion of sin.

Sin—Foundational Points

Richard Connors and Patrick McCormick begin their exploration of sin by noting that it is a specifically religious concept which refers to the harm done to the relationship between a person and God and which has a close link with morality.[123] They go on to note that the Biblical tradition understands sin in a twofold manner—as a rift in relationship between God and neighbor.[124] For Gascoigne, an understanding of sin begins with an awareness of the difference between good and evil. He argues that "evil cannot exist in any 'pure' form" but rather that "it is always the distortion of something good."[125] In support of this, Judith Merkle argues that "to sin is to choose to be twisted, to pretend to be something other than what one is. It is a rebellion, a denial of reality."[126] On this view, sin is a choice or disposition which distorts or destroys what is known to be good and which has as its consequence the harming or breaking of one's relationship with God or neighbor.[127]

It is here that we can show the relationship between sin and the theory developed by Porter thus far. That is, whilst we are naturally oriented

---

122. See (respectively) *GS*, 2, 13, 15, 25.
123. Connors and McCormick, *Character, Choices and Community*, 203.
124. Ibid., 205.
125. Gascoigne, *Freedom and Purpose*, 97.
126. Merkle, "Sin," in *New Dictionary of Catholic Social Thought*, 883.
127. Gascoigne, *Freedom and Purpose*, 101. See also chap. 3.

towards flourishing and happiness, we are also constituted in such a way as to be vulnerable to re-orientation, either through our own choice or through factors outside of our control. Timothy O'Connell suggests that this phenomenon can be understood in three ways, as "a *fact* of life, an *act* of persons or communities, and a fundamental *orientation* towards evil."[128] His threefold distinction is a helpful framework within which sin can be understood, and I will develop each aspect of it here.

Original Sin

When O'Connell suggests that one component of the category of sin points towards a *fact* of life, he is referring to what the tradition has called *original sin*.[129] Contemporary moral theologians, such as Connors, McCormick and Gascoigne, understand original sin as the fact that a person's choices are unavoidably influenced by factors outside of their control and that these factors can contribute to the person acting in a way which does not correspond with the good.[130] This corresponds with Rahner's explanation of original sin as those factors which are imposed on a person and co-determine their capacity for freedom.[131] Clearly, the individual cannot be held responsible for these factors, but this does not change the fact that they limit his ability to be well disposed and act in accordance with the good.[132]

This helps to clarify the point that sin is a dimension of what it means to be a human person—it is as if we find ourselves as broken persons, aware of the good but conflicted in our consideration of how to respond to it. Rahner explains the phenomenon in this way: "There are no islands for the individual person whose nature does not already bear the stamp of the guilt

---

128. Connors and McCormick, *Character, Choices and Community*, 206. See O'Connell, *Principles for a Catholic Morality*, 82–87.

129. O'Connell, *Principles for a Catholic Morality*, 81, 87. Given that this explanation of sin is a component part, and not the focus, of the book, our explanation of each aspect of sin will be necessarily brief. The works cited here, and further works on this topic noted in the bibliography, provide helpful avenues for further research in the area.

130. References to these authors' understanding of original sin are included below. See also Henry, "Original Sin: A Flawed Inheritance," 10.

131. In Rahner's own words, the human person "exercises his personal, inalienable and unique acts of freedom in a situation which he finds prior to himself, which is imposed on him, and which is ultimately the presupposition of his freedom. It means that he actualises himself as a free subject in a situation which itself is always determined by history and by other persons." Rahner, *Foundations of Christian Faith*, 107. Cf. Merkle, "Sin," 884.

132. Gascoigne, *Freedom and Purpose*, 100.

of others, directly or indirectly, from close or from afar."[133] As Connors and McCormick point out, we are not responsible for this aspect of sin but we are still charged with the responsibility of dealing with it.[134] We will return to this point below.

Sin as Action

Where O'Connell refers to sin as an *act* he refers to those actions which cause harm to one's relationship with God through distorting the good.[135] Connors and McCormick point out that this 'acting' aspect of sin should include both *actions* and *character dispositions*, and their suggestion is valuable given that such an approach aligns with the virtue ethics approach taken in the book.[136] Indeed, we have already explored something of the concept of sin as it pertains to character dispositions in chapter 3, at which point we developed the Thomistic understanding of sin in relationship with the concept of vice as understood through the paradigm of virtue ethics. In terms of disposition, this approach holds that sin refers to those vices which are deficient when compared to the virtues. I would argue, however, that it is important to draw a distinction between sin as action and character disposition (without denying their essential relationship with one another) which is not reflected in Connors and McCormick's suggestion. This is because such a separation allows for a distinction between sin which occurs on the *categorical* level and sin which occurs on the *transcendental* level.[137] We will explore the categorical level of sin in this section, and the transcendental in the next.

Put quite simply, the 'act focused,' or categorical, aspect of sin refers to those "words, actions or deeds that express and embody a decision to say no to God."[138] As Kelly notes, however, such an approach to sin is more

---

133. Rahner, *Foundations of Christian Faith*, 109.

134. Cf. Connors and McCormick, *Character, Choices and Community*, 219; Rahner, *Foundations of Christian Faith*, 109.

135. O'Connell, *Principles for a Catholic Morality*, 85–86.

136. See Connors and McCormick, *Character, Choices and Community*, 213.

137. Cf. Rahner, *Foundations of Christian Faith*, 95. As we will see below, Rahner's understanding of the links (or, according to some, lack thereof) between transcendental and categorical freedom has been the cause of significant debate in terms of the concept of *fundamental option*, to which we turn below.

138. Connors and McCormick, *Character, Choices and Community*, 213. The discussion of sinful action links closely with the question of whether or not particular actions can be considered as gravely sinful in themselves and, therefore, subject to prohibition through an absolute moral norm. While important, this discussion falls

complicated than simply determining the rightness or wrongness of actions in themselves.[139] This is because for an action to be considered sin it must also involve some form of subjective commitment on the part of the acting agent and so should be distinguished from those actions which come as a result of some form of impediment or misunderstanding, or are simply accidents. As such, an action which distorts the good must be combined with a subjective *intention* to commit the action as well as the *knowledge* that it is damaging if it is to be considered sinful.[140]

A further point should be made here which follows from the simple observation that damaging actions can be *more or less* damaging depending on their seriousness or, in more traditional language, gravity. For example, the act of over-eating once in a lifetime is clearly far less damaging with reference to what is due to self and others than the act of adultery. Furthermore, there are some actions which go beyond damage and embody sheer destructiveness: they not only damage one's relationship with self, others and God, they have the capacity to destroy these. Traditionally, the categories which have been used to describe the seriousness of specific acts are *grave* and *light matter*, the former referring to actions which are seriously damaging or destructive, the latter referring to those which are only mildly so.[141] As noted above, such actions must be combined with a level of subjective commitment in order for them to be considered sinful, and it is here that moral theology has spoken of *mortal* and *venial* sin. For an action to be considered mortally sinful (in other words, destructive for one's relationship with self, others and God), it must be an action which constitutes grave matter which is committed with full knowledge and intent. If any of these factors are lacking, the action is considered venially, or less, sinful.[142] This traditional understanding which focuses on specific *actions* can be complemented by turning to an understanding of sin which is informed by a focus on character disposition. For this purpose, we turn now to the theory of the fundamental option.

---

outside the scope of the current work. A number of responses can, however, be traced through the following resources: Finnis, *Moral Absolutes: Tradition, Revision and Truth*, 1–9; Gula, *Reason Informed by Faith*, 283–97; O'Connell, *Principles for a Catholic Morality*, 187–214.

139. Kelly, *New Directions in Moral Theology*, 17.

140. Gascoigne, *Freedom and Purpose*, 184.

141. Ibid., 104.

142. For further explanation of this understanding of sin, including its strengths and weaknesses, see Connors and McCormick, *Character, Choices and Community*, 202–24; Gascoigne, *Freedom and Purpose*, 96–109; Gula, *Reason Informed by Faith*, 109–16.

Sin as Fundamental Option

As we saw previously, Janssens understood the human person as an historical and developmental being and part of Kelly's exploration of this dimension of the person involved an emphasis on the continuity of human life. Following from this, he argued that human moral life is not made up of a series of disconnected actions, but rather an ongoing development of character which takes place across a lifetime. As we noted earlier, Kelly relates this point both to the theory of the 'fundamental option,' which refers to the fundamental stance of one's life considered as a whole—whether one has chosen, at the deepest levels of their subjectivity, to be oriented towards God and the good, or away from these.[143]

The concept of a fundamental option was originally developed by Karl Rahner and influenced by his reading of Jacques Maritain and Joseph Marechal.[144] Rahner, out of his theological anthropology of the human person as 'transcendental existential,' argued that freedom is actualized not through specific acts, but rather through the person's subjectivity itself.[145] Salzman and Lawler provide a helpful distinction here with regards to the kind of freedom one's fundamental option engages. Until this point, we have been largely focused on specific acts which Salzman and Lawler argue refer to 'categorical freedom,' understood as the freedom to do this or that, "to stand or sit, to kill or not to kill, to read or to sing, in space and time."[146] This is distinct from 'transcendental freedom,' understood as a "personal, subjective responsibility for self-realization in the affirmation and love of self, of God, and of neighbour."[147]

This kind of freedom refers not to a specific choice, but to the "total project of human existence" understood in its manifestation across a lifetime, and it is this freedom with which the theory of the fundamental option is concerned.[148] It is, as such, not the freedom to *do* this or that, but to

---

143. Kelly, *New Directions in Moral Theology*, 51.

144. See Rahner, *Foundations of Christian Faith*, 90–115. Cf. Porter, "Moral Theology and the Language of Grace," 170. As O'Connell notes, the specific terminology of *fundamental option* is not to be found in this specific text, but the theological anthropology that gives rise to the concept certainly has its foundation here. O'Connell, "The Question of Grundentscheidung," 151. It should be noted that there is some disagreement on the origins of the concept of a fundamental option. Others find its foundations in the work of Louis Janssens, Piet Fransen, Bernard Häring, or Joseph Fuchs. See Keenan, *A History of Catholic Moral Theology*, 186.

145. Rahner, *Foundations of Christian Faith*, 97.

146. Lawler and Salzman, "Karl Rahner and Human Nature," 396.

147. Ibid.

148. Rahner, "Theology of Freedom," 185. Quoted in Lawler and Salzman, "Karl Rahner and Human Nature" 396.

be this or that.¹⁴⁹ This means that one's fundamental option is concerned less with one's specific actions at any given moment in time, and more with the consistent disposition towards or away from the good that one has embodied across a lifetime.¹⁵⁰ This is not to suggest that the two are not related. As Salzman and Lawler point out, one's fundamental option and one's specific actions are inherently related—the fundamental option provides the condition of possibility out of which specific acts arise, and specific actions necessarily have an influence on the orientation of the fundamental option.¹⁵¹

In its focus on the consistent disposition of a human person's moral life, the fundamental option shares many of the characteristics of virtue ethics, as Kelly has noted.¹⁵² Furthermore, the theory of the fundamental

---

149. Lawler and Salzman, "Karl Rahner and Human Nature," 396.

150. Coffey, "Rahner's Theology of Fundamental Option," 256. See also Qureshi, "Sin, Fundamental Option and Conversion," 277–78.

151. Lawler and Salzman, "Karl Rahner and Human Nature," 396. As noted above, this issue has not been without controversy. The most well-known critique of the approach can be found in the concern *Veritatis splendor* expresses that the theory of the fundamental option presents the danger of a separation between one's fundamental disposition and specific acts, see VS, no. 65. Indeed, Porter has argued that the concept is problematic in terms of what it contributes to moral theology because Rahner does not, in his description of the fundamental option, provide a clear enough link between the transcendental freedom that the concept refers to and the categorical freedom that people are familiar with in the moral life. According to Porter, this makes it difficult to identify and to exemplify what an expression of a good (or an evil) fundamental option might look like in practice. As such, she argues that the concept requires further revision before it can make a helpful contribution to moral theology and then proceeds to suggest an alternative in Aquinas's virtue of charity. See Porter, "Moral Theology and the Language of Grace," esp. 173 and 175. David Coffey is critical of Porter's suggestions and provides a direct response by showing how the transcendental freedom of fundamental option and categorical action are linked in Rahner's work, especially in terms of his emphasis of the love of neighbor. See Coffey, "Rahner's Theology of Fundamental Option," especially 264, 270, and 271. Another more recent work challenges Porter's critique of fundamental option on its own terms and suggests that her alternative can be critiqued on some of the same points that she originally raised concern in relation to fundamental option. See Linnane, "Rahner's Fundamental Option and Virtue Ethics,." Salzman and Lawler also note, and respond to Porter's criticism in a similar way to Coffey. See Lawler and Salzman, "Karl Rahner and Human Nature: Implications for Ethics," 405–7. While it is not the task of this work to adjudicate on this matter, I would argue that Coffey, Linnan, and Salzman and Lawler provide a sufficient response to Porter's concern, which supports the understanding of the link between fundamental option as transcendental freedom and the categorical freedom that concrete actions engage with as described above.

152. Kelly, *New Directions in Moral Theology*, 51. Note also that this has led to a reframing of the categories of mortal and venial sin. It would take us too far afield to consider this here, but it is well summarized in McCormick, *The Critical Calling*, 179–80.

option allows us to acknowledge that an individual's disposition towards or away from the good can change gradually over time, in the same way that a virtuous disposition can change into a vicious one if it is not consistently reinforced, and vice versa.[153] The possibility of a *change* in one's fundamental option introduces us to the possibility for moral conversion.[154] Conversion here refers to a reorientation of "our way of seeing, thinking, feeling, judging, and acting."[155] Understood as such, moral conversion is ambivalent: it can refer either to a conversion towards or away from the good.[156] Herein lies the value of a virtue ethics approach which has, as its pedagogical function, the orientation of human character towards that which is virtuous.

CONCLUSION

In this chapter, we have been developing an anthropological vision which is informed by the Catholic tradition. Our purpose in doing so has been to create a refined understanding of what is due to the human person, in order to inform the practice of the virtue of justice which, as we have seen, is concerned with giving each what is her or his due. To develop this anthropological vision, we turned first to the understanding of human dignity in the Catholic tradition, further developed this by means of Pope Paul VI's concept of 'transcendent humanism,' and built on this foundation in more detail by means of Louis Janssens's eight dimensions of the 'human person integrally and adequately considered.' These explorations provided us with a robust and holistic understanding of the human person and, correlatively, a more adequate understanding of what is due to her, by means of what Janssens described as the 'personalist criterion' for moral action. We noted that the vision of the human person, outlined above, lacked an articulation of those dimensions of the person which open us up to, and can cause, harm: vulnerability and sin.

Throughout this chapter, we have a number of times noted the sheer complexity of the human person, and the great diversity of ways in which each might be encountered. A number of times, too, we have noted that this complexity and uniqueness carries with it a need for careful attentiveness

153. Kopfensteiner, "The Theory of the Fundamental Option and Moral Action," 128.

154. See Qureshi, "Sin, Fundamental Option and Conversion," 279, 283.

155. Gula, *Reason Informed by Faith*, 176.

156. On the importance of conversion for moral theology, see for example Crysdale, "Heritage and Discovery: A Framework for Moral Theology," 569–73; Curran, *A New Look at Christian Morality*, 25; Hanigan, "Conversion and Christian Ethics," 25; O'Connell, *Making Disciples*; Rahner, *Foundations of Christian Faith*, 109.

An Anthropological Vision Informed by the Catholic Tradition

to each individual person, in order to ascertain what is due to *this* person in *this* context. Far from being some form of ethical relativism, this is an acknowledgment of the irreducible complexity and uniqueness of the human person, reflected in the imperative to be attentive to her in order to come to a just response. In chapter 5, we turn to the virtue of prudence which is charged with the task of responding to this uniqueness. Beyond this, we will explore the virtue of solidarity in chapter 6 which, I will argue, can provide helpful guidance in directing the attentiveness of prudence still more adequately.

5

The Virtue of Prudence and the Importance of Attentiveness for Moral Reasoning

INTRODUCTION

THIS CHAPTER FOCUSES ON Porter's understanding of the virtue of prudence. Methodologically, this means moving from the anthropological vision of chapter 4 back to a focus on Porter's theory that is more akin to Chapters Two and Three; this is because the virtues of fortitude, temperance and justice are all articulated and applied by means of the virtue of prudence. As such, it was logical to include this consideration of prudence after the others had been explored.[1] In its relationship with the book's argument considered as a whole, this chapter continues to develop the exploration of Porter's theory that began in Chapters Two and Three and frequently cross references these to show their relationship. It also continues to fulfill the task set out at the beginning of the book by developing yet another link between Porter and Levinas by way of a careful discussion of the former's understanding of reason. Furthermore, its discussion of prudence includes the beginnings of an analysis of the importance of attentiveness for moral reasoning which both fulfills a part of the hypothesis the book has not yet

---

1. This structure is also reflected in *Nature as Reason*, see Porter's table of contents: *NR*, vii–viii.

dealt with and also provides the means by which the virtue of solidarity can be integrated into the developing theory.

This chapter begins by exploring Porter's understanding of reason. Linking back to chapter 3, the chapter then discusses the relationship between the passions, the will, speculative reason and practical reason, before suggesting further links between Porter and Levinas on the grounds of the former's understanding of practical reason and its relationship to the first principles of natural law. The chapter then introduces prudence, and considers what role prudence plays in determining the mean of the virtues in the face of complex ethical situations. It then builds from this point and highlights the relationship between prudence and attentiveness, suggesting that the virtue of solidarity, as expressed in CST, will be able to further clarify the nature of this attentiveness. This then becomes the focus of chapter 6.

PRACTICAL AND SPECULATIVE REASON

Contemporary Thinking around Practical Reason and Porter's Approach

At the outset of our discussions regarding Porter's understanding of reason, it is important to point out that her theory of natural law focuses largely on 'practical reason.' There is, however, something of a lack of clarity in her work in this regard. Porter tends to use the shorthand 'reason' to refer to 'practical reason,' which causes some confusion in distinguishing the operations of practical and speculative reason. This would not be of major consequence were it not for a second issue, which is that Porter seems to overlap her discussions of the operations of practical reason with operations that belong to speculative reason without providing a clear distinction between the two.[2] It is possible that she has done this deliberately to reveal the close link she sees between the operations of practical and speculative reason which we will explore in detail below. Desirable as this may be, my concern is that it does not allow for a sufficient critical discussion of Porter's understanding of practical reason, the way it contrasts with other contemporary understandings, and the unique role it plays amidst the other dimensions of the human person she names in her approach. This can also lead to some confusion regarding the role of prudence. As such, in what follows, I have made a considered effort to show the links between practical and speculative reason and to name them clearly throughout to prevent confusion. In some

---

2. See for example *NR*, 248–68. For an excellent and concise explanation of the differences between these two dimensions of reason, see McCabe, *On Aquinas*, 88–91.

places I have included parentheses in quotes from Porter to indicate which dimension of reason I believe she is referring to, and have been careful to be accurate in this regard. Where I use the term 'reason' on its own I am using this as a broad term to refer to both practical and speculative reason, and I have left quotes from Porter unadjusted where I believe she is doing the same. We begin now with an exploration of reason, broadly considered, in Porter's approach.

When Porter turns to her consideration of practical reason, she begins by noting that this dimension of her approach to natural law will come across as far more familiar to us, given that many contemporary moral theories understand moral discourse as a characteristic of reason, rather than something which is aligned with our prerational nature.[3] She argues, however, that the role of reason in the contemporary sense was not absent from the scholastic approach, but rather that its operations were closely intertwined with prerational nature:

> While they (the scholastics) distinguish between the rational and the natural more comprehensively understood, they also insist on the continuities between reason and the intelligibilities inherent in prerational nature. Reason stems from these intelligibilities, even as it determines the appropriate forms for their expression. By the same token, however, reason never operates in isolation from the intelligibilities informing prerational nature, nor can the normative force of reason be understood apart from its grounding in wider forms of intelligibility.[4]

Porter argues that such an approach is distinct from a broadly Kantian understanding which is grounded in the belief that norms of moral action come from the deliverances of practical reason in isolation from any speculative or prerational influences, and are therefore applicable in all contexts regardless of any other factors.[5] Immanuel Kant achieved this position by arguing that "practical reason generates moral norms through a self-reflective and discursive unfolding of its own exigencies."[6] Porter argues, however, that there is a major problem with this argument in the following:

> No one has yet shown how norms of self-consistency, taken by themselves, can yield practical principles specific enough actually to guide conduct. What appear to be the exigencies

---

3. *NR*, 231.
4. Ibid., 232; parenthesis added.
5. Ibid., 235.
6. Ibid., 236.

of practical reason turn out, on close inspection, to be expressions of commitments for which we can account in other terms, usually through a close inspection of the values implicit in the philosopher's social setting—or so, at least, the arguments go.[7]

Porter then looks towards the widely held alternative to such a view in contemporary thought, which can be understood as a broadly sentimentalist approach in which practical reason is understood only inasmuch as it has instrumental value for achieving the ends of desires.[8] When there is a situation in which desires are in conflict, such a perspective would argue that practical reason's role is to determine the greatest good for the greatest number of desires and thus look for compromise. In a theoretical sense, this perspective finds its manifestation in various forms of consequentialism and utilitarianism. Porter believes that the scholastic approach develops a convincing middle ground between these two understandings of the operations of reason, and we now turn to her development of this.

Porter and Aquinas on Practical and Speculative Reason

Porter begins her discussion of practical reason with Aquinas' observation that "practical reflection and action always take their starting points from some desire" and this follows from the understanding of the natural intelligibility of the human person as oriented towards flourishing that we have been developing thus far.[9] On this view, given our exploration of the desires proper to the human person and their status as intelligible expressions of our orientation towards flourishing (see chapter 3), the motivation for practical action is a sense of attractiveness as distinct from a sense of duty.[10] For Aquinas, and Porter following him, the virtue which is charged with the task of specifying the most appropriate expressions of practical reason is prudence which, properly understood, is a virtue of the intellect (as distinct from the virtues of passions, temperance and fortitude, and the virtue of the

---

7. Ibid., 239. Porter points toward the work of Simon Blackburn for further development of this argument. See Blackburn, *Ruling Passions*, 214–24. As an example of this line of criticism we can turn to the New Natural Law Theory, which, I would argue, is concerned with using supposed isolated exigencies of practical reason as proofs for the authors' specific commitment to the norms promulgated by the Roman Catholic magisterium. See Stephen Pope's critique of this approach, which we will return to below, Pope, *Human Evolution and Christian Ethics*, 53.

8. *NR*, 240.

9. See especially chap. 3. Ibid., 249. Porter points toward *ST* I-II 9.1, especially *ad* 2; II-II 47.4.

10. *NR*, 149.

will, justice, all of which are specifically moral virtues). Porter argues, however, that it "cannot operate apart from the moral virtues properly so called" because these "rectify the desires which provide practical deliberation with its starting points and aims."[11] As such, the operations of prudence are limited in their scope given that they are concerned with "directing choice at the level of particular acts."[12]

This means that Porter's approach to practical reason tends towards a calculative understanding which seeks to determine specific courses of action which represent "a sound or appropriate way to attain, safeguard, or enjoy some further end" which is presented to practical reason by natural desires and mediated through the virtues appropriate to these.[13] As such, prudence is *not* the virtue which determines the objects of the virtues (as we noted in chapter 3, the specifically moral virtues do this), but rather the virtue which determines "what counts, concretely, as attaining the mean of the virtues in particular instances of choice."[14] There is thus an indelible link between the functions of practical reason and the prerational nature of the human person, and therefore an indelible link between the virtues of the appetites and the will and the virtue of prudence, a point which we will explicate further below.

For now, it is worth turning back briefly to the virtue of justice in order to understand a further link—the one which exists between practical reason and speculative reason in Porter's theory. As we noted in chapter 3, the virtue of justice requires that the desires which are proper to the human person

---

11. Ibid. Porter points toward *ST*, I-II 58.2, 5; II-II 47.6. She also points out that prudence is numbered along with the moral virtues at *ST*, II-II 47.4 even though it is, strictly speaking, an intellectual virtue.

12. *NR*, 250. See *ST*, II-II 47.1–3

13. *NR*, 250.

14. Ibid. James Keenan develops a slightly different argument which, rather than emphasizing choice of particular acts as Porter's approach does, understands prudence as an integrative virtue: "Prudence functions to perfect a person's natural inclinations through integrating them into a coordinated way of acting and living in a right manner. From the outset, prudence is not simply the virtue that makes particular choices. Rather, prudence has a privileged position among the cardinal virtues: it recognizes the ends to which a person is naturally inclined, it establishes the agenda by which one can pursue those ends, it directs the agent's own performance of the pursued activity, and, finally, it measures the rightness of the actions taken. Prudence, in short, guides the agent to living a self-directed life that seeks integration." Keenan, "The Virtue of Prudence," 259. While Keenan's broader vision of prudence is not reflected in the specific part of Porter's theory that has been developed thus far, what follows reveals that Porter's understanding of prudence is broader than this part of her work suggests. Cf. also Terence Irwin's exploration of the same which errs on the side of Porter's argument, Irwin, *The Development of Ethics*, 1:571–72.

be ordered in accordance with the good of the human creature, comprehensively considered, so as to ensure that each is given his due. When it came to Porter's argument, this meant turning to a speculative understanding of the human person in order to specify a criterion by which what is 'due' can be known.[15] In chapter 4, we developed such a paradigm and, as noted there, this can be understood as a 'personalist criterion' for understanding the implications of justice.

In view of this and the comments above regarding the relationship between prudence and all other virtues, it is now possible to understand the link Porter's theory makes between practical and speculative reason. That is, the operations of prudence (the virtue which specifies the operations of practical reason) will necessarily be informed by the operations of justice (the virtue which appeals to and is informed by speculative reason). The link is such that prudence, in its drawing on the virtue of justice, will necessarily also draw on the moral wisdom (or not) of speculative reason, a point to which we will return below.[16]

To illustrate the contrasts between this understanding of the relationship between practical reason and the other dimensions of the human person, including speculative reason, Porter turns to a metaphor used by Simon Blackburn in his book *Ruling Passions*. If we imagine the human person as a ship wherein the crew represent the passions and the captain represents practical reason, the broadly Kantian approach outlined above would have the captain separated from the ship's crew in a form of splendid isolation, able to determine the appropriate direction of the ship and override the inclinations of the crew below. The captain, from this perspective, also generates his own map without recourse to any speculative knowledge about the context in which he is navigating. The broadly sentimentalist account we noted, on the other hand, would have the captain's role as a minor one, reduced to achieving compromise between the conflicting desires provided by the ship's crew. The course of this ship would be a result of the compromise achieved, as distinct from the specific deliberations of its captain, practical reason.[17]

As we have noted, the Thomistic account of the human person Porter is developing would not align itself directly with either of these approaches, and this is for two reasons which we will name briefly here and explore in

---

15. Remembering that the terminology of "speculative" was used here not because it is *merely* speculation, but because it belongs to the epistemological functions of speculative reason, namely the apprehension of things as true.

16. See *NR*, 252.

17. Ibid. Here Porter builds on Blackburn, *Ruling Passions*, 245–46. Cf. Fleming, "Intelligibility in the Natural Law," 13.

more detail below.[18] The first lies in Porter's observation, following Aquinas, that the passions themselves are intelligibly oriented towards the overall good of the human person and that they have an inseparable relationship with the functions of the will. Through the will, the passions thereby have an influence on the functions of reason. The second is that the 'engine room' of the human person—the will—desires objects that are good as apprehended by speculative reason and, as such, provides a link between the operations of practical and speculative reason that is not found in the accounts noted above. The following represents how this can be exemplified through the metaphor that we have been building on thus far:

> The crew (the *intelligible* inclinations of the human person) provide their captain (practical reason) with promptings and suggestions on which course to take and the captain builds on these when navigating the vessel. Furthermore, the captain appeals to knowledge about the environment the ship is travelling in as well as her own orientation toward the overall goal of the ship (happiness) to specify the most appropriate course of action.[19]

As we can see, the navigation of this metaphorical ship draws on Porter's understandings of the roles of prerational nature, speculative reason and practical reason. We can further this understanding about the links between these dimensions of the human person with a consideration of Porter's approach to the relationship between the passions, the will, speculative reason and practical reason.

The Relationship between the Passions, the Will, Speculative Reason and Practical Reason

As we noted in chapter 3, Porter follows Aquinas in arguing that the will is a kind of desire.[20] There is, however, a critical difference between the will and the passions, even though both express themselves in terms of desire, and

---

18. In what follows I extend Porter's use of the ship metaphor in a way that she does not. However, I believe that the following is faithful to her theoretical approach overall. Cf. Fleming, "Intelligibility in the Natural Law," 13.

19. Fleming, "Intelligibility in the Natural Law," 13. Aquinas himself, in his consideration of the relationship between reason and the irascible and concupiscible appetites, uses an analogy that would correspond well with the ship metaphor. That is, he argues that reason rules these appetites not as a despotic ruler, which rules his slaves with no resistance from them, but as a politic power, which emphasizes coordination instead of subjugation. See *ST*, I 81.3 ad. 2.

20. *NR*, 253.

our explanation of this furthers some of the points noted above. Whereas the passions are oriented towards objects that are desirable according to the mediation of the senses and the imagination, the will is oriented towards goods as understood by speculative reason.[21] According to Porter, this means that the will "takes its objects from a rational judgment according to which this or that is in some way good, and therefore a fitting object for pursuit or enjoyment."[22] On this view, speculative reason has a *certain* degree of primacy because it has the role of presenting the will with its objects. As such, the orientation of the will towards the good will be tied up with speculative reason's understanding of the good, and so "its overall orientation will only be as sound as the judgments of the intellect presenting it with its objects."[23] This re-emphasizes the importance of the speculative account of the good concerning the human person which we developed throughout chapter 4 (including the need for an ongoing refinement of this in light of new insights as they come to light), and we will continue to link back to this point in the next few paragraphs. As such, speculative reason and the will are in consistent dialogue, and whilst it is true that the will "never operates except on the basis of some rational judgment or other," this does not mean that the will is under the complete *control* of speculative reason.[24]

According to Porter and Aquinas, the reason for this is that the will and the passions are forms of appetite and, according to the account of the human creature as intelligibly oriented towards the flourishing proper to her, each of these aspects of the person is oriented towards flourishing according to its own specific mode of operation.[25] As such, the will must be understood with reference to its grounding in the nature of the human person, comprehensively considered, and the person's overall orientation towards the flourishing proper to the human creature. This means that the will can only respond to those objects presented to it by speculative reason which correspond in some way to the intelligible nature of the person. In other words, speculative reason cannot "coherently present anything whatever to

---

21. Ibid., 254.

22. Ibid. On the will, Porter points toward *ST*, I-II 8.1; 9.1, 2. On the passions, Porter points toward *ST*, I-II 22.2, 3.

23. *NR*, 255. See *ST*, I-II 8.1. Porter continues with this point and draws a relationship between this understanding and the Catholic understanding of the importance of the correct formation of conscience: "That is why it is so important for someone to have a correct appraisal of that in which her happiness truly consists, because otherwise she will not direct her will toward her genuine perfection, much less orient her actions accordingly." *NR*, 255. See *ST*, II-II 4.7; cf. *ST*, I-II 5.8; *ST*, II-II 25.7

24. *NR*, 259.

25. Ibid., 256. See *ST*, I-II 8.1.

the will as an object of desire and enjoyment."[26] This is a point to emphasize, because it highlights another indelible link in Porter's theory—the link between the prerational nature of the human person and the operations of speculative reason, hence the title of her book *Nature as Reason*. To redeploy the analogy used above, if the will is the engine room it is already pushing the ship in a particular direction, which is set by the operations of the crew.

Furthermore, the human person cannot flourish simply by *knowing* the good through the means of speculative reason. She can only achieve flourishing by acting in the world, she must *do* the good, and when we move from the domain of knowing something to doing something, we move from a consideration of speculative reason to a consideration of practical reason.[27] We will return to practical reason in more detail below, but for explanation's sake it is important to note for now that the possibilities for action to which practical reason is drawn are influenced by the prerational nature of the human person precisely because of the close relationship between these and the will. As such, there is a constant interplay between the operations of practical reason, speculative reason, the will, and the passions, which means that reason is closely linked to the constitution of the human person through the will. Porter specifies this further:

> What this means, practically, is that reason and will are always in a process of dynamic interaction. As reason presents the will with possible objects for pursuit and suggests courses of action directed toward these goods, so the will prompts reason to consider this or that alternative, to deliberate on the best way to attain this or that end, and the like.[28]

At this point, we can see the link between these activities and the understanding of the human person we have been developing thus far:

> The agent's persistent dispositions of intellect, will, and passions—his virtues, in other words, or perhaps his vices—together with his overall beliefs, desires, and commitments as shaped by his particular history and circumstance, all come together to inform the exercise of will and reason at any given point in time.[29]

---

26. *NR*, 257.

27. Westberg, *Right Practical Reason*, 4. Noted in Keenan, "The Virtue of Prudence," 265.

28. *NR*, 259.

29. Ibid., 260.

The Virtue of Prudence and the Importance of Attentiveness 185

To further the argument we have been developing throughout, this means that reason never operates in isolation from the prerational intelligibilities which enable its action. We will now consider the implications of this in relationship to specifically practical reason as yet another link between Porter and Levinas.

The Operations of Reason and the Levinasian Insight

In view of the argument developed thus far, that reason is in consistent dialogue with the will and—by implication—the human person's natural intelligibility, the appetites and the virtues associated with them, we can provide substantial support for Levinas's argument that ethics is the first philosophy. That is, it is now possible to argue that Levinas was correct in his argument that ethics, understood as an optics which sees the human person as always constituted by a relationality that is profoundly affected by the presence of the Other, is always fundamental for the operations of reason. Given that we have turned to Andrew Tallon's use of affective neuroscience to demonstrate the plausibility of this claim on the level of scientific insight into the person, Porter now provides the link to show how this part of our prerational nature undergirds the very function of reason which means that any activity undertaken by reason is always permeated by this. In other words, when Levinas and Porter's insights are combined here we can see that *any* activity of reason always has something to do with our prerational orientation towards being affected by the Other and, if this is the case and Porter is correct that our prerational nature reveals something of the teleological goal towards which we are intelligibly directed, any natural and truly human use of reason should reflect this fact of human nature, rather than ignore it (as Levinas suggests philosophy has done in the main). Porter provides further clarification on this point:

> Reason takes its starting points from inclinations which are not simply blind surges of desire, but intelligibly structured orientations towards goods connatural to the human creature, and it is informed through a process of ongoing reflection on those intelligibilities. In this way, the natural law as Aquinas understands it stems from and respects the intelligible order of nature—not (primarily) by tracking a natural or moral order to be found in relations or states of affairs outside the creature, but by respecting and bringing coherence to the intelligible order of the human creature itself.[30]

30. Ibid., 262.

In view of this, we can see that reason is, as it were, underdetermined by the prerational intelligibility of the human creature and that, when our understanding of this intelligibility includes the Levinasian insight, ethics as an optics is both fundamental and foundational for the operations of reason. It is noteworthy that, in Porter's theory, we find a point at which she reveals the kind of methodology that Levinas points towards in that she locates the so-called first principles of natural law within this understanding of this link between nature as nature and nature as reason. Thus, the first principles *reflect* the constitution of the human person, in the same way that Levinas argued that the operations of consciousness would be founded in and reflect something of the human person's pre-intentional constitution. We turn now to a consideration of how Porter develops this point, and how it is distinct from the approach found in Kant and the New Natural Law Theory.

Practical Reason and the First Principles of the Natural Law

As we have seen, Porter sees a dynamic interplay between the operations of reason and the prerational intelligibility of the human person and, as we indicated at the end of the last section, it is this interplay that Porter sees as foundational for the so-called 'first principles' of natural law. As we have also seen, other natural law theorists (such as the New Natural Law theorists) associate these first principles with the exigencies of practical reason. Porter, too, sees them as associated with the activity of practical reason, but rather than being the *creation* of practical reason they are *constitutive* of its operations. This means that, rather than coming out of a conclusion of the process of practical reason, the first principles of natural law are intuitive reflections of the fundamental orientation of the human creature towards her flourishing.[31] In other words, because the person is intelligibly oriented towards what is good for her at a prerational level and the function of practical reason arises out of the natural, its operations are bound up with and reflective of this fundamental orientation whilst at the same time able to introduce a degree of creativity in its expression.[32] From this perspective,

---

31. Ibid., 264. Irwin makes the same point regarding Aquinas's understanding of the first principles, see Irwin, *The Development of Ethics*, 579.

32. This is distinct from the Kantian approach, which would have practical reason separated from the natural and would see the will being motivated by prerational dispositions as a form of heteronomy. As such, the perspective Porter is advancing here would argue that practical reason and its capacity for "free choice" is "better construed as a capacity to select from influential factors rather than as a complete transcendence of them. It is a modification of the ordering of nature, not a suspension of it." Pope, *Human Evolution and Christian Ethics*, 183.

the first principles of natural law are grasped as such because they are natural to the human creature. From a Levinasian point of view we can make a further argument here to say that our orientation towards valuing the Other is primary precisely because it is constitutive of the person and, as such, will be intuitively grasped in all of the operations of both practical and speculative reason.

Turning back to the scholastics, Porter notes that the most commonly cited first principle is that good is to be done and evil is to be avoided and this is frequently linked with the commandments to love God and neighbor.[33] The latter of these, of course, should be of no surprise to us at this point because—as Porter argues—the love of neighbor is intelligible precisely because it is the most perfect expression of what it means to be a social animal.[34] This draws us towards Porter's distinctive understanding of moral norms. As we noted earlier in chapter 2, the New Natural Law Theorists require too much specification from the operations of practical reason alone for their theoretical approach to be convincing without some recourse to their broader social and philosophical commitments. Stephen Pope articulates this criticism strongly:

> Though this position (NNLT) does not rely on faith in any explicit way and in fact claims to be purely rational, it has been used by many Catholics to provide a contemporary theoretical defense of the moral code taught by the official teaching authority of the Catholic church. It is no coincidence that the content of the "new natural law" happens to agree with almost every item of moral teaching found in the *Catechism of the Catholic Church*.[35]

Porter, in contrast, understands moral norms as the result of communal reflection on the most appropriate expressions of the basic principles of natural law in dialogue with the understanding of the virtues that we have been developing, which are reflective of our common prerational nature.[36] In view of this, one can expect and affirm the diversity of practical conclusions which arise out of this process. As Porter also notes, however, and as we explored in chapter 3 and chapter 4, the Christian tradition has emphasized that humankind is wounded by sin and, as such, looks towards a way of correcting and completing this communal reflection in dialogue

---

33. *NR*, 263.
34. Ibid., 264–65.
35. Pope, *Human Evolution and Christian Ethics*, 53.
36. *NR*, 267.

with the sources of revelation.[37] As we noted in chapter 3, and demonstrated throughout chapter 4, Porter allows for an appeal to a wider speculative understanding of what counts as the good and, following the scholastics, gives room for an appeal to Tradition founded in Scripture as a way of correcting and completing the necessary limitations of this communal reflection.[38]

In view of all that has been developed above, we can make the following concluding statements about Porter's understanding of practical reason. In the first instance, practical reason's role is more limited in Porter's theory than it is in—for example—the Kantian approach and the New Natural Law Theory and also has a close link to the operations of speculative reason. In the second instance, practical reason's operations are informed by the human person's prerational intelligibility and are, as such, not arbitrary but rather directed by the overall natural orientation of the human person, comprehensively considered. In the third instance, her understanding of reason (broadly considered) provides a strong argument for the plausibility of Levinas's claim that ethics is first philosophy and, following on from this, we have seen how Porter's approach can account for the first principles of natural law in a way which aligns itself with the rest of her theory and is more convincing than the NNLT approach. Finally, we have touched briefly on Porter's understanding of the development of moral norms and have linked this with the theological understanding of sin and the necessary appeal to a speculative, communal account which is informed by revelation in order to correct and complete the resources on which practical reason can draw for the task of engaging in action and have noted that such an account has been developed in chapter 4.

Practical reason, therefore, is charged with the task of answering the question "what must be done?" in specific situations and informed by the prerational intelligibilities and speculative accounts of the good noted above. As with the other capacities of the human person in Thomistic moral psychology—the appetites and the will—its proper function is understood as bound up with a virtue which has the capacity to specify how it goes about its operations in the most excellent way possible, all things considered. This virtue is prudence, and we turn to a detailed consideration of it now.

---

37. Cf. Vatican I, *Dei Filius: On Faith and Reason*, no. 4.
38. *NR*, 267.

THE VIRTUE OF PRACTICAL REASON: PRUDENCE

Foundational Points about Prudence in Porter's Theory

As we have noted, practical reason operates at the level of judgment and is informed in its operations by both the passions and the will. As with all of the capacities of the human person, practical reason is oriented towards the operations of a particular virtue which Porter and Aquinas name as prudence.[39] The role of prudence is thus closely aligned with the understanding of practical reason that we developed above:

> its central actions are to inquire with respect to what is to be done in a given situation, to form a judgment based on that inquiry, and to command the action or actions so determined (II-II 47.8). Moreover, the moral virtues properly so called (that is, temperance, fortitude, and justice) cannot exist without prudence (I-II 58.4), nor can prudence in its turn exist without the moral virtues (I-II 58.5).[40]

The operations of prudence are especially significant in view of the complex situations which the human person encounters, and here I quote Porter at length for her clarity of expression in this regard:

> While there may be circumstances in which the virtuous individual knows clearly what he needs to do in a given situation, and is puzzled about the means by which to carry out his good aim, normally the uncertainties of the well-meaning, virtuous person will not be like that. Compare, for example, the uncertainties of the individual who feels moved to give something to a charity but cannot decide which charity is most effective, to the uncertainties of the father who wants to be generous to his son but is worried that a large present of money would really be ungenerous, because it would encourage dependency and passivity on the boy's part. In the latter case, unlike the former case, what is uncertain is precisely what would count as a generous act, all things considered. What prudence provides in the latter sort of case, in other words, is a determination of what would count as a virtuous action in a specific situation; that is what it means to

---

39. Ibid., 311. Porter notes that prudence is also known as the virtue of practical reason. For clarity's sake, I will use "practical reason" to refer to the human person's ability to make concrete, practical decisions in view of a particular situation, and "prudence" to refer to the virtue that expresses this inclination in the most perfect way.

40. *NR*, 312. See also Keenan, "The Virtue of Prudence," 264, 266.

say that prudence determines the concrete content of the mean of the virtue, in specific instances of choice.[41]

As such, prudence has an inseparable relationship with the other virtues. This is founded in its appropriate field of operation which determines the mean of each virtue in a concrete situation. We move now to a consideration of this point in more detail.

Prudence and its Relationship to the Other Virtues

As we have seen, prudence performs the function of determining the mean of each virtue at the level of concrete choice. The function that prudence performs and its field of operation will be largely dependent on the particular virtue that it is attempting to express in any given situation. For example, the virtue of temperance—as we have seen in chapter 3—determines the expression of concupiscible appetites according to criteria which are largely referential to the agent himself and his own individual good.[42] We have also seen, however, that such an expression cannot be considered truly virtuous unless it accounts for the human person adequately considered, including their profoundly social nature, and that the virtues should therefore not be understood as operating in isolation. As such, prudence will also need to be informed by the other virtues, including justice, which is necessary for the good of both individual persons and those with whom they are in relationship.[43]

On this view, prudence is not a virtue which operates in dialogue with only one virtue at a time, given that such an approach could lead to actions which are deficient in their reference to other virtues, the human person as a whole and to the common good.[44] The disposition of prudence therefore requires a critical awareness and balancing of diverse considerations

---

41. *NR*, 313.

42. The disposition of temperance will thus produce different concrete outcomes for an adult than it would a child. See ibid.

43. Hence the comment in chap. 3 that temperance could not be considered virtuous if it involved consuming food at the expense of another's survival. Porter synthesizes this further at this point of her book: "[Justice therefore] directs the individual to the common good, which for Aquinas is necessary for the full perfection of the individual himself (I-II 56.6; II-II 47.10; 58.12); at the same time, it qualifies both temperance and fortitude, providing norms by which true temperance and fortitude can be distinguished from incomplete or counterfeit forms of these virtues (II-II 58.5, 6)." See *NR*, 314; parenthesis added. See also Kent, "Habits and Virtues," 121.

44. Cf., for example, our description of the "temperate" individual who eats in moderation, but does so at the expense of another's survival in chap. 3.

in order to, as Porter states, "arrive at a choice which is not only virtuous in this or that respect, but virtuous without qualification."[45] The paradigmatic example of a person who is prudent will therefore be the "ability to balance diverse considerations in order to arrive at a settled judgment concerning the best course of action, all things considered."[46]

Such an approach requires that we draw on a framework within which these diverse, and often complex, considerations can be prioritized by their relative value in any given moral situation. Porter argues that higher-level categories of virtues (such as justice) provide such a framework, and we have seen in chapter 4 how a paradigm of this particular virtue can be developed.[47] Virtues in such higher-level categories enable us to understand the interrelationship among the virtues which can provide us with ways of analyzing how diverse considerations can be ranked on a scale—"that is to say, the claims of the higher virtues, and particularly justice and (where applicable) charity, shape and direct the exercise of the lower virtues."[48] It should be made clear that this approach is distinct from a simple mathematical equation which would enable the human person to rank goods in isolation from any particular situation.[49] As we have already noted, the disposition of prudence specifies practical reason in accordance with human happiness. Practical reason, furthermore, is a dimension of the human person which cannot operate apart from some form of dialogue with context. As such, a mathematical equation which develops a hierarchy of goods in a way that is separated from contextual considerations would be deficient because its outcome would always be predetermined from within and simply applied in this or that particular situation.[50] As distinct from this approach, prudence is always informed by unique situations, and the ordering of priorities it develops will necessarily be informed by the morally salient features of these

---

45. *NR*, 314. Cf. Pope, *Human Evolution and Christian Ethics*, 179. In this sense, as Keenan notes, Aquinas argues that prudence has a certain degree of primacy in its relationship with the other cardinal virtues, given that their correct expression could not be achieved without its function. See Keenan, "The Virtue of Prudence," 260–61. Aquinas follows Aristotle on this point, see Dunne, "Virtue, *Phronesis* and Learning," 51, 62.

46. *NR*, 314.

47. See ibid., 315: "a higher level category provides a framework within which to assess the significance and relative value of different considerations, and as such, it enables me to make a choice informed by reasons, brought together in some kind of comprehensible order—in other words, a nonarbitrary, rational choice."

48. *NR*, 316. See *ST*, II-II 23.8; 58.12.

49. *NR*, 316, cf. 318. See also Kupperman, "Virtues, Character and Moral Dispositions," 207.

50. Cf. Levinas's description of "totalization" in chapter 1.

situations.[51] In the next section, we will consider two such situations in order to provide an example of the operations of prudence in the concrete.

Prudence in Action

We can look at two examples which reveal the thrust of the argument that the operations of practical reason, and therefore prudence, cannot be understood without an appeal to the context in which they operate. In the first instance, we return to the father (in the example we took from Porter above), who wishes to be generous to his son, but is unsure as to whether the gift of a large sum of money would actually count as generosity or not. In the first place, we can see how difficult it is to consider act A (a gift of large sum of money) to be an instance of the virtue of generosity G. Whilst A = G might be true, we are unable to determine its truth without some attention to the context in which A will occur. In this case, such attentiveness would need to consider (among other things) the son's financial situation; his level of responsibility regarding the use of money; whether or not the gift would hinder rather than help the development of necessary autonomy; and so on. Furthermore, recall that for Porter the role of prudence is not only to consider whether this or that act is an instance of an individual virtue because the virtues themselves do not operate in isolation. To determine whether A = G, then, also invites a broader consideration of how A aligns itself with the other virtues, especially the higher-level virtues such as justice. From this perspective, the father might find out that A does not constitute a generous action at all because the gift of a large sum of money would effectively isolate his son from an awareness of what it means to work for a living or, perhaps, because his son is in recovery from a gambling addiction and the father fears that a large sum of money could be the catalyst for a relapse. On the other hand, if the father's son has recently lost his job and is unable to care adequately for three growing children, then it may turn out that act A is in fact an instance of G. So, does A = G? According to what has been developed, this is actually the wrong question. It would be more appropriate to ask, what features of this unique ethical context will determine whether A counts as an expression of G?

Porter notes that Aquinas provides another poignant example of this in terms of religious devotion and filial piety. The latter should be subordinated

---

51. This same point appears in Aquinas's understanding of prudence, see *ST*, II-II, 47.7 (ad 3); II-II, 47.15.
Keenan, "The Virtue of Prudence," 261. The same point is made by Nancy Sherman from a purely Aristotelian point of view, see Sherman, "Character Development," 38.

to the former, Aquinas argues, unless the situation of one's parents requires that they be cared for and provided the necessities of life, in which case the hierarchy is adjusted and care for one's parents becomes a priority.[52] In this instance, recourse to a paradigm of justice (such as the one we developed in chapter 4 in dialogue with our understanding of the human person adequately considered and Paul VI's transcendent humanism) acknowledges that an awareness of the value of others requires a commitment to ensuring that the basic goods necessary for them to live and flourish are provided first of all, before moving towards the higher goods such as the spiritual life. This is not a simple mathematical equation, however, and as an example of this, moral theology (and the official teaching of the Church), has recognized that the duty to sustain and prolong life has limits and, where necessary, can be subordinated to the relief of pain in order to focus on care for the emotional, psychological and spiritual dimensions of the human person when death has been accepted as imminent.[53]

In both instances, the outcome cannot be absolutized ahead of time, and an accurate understanding of the ethical situation is thus essential in order for prudence to specify this action and determine the best possible action, all things considered. We turn now, therefore, to a development of what it means for prudence to be attentive in the context of concrete ethical situations.

Prudence and the Need for Attentiveness

As we have seen, prudence operates in dialogue with the other virtues and with the concrete context in which it operates. Given the complexity of both sides of this dialogue, we have also seen that it is impossible for the operations of prudence to be understood as a simple mathematical equation for coming to an adequate moral judgment.[54]

The fact that moral discernment calls for the virtue of prudence also implies that there can be no truly virtuous action without it. As we have

---

52. *NR*, 316–17. See *ST*, II-II 101.4, ad 3: "And so if our observances are necessary to our parents in the flesh, in such a way that they cannot be sustained without it, then neither do they lead us to something contrary to God, and we ought not to leave them in order to enter religious life. If however we are unable without sin to be free to fulfill our observances towards them, or if they can sustain themselves without our aid, it is licit to leave off our observances towards them, in order that we might more readily be free for religious life."

53. See for example *EV*, 64–67; Connors and McCormick, *Facing Ethical Issues*, 285–305.

54. *NR*, 320.

indicated above, a person may well be disposed to act in a virtuous way, but the extent to which this actually occurs depends largely on the capacity that prudence has to be attentive to the context in which it operates.[55] Bonnie Kent provides the following in support of this argument, and her words can also help in our understanding of prudence and its relationship with our prerational orientation towards goodness, as well as the moral virtues which arise out of this:

> The argument that no proper moral virtue can exist without prudence makes more sense if one recalls that a virtue cannot be put to bad use. The ability to face danger, in its own right, would go just as well to make a daring bank robber as an admirable war hero. A person needs prudence to judge correctly which dangers would be *good* to face. As a moral virtue requires prudence, so, too, prudence requires moral virtue. A fearful person, with an excessive desire for safety, will naturally tend to judge too dangerous by half situations that it would actually be good to face. Someone's sense of justice cannot consistently govern her actions if she often lacks the courage to do the right thing.[56]

The functions of prudence are thus essential to an adequate understanding of the concrete ethical implications that the understanding of the human person we have developed throughout the book implies. As such, they have an insatiable influence on the moral life. Porter's approach to prudence has revealed the importance of both its expression of the moral virtues and its ability to be attentive to the context in which it operates. Without the latter of these, the virtue is deficient, and I would like to suggest that Porter's discussion of this can be complemented further with a return to reflection on what Levinas calls "totalization," and beyond this towards a virtue which can be understood as the disposition which shows an awareness of the problem of 'totalization' and a willingness to avoid it in a very practical way through a commitment to, and practical guidelines for, attentiveness.

---

55. For further discussion on this point, albeit from a more Aristotelian point of view, see Curren, "Cultivating the Intellectual and Moral Virtues," 71; Sherman, "Character Development," 38.

56. Kent, "Habits and Virtues," 123.

PRUDENCE AS ATTENTIVENESS

The Complexity of Ethical Situations and the Priority of Attentiveness

One picks up in Porter's theory as a whole, and especially her discussion of prudence, an awareness of the complexity of ethical decision making and the uniqueness of the contexts in which this occurs. This same point was made by Louis Janssens in his reflections on the anthropology of *Gaudium et spes*, firstly in terms of the human person as an agent who comes to ethical decisions in a necessarily unique historical and developmental context which can provide both limitations for how one understands any given situation, and also unique insights (see chapter 4). Furthermore, Janssens noted a theme that Levinas articulated strongly and which we spent some time developing in chapter 1—that the human person is fundamentally unique, an infinity which cannot be reduced to any particular conception. Any attempt to control or tame this infinity was called a 'violence' by Levinas, and we noted that Janssens acknowledged the same whilst holding this in tension with the fundamental equality that exists among all human persons. This places in sharp relief the problems associated with deductive theories of morality which, as we noted in dialogue with the New Natural Law theory, fail to take into account the uniqueness and complexity of the encounter with the Other and are thus prone to damaging 'totalizations' and the violence that results from these.[57]

As we have seen, Porter shows an awareness of this problem throughout her theory and its very composition is a testament to that. It is, however, most apparent in her discussion of prudence in which she shows convincingly the importance of an 'all things considered' understanding of each ethical situation in coming to an adequate moral response. Such an awareness can further the Levinasian critique of the ego which simply stays "at home with itself" and acts out of this conceptual framework: organizing, categorizing and reducing all that it encounters according to the rigid walls of the home which is closed to what is Other than itself. Whilst one might have a stunning grasp of the virtues and their proper operation, Porter shows us that this alone is not enough, just as Levinas reveals the deficiencies of 'totalization.' As we have seen, the virtues are not a mathematical equation for ordering the goods which apply to the human person and her environment. They hinge, rather, on the inductive functions of prudence which are

---

57. Keenan furthers this argument by pointing out that a focus on prudence can also help to avoid the problems with highly deductive forms of morality, which we explored early in chap. 2. Keenan, "The Virtue of Prudence," 265.

only as effective as their alignment with the reality of the complex ethical situations that the human person encounters. As James Keenan notes, it is the virtue of prudence which places our entire discussion of moral reasoning into an inherently anthropological context, along with all the complexities encountered therein.[58] In view of this, there is a certain sense in which the operations of prudence are only as adequate as the person's ability to be *attentive* to what is encountered.[59] In the next section, we will build from this point and use it to argue for the introduction of the virtue of solidarity into Porter's discussion of prudence.

Links between Prudence, Attentiveness and Solidarity

As we have seen, Porter's understanding of prudence carries with it a certain priority for attentiveness to the unique ethical context in which it operates. As a virtue then, prudence is able to avoid 'totalization' because its starting point is not only within the human person, the "I" at home with itself, but also as an openness to the uniqueness of what it encounters. As we have seen, to avoid 'totalization' in any sense there must be an openness to 'infinity,' and such an openness is only possible if the disposition provided by the virtue of prudence is not only to apply a certain grasp of what should be done when an Other is encountered, but also to be attentive to *this* Other and *this* situation in all of its complexity. This is something a mathematical or 'totalizing' approach is unable to do. Only then, as Porter has argued, will one be able to make the best possible decision, "all things considered." As Diana Fritz Cates argues, "the prudent person must perceive when a law or a rule is appropriate to a situation, and he or she must apply all guidelines in a context-sensitive manner, attending with special care to the irreducibly particular features of the situation."[60] This requires us to spend some time developing what it means to be attentive in view of complex ethical situ-

---

58. Keenan, "The Virtue of Prudence," 259.

59. Diana Fritz Cates makes this same point about prudence as it is expressed in Aquinas's own approach. See Cates, "The Virtue of Temperance," 325. This observation aligns well with *Veritatis splendor's* argument that "The Church is always and everywhere at the *service of conscience*." VS, no. 64. In this context, the argument highlights the importance of the magisterium's function in helping people to grow in wise judgment and, in view of the book's argument, careful attentiveness. Cf. Gleeson's emphasis on the magisterium's primary role in moral teaching as "the exhortation of moral goodness, to the formation of conscience and the exercise of prudence in searching for right ways of living." Gleeson, "The Scope of the Church's Moral Teaching," 267. For further discussion on the nature of the kind of service that can assist in the formation of conscience in this way, see Gleeson, "Prophecy, Patience and Pardon," 207–11.

60. Cates, "The Virtue of Temperance," 325.

ations. It is at this point that the book takes a unique turn with the link it makes between the proper functions of prudence and the virtue of solidarity, which has been developed in Catholic Social Teaching, as *the* paradigm for moral reasoning when the complexity of social situations is such that one cannot offer solutions without first embodying a genuine openness to the uniqueness of what is encountered.[61]

CONCLUSION

In this chapter, we turned from the anthropological vision of the human person informed by the Catholic tradition developed in chapter 4, to a close consideration of Porter's understanding of that dimension of the human person which seeks to navigate human activity, practical reason. The chapter began with a consideration of practical reason, and developed yet another link with Levinas through the first principles of natural law by proposing an argument for a complementarity between Porter and Levinas on this point. In view of its discussion of practical reason, the chapter introduced the virtue of prudence. By considering prudence in relationship with the other virtues, it developed an understanding of the virtue which was used to demonstrate what influence it has on the moral reasoning of the prudent person. This development of prudence led to an emphasis on the need for attentiveness in moral reasoning and, indeed, to the proposition of an argument for the priority of attentiveness. This last point enabled the chapter to propose a link between prudence, attentiveness and solidarity, which now becomes the focus of chapter 6, and which moves us to the last part of the task that the book is undertaking.

---

61. This is not to say that other authors have not highlighted the importance of considering solidarity in fundamental ethical theory. As an example, Lisa Sowle Cahill's book on fundamental sexual ethics, *Sex, Gender and Christian Ethics*, makes a clear point of integrating solidarity into any Christian ethics that refers to human relationality. However, it should be noted that Cahill tends to see solidarity as a social virtue and compassion as its interpersonal correlate. See for example Cahill, *Sex, Gender and Christian Ethics*, 162. As we will see in chap. 6, the way in which I develop the virtue of solidarity can incorporate the more personal disposition of *compassion* whilst retaining its concern for solidarity in the social order. On Cahill's general reasons for including solidarity in her approach, see Cahill, *Sex, Gender and Christian Ethics*, 109, 117.

6

The Virtue of Solidarity and Attentiveness to Vulnerability

INTRODUCTION

THIS IS THE LAST substantial chapter of the book. Methodologically, it moves from a consideration of Porter's understanding of prudence and the argument regarding the importance of attentiveness that were the focus of chapter 5, towards the proposal of an argument for the usefulness of the virtue of solidarity in directing the attentiveness of prudence. In order to do this, it first builds up an understanding of solidarity in dialogue with the body of thought known as Catholic Social Teaching (CST) and a number of authors who have commented on this, before analyzing the virtue of solidarity itself more closely and showing how it relates to the rest of the book's argument. In terms of this argument as a whole, this chapter focuses on the incorporation of the virtue of solidarity into the approach that has been developed in Chapters One through Five. In order to fulfill the final parts of the task set out at the beginning of the book, it uses solidarity to provide clarification on how the attentiveness of prudence can be directed. Further to this, it proposes an argument for a careful consideration of vulnerability in moral reasoning which draws in the discussion of vulnerability as a dimension of the human person from chapter 4. This, it argues, also has implications for understanding the principle of the preferential option for the poor, which is closely related to solidarity in CST. Finally, the chapter proposes an argument which identifies three vices associated with the virtue of solidarity. Among these can be found the 'vice of totalization,' the critical analysis of which reveals how the approach developed throughout the book—when it includes the virtue of solidarity—can avoid what Levinas refers to as 'totalization.'

THE VIRTUE OF SOLIDARITY: BACKGROUND AND FOUNDATIONS

Catholic Social Teaching

As we argued in chapter 5, Porter's understanding of prudence includes a certain priority for attentiveness to unique ethical situations and, as noted above, some time will now be spent engaging with the virtue of solidarity as a paradigm for what it means to be attentive in complex ethical situations in such a way as to prevent 'totalization.' The virtue of solidarity is expressed within the teaching of the Church's magisterium as part of the body of thought known as Catholic Social Teaching (CST). As such, we will begin our consideration of this virtue with some very brief comments about CST in general and then move into an analysis of how solidarity is expressed in this body of thought. This foundational understanding of the virtue will then be integrated into the understanding of justice and prudence that we have been developing with Porter and in dialogue with Levinas thus far.

It is widely agreed that the beginnings of CST can be found in Pope Leo XIII's 1891 encyclical *Rerum Novarum* which, for the first time in official Catholic teaching, developed the implications of human dignity in relationship to the modern social order.[1] CST would develop much further from Leo XIII's original observations and, in the middle of the twentieth century, found itself well positioned to respond to the emerging challenges of globalization. This can be seen in Pope Paul VI's 1967 encyclical, *Populorum Progressio*, with which we have already engaged for its understanding of 'transcendent humanism' (see chapter 4). Paul VI's encyclical warmly welcomes the beginnings of globalization and comes across as optimistic and inspiring, providing a window of insight into the positivity about globalization that was common in the 1960s. In it, the Pope argues that the emerging globalization has the potential to lead humankind to peace if it is navigated successfully with an orientation towards the good of all human

---

1. See *RN*. For a detailed exploration of the historical context out of which the encyclical arose, see Aubert, *Catholic Social Teaching*, 181–98. See also Sniegocki, *Catholic Social Teaching*, 105–9.

persons.² Yet, when the *Compendium of the Social Doctrine of the Church* was published some 37 years later, it would begin its discussion of solidarity with the observation that globalization had brought people together in practical terms but had not necessarily made them more equal.³ Paul VI's optimistic outlook for the future of globalization had not been fulfilled and in the most recent of the social encyclicals, Pope Benedict XVI follows the lead of the *Compendium* by arguing that globalization "makes us neighbours but does not make us brothers."⁴ More recently, Pope Francis has led a sustained and provocative analysis of what actually characterizes our current globalization. Far from the hopes articulated by Paul VI, Francis sees our current globalization primarily in terms of the export of inequality, technocratic paradigms, and unjust economic models, all of which undermine the capacity for the kind of global movement that assures all people of the flourishing that their dignity deserves.⁵ What is missing in making the global family an authentically human one is the virtue of *solidarity*.⁶

The Origins of the Principle of Solidarity

Pope John XXIII was the first to invoke the word 'solidarity' in official Catholic teaching in his 1963 encyclical *Pacem in Terris*, which is a plea for greater solidarity between nations and between socio-economic classes.⁷ Pope John Paul II, true to his emphasis on the continuity of Papal teaching, develops an argument in his 1991 encyclical *Centesimum Annus* to suggest that the principle had been present consistently throughout CST, albeit under different names: "friendship" in the writing of Pope Leo XIII; "social charity" from Pope Pius XI; and Pope Paul VI's "civilization of love."⁸ It is clear, however, that Pope John Paul II develops CST's understanding of the word as a principle and its practical implications considerably—both *Centesimus Annus* and *Evangelium Vitae* place an emphasis on the principle, and *Sollicitudo Rei Socialis* uses the term 27 times.⁹ In Pope Benedict XVI's

---

2. Ward, "Looking Back on *Populorum Progressio*," 130.
3. *CSDC*, no. 192.
4. *CV*, no. 19.
5. *LS*, nos. 106–14, 144.
6. Which was also emphasised very strongly by Pope Paul VI in *PP*, nos. 67–69.
7. *PT*, no. 98.
8. *CA*, no. 10. Aubert finds the same continuity in the *CST* encyclicals, see Aubert, *Catholic Social Teaching*, 205.
9. On the centrality of solidarity in the social encyclicals of Pope John Paul II, see Curran, Himes, and Shannon, "Commentary on *Sollicitudo Rei Socialis*," 426; Dorr,

2009 encyclical *Caritas in Veritate* the principle is invoked 41 times.[10] The principle sits at the heart of Pope Francis' 2015 encyclical *Laudato Si'* midst his urgent appeal for focus on the ecological crisis and all of the human crises that go along with it. Francis argues that "We require a new and universal solidarity."[11]

The origins of the principle of solidarity are, however, not to be found within the Catholic tradition.[12] Rather, the principle was first developed during the industrial revolution with thinkers who were looking for a middle way between the extreme forms of socialism and liberalism. In attempting to avoid the collectivism and individualism that were seen as so problematic in these approaches (respectively), they oriented themselves towards an approach which emphasized both the value of the individual and of the broader community. This led them to employ the concept of an organic community in which all members have a responsibility to each other and themselves for the good of the community as a whole.[13] Given the complexity of industrial societies (and now post-industrial societies), however, this somewhat vague concept could not, of itself, provide an adequate framework for understanding social order, let alone critiquing it, or for moral decision making. As such, the Catholic understanding of solidarity built on the concept of an organic community by adding to it many of the key components of the Catholic understanding of the human person that we developed in chapter 4: the individual human person as fundamentally unique but equally dignified with all other persons, the importance of the social aspect of the human person for individuals and for communities, and those goods understood to be universal through reflection on the theory of natural law.[14]

This brief background history of the concept of solidarity provides us with a foundational understanding of the principle's development. What is particularly attractive about this history for our purposes is that the principle and the virtue of solidarity arose out of an awareness of the complexity, diversity and particularity of social situations. As such, we can expect that

---

Option for the Poor, 326; Sniegocki, *Catholic Social Teaching*, 141; Verstraeten, "Solidarity and Subsidiarity," 140. *CA* and *EV* invoke the term "solidarity" 15 and 16 times, respectively.

10. See *CV*. On the continuing importance of solidarity in the social teaching of Benedict XVI, see Sniegocki, *Catholic Social Teaching*, 152.

11. *LS*, 14.

12. Verstraeten, "Solidarity and Subsidiarity," 133.

13. Njoku, *Examining the Foundations of Solidarity in the Social Encyclicals of John Paul II*. See also Verstraeten, "Solidarity and Subsidiarity," 134.

14. Lamb, "Solidarity," 908.

solidarity will have something to say about how to grapple with the complexity of concrete ethical situations. In order to see exactly what this is, we turn now to a consideration of solidarity as a principle and a virtue.

Interdependence and Solidarity as a Principle and a Virtue

In light of this brief historical overview of the development of the principle and virtue of solidarity, we are now in a position to consider how CST understands it more specifically. At the outset, it is necessary that we begin with a definition of 'interdependence' which can be understood as the condition within which a change in one part of a whole has an effect on the rest, which necessarily means that the good of the whole is closely intertwined with the good of each. In CST, interdependence is understood as the condition of the human family as a whole and, in practical terms, it is simply the observation that we are now more dependent on more people who live in more locations that ever before.[15] This interdependence is the condition out of which solidarity arises, but it is not the same as solidarity, because interdependence can manifest itself both positively and negatively.[16] David Hollenbach has explored these two different types of interdependence, and we turn to him now for further clarification.

Hollenbach gives the name 'unequal interdependence' to the negative form of interdependence. Unequal interdependence is characterized by abusive or subversive relationships wherein each participant (understood as either individuals or groups) is reliant on the other in an unhealthy way.[17] To use Porter's terminology, we might describe this as a social situation which exists in such a way as to prevent, rather than promote, authentic human happiness. Hollenbach contrasts this with 'equal interdependence,' in which "the agency and well-being of all" are enhanced.[18] Solidarity, therefore, refers to the movement from independence to awareness of interdependence and beyond the negative forms of this towards genuine concern for, and action towards, the common good, expressed in Hollenbach's 'equal interdependence.'[19] As such, solidarity has two aspects and these can be understood as a goal for society (the condition of the common good) and a

---

15. For a more thorough exploration of this point, see Fleming, "Understanding Trade," 11–13. See also Verstraeten, "Solidarity and Subsidiarity," 142.
16. *CSDC*, 193.
17. Hollenbach, *The Common Good and Christian Ethics*, 188.
18. Ibid.
19. Himes, *Responses to 101 Questions on Catholic Social Teaching*, 38–39.

moral virtue, which is made up of the social characteristics and dispositions which facilitate the movement towards this goal.[20]

As a social goal, solidarity is the condition which allows for the common good to be achieved. More specifically, this involves the establishment of what CST has called 'structures of solidarity.' To clarify, the language of structures refers to social structures, which can be understood as "institutionalized sets of interdependent human relationships that influence social behavior and regulate the life-chances of people at a given time and place."[21] In view of this, 'structures of solidarity' are understood as the social structures which enable the flourishing of all for the common good.[22] These contrast with what are described as 'structures of sin,' understood as the "actions and attitudes opposed to the will of God and the good of neighbor, as well as the structures arising from such behaviour" which act as obstacles and impediments in the movement towards the common good and therefore impede, rather than promote, human flourishing.[23]

In this section we have been exploring the foundations and basic understanding of solidarity as it is expressed in CST. A consideration of the background of solidarity in CST, the principle's development, and its dimensions as a both a principle and as a virtue has revealed that solidarity is a firm and persevering commitment to achieving the common good through overcoming structures of sin and moving them towards structures of solidarity.[24] In the next section, we turn specifically to the *virtue* of solidarity, understood as the character disposition (either of an individual or a community) which enables the movement towards the common good to occur. Given that the common good accounts for all dimensions of what it means to flourish as a human person, it is worth restating here that it will include a commitment to avoiding 'totalization' and reducing any person to a passive object in the social system. As we will see, solidarity as a virtue can inform

20. *CSDC*, no. 193. Cf. *CCC*, 1939–42. The virtue of solidarity therefore corresponds to the definition of a virtue employed in this book as a consistent disposition of character that is oriented toward flourishing, but extends this to apply to society as a whole.

21. Merkle, "Sin," 886.

22. *CSDC*, no. 193. Cf. Hollenbach's equal interdependence and the comments made about the link between such a disposition and the definition of virtue that we have been building on throughout.

23. Ibid., no. 193. Cf. Hollenbach's unequal interdependence. Merkle's discussion of structural sin is helpful in clarifying the relationship between actions, attitudes, and social structures indicated, but not explained, in the quote from the *CSDC*. She argues that structures of sin, rather than sinning in themselves (this would be impossible because they are anonymous social entities), reflect and incarnate "the sinful condition of humanity and the sinful choices of individuals." Merkle, "Sin," 886.

24. Cf. *SRS*, no. 38.

prudence's attentiveness in the face of the complexity of ethical situations in such a way as to avoid 'totalization' through an acknowledgment of the need to begin with a consideration of the Other, in contrast to the stance of the "I" which is merely at home with itself.

THE VIRTUE OF SOLIDARITY

The Virtue of Solidarity Defined in Dialogue with Levinas

As a moral virtue, which is our focus here, solidarity is understood as the disposition which enables both individuals and groups of individuals to develop equal interdependence and thus move towards the common good which, as we have noted, includes the commitment to avoiding 'totalization.' Pope John Paul II specifies this in his definition of the virtue of solidarity:

> [Solidarity is] a *firm and persevering determination* to commit oneself to the *common good*. That is to say the good of all and of each individual, because we are *all* really responsible for *all*.[25]

With this as our foundational understanding of the virtue of solidarity, we now focus specifically on how the virtue relates to the philosophy of Levinas, and beyond this towards a consideration of how it can complement the attentiveness that is so crucial to the operations of prudence.

As a virtue, we can expect that solidarity will possess the general characteristics of a virtue that we noted in chapter 3, namely, that it is a consistent character disposition which enables the human person (or, in the case of its social manifestation, a community) to act in a way which corresponds to the good. Our exploration of solidarity as a virtue begins with Charles Curran

---

25. *SRS*, no. 38; emphasis in original. Note the link between this definition and the broad definition of virtue that we explored in cahp. 3, especially in terms of its highlighting stability (firm), consistency (persevering), and motivation (determination). In *Laudato Si,*' Francis adds an important dimension to this definition of solidarity, namely, that it is also concerned with "time." He argues for a virtue of "intergenerational solidarity," which is able to commit to what John Paul II identifies not only in the present time, but into the future as well: "The global economic crises have made painfully obvious the detrimental effects of disregarding our common destiny, which cannot exclude those who come after us. We can no longer speak of sustainable development apart from intergenerational solidarity. Once we start to think about the kind of world we are leaving to future generations, we look at things differently; we realize that the world is a gift which we have freely received and must share with others. Since the world has been given to us, we can no longer view reality in a purely utilitarian way, in which efficiency and productivity are entirely geared to our individual benefit. Intergenerational solidarity is not optional, but rather a basic question of justice, since the world we have received also belongs to those who will follow us." See *LS*, no. 159.

who describes solidarity in a way that, significantly, links with the argument we developed through Levinas in chapter 1. Curran argues that solidarity as a virtue orients us towards the common good through a careful and attentive consideration of the other (person or community), a standing with the other, and an acknowledgment of and commitment to acting in a way which promotes the fullness of their flourishing.[26] It is what William O'Neill refers to as the disposition which is willing to pass over to the Other's side, in the sense which we see embodied in the parable of the Good Samaritan, in order to be attentive to the Other in her "concrete moral truth."[27]

What is core in this understanding of the virtue is its emphasis on a disposition of empathetic attentiveness to the Other in which the first movement is a standing with, empty of all preconceived judgments, with a commitment to discovering what exactly would count as a moral response to *this* person (or these persons) in *this* situation.[28] This is a disposition which cannot simply be an intellectual exercise, but will also involve other faculties such as imagination and emotion.[29] Furthermore, solidarity is closely aligned with a disposition of humility which acknowledges that, in Hollenbach's words, "one is not the centre of the universe precisely because one feels reverence for the inherent worth of realities beyond the self."[30] As Hollenbach notes, such a disposition can be exemplified as follows:

> [In the] experience of solidarity and genuine 'listening,' particularly to fellow suffering human beings, as well as setting out with the acknowledgment that one does not have ready answers to all questions of how people ought to live together.[31]

26. Curran, *Catholic Social Teaching*, 36. See also Cahill, *Sex, Gender and Christian Ethics*, 163; Sniegocki, *Catholic Social Teaching*, 144.

27. O'Neill, "Christian Hospitality and Solidarity with the Stranger," 150.

28. It is at this point that we can account for the suggestion above that solidarity incorporates the virtue of compassion in response to Cahill's separation of the two. The incorporation of compassion within solidarity can be seen here with solidarity's emphasis on empathy, which, in the original Greek, means to "suffer in" and is thus closely linked with the word compassion, which derives from the Latin words for "suffering with." See Gascoigne, *Freedom and Purpose*, 201. While it is true that Cahill's book separates these terms, it should also be noted that they are frequently placed next to one another, indicating the strong link between them. See for example Cahill, *Sex, Gender and Christian Ethics*, 43, 109, 117, 153, 162, 163, 183, 210, 256, 257.

29. Ibid., 43. Here Cahill is creating a link between the understanding of the crucial role that empathetic imagination carries for moral discourse which is found in the work of Seyla Benhabib and the understanding of solidarity developed in the work of the feminist theologian Sharon D. Welch. See Benhabib, *Situating the Self*; Welch, *A Feminist Ethic of Risk*.

30. Hollenbach, *The Global Face of Public Faith*, 45.

31. Hollenbach, *The Global Face of Public Faith*, 46. See also John Battle's exploration

Roger Burggraeve argues that this aligns closely with the kind of ethical approach that arises out of taking Levinas seriously, for it encourages the attention of "individual consciences who in their corporeal affectivity are sensitive and vulnerable to the suffering of the separate and unique Other."[32] In these ways, the virtue has the capacity to avoid "totalization," objectification, and a lack of concern for the uniqueness of any Other because it begins *with* the Other and with a commitment to doing what is required to be open to them *as* and *where* they are.

Furthermore, Curran (along with Kenneth Himes and Timothy Shannon) argues that the virtue of solidarity acknowledges the subjectivity of all human persons by emphasizing the cooperative nature of ethical action, as distinct from any response that is imposed as if persons were simply passive and receptive objects.[33] Building on the argument we have developed above, this means that the virtue of solidarity is quite the opposite of a disposition which would see more powerful, wealthy or influential individuals or groups providing and imposing solutions for weaker individuals or groups. Rather, the goal towards which the virtue is oriented requires the active participation of all and, as such, the virtuous disposition must facilitate the active participation of all in the movement towards the common good rather than reduce anyone's role to a passive recipient of the gifts or actions of another.[34] This is yet another point of correlation with the Levinasian warning against 'totalization' which we developed in chapter 1. As we noted there, Levinas pointed out the violence that occurs when the Other is reduced to an element over which the "I" can claim control. Clearly, this is distinct from allowing for the absolute uniqueness—the Infinity—of the Other, which would encourage a disposition that values the unique participatory potential of all and the prohibition of reducing any to a passive object over which the self, or a society, has control. This also reinforces the

---

of the importance of humility for moral theology (specifically as it occurs in the political sphere) and the links he draws between humility and solidarity in dialogue with Hollenbach and the moral theology of Kevin Kelly throughout. Battle, "Kevin Kelly and Political Humility," especially 265–68.

32. Burggraeve, *The Wisdom of Love*, 179. Indeed, Burggraeve points out that Levinas pleaded for a form of "noble casuistry," which could honor the uniqueness of each situation and, more importantly, individual encountered, because such an approach can be seen as "essentially a search for an adequate basis to render judgment, understood to remain within the limits of the relation and actions of a unique situation. It is above all a recognition of the fact that the being I find before me is completely now, or *hapax*: someone who is there but once, here and now." Burggraeve, *The Wisdom of Love*, 178.

33. Curran, Himes, and Shannon, "Commentary on *Sollicitudo Rei Socialis*," 423. See also Cahill, *Sex, Gender and Christian Ethics*, 129.

34. Hollenbach, *The Common Good and Christian Ethics*, 188. See also *JW*, no. 59.

paradigm for justice we developed in chapter 4, especially in its emphasis on the subjectivity and uniqueness of the human person.

The virtue of solidarity, therefore, has a commitment to stand with *this* Other and in *this* ethical situation with a view to honoring her infinity and avoiding objectification and "totalization," and its further commitment to enable the active participation of all. As such, it can avoid the temptation to reduce the other person to a passive object over which the "I" can claim control and respond to the challenges to ethical decision making posed by the problem of 'totalization.' Correlatively, it can respond to the personalist criteria and paradigm for justice developed in chapter 4. Critically, it is a disposition which can inform prudence of the morally relevant features of a situation in a Levinasian way, because it begins with openness and receptivity to the Other rather than from a preconceived judgment about what might count as a moral response to him. Furthermore, and as we will see below, CST links solidarity with the methodological tool known as the 'preferential option for the poor' which, when combined with the empathetic attentiveness of the virtue of solidarity, can assist in prioritizing prudence's moral attentiveness. In the next section, we will briefly consider solidarity's relationship with the other virtues and, from this foundation, also consider some limitations on its operations which come out of the anthropological vision we developed in chapter 4.

Solidarity: Limitations and Possibilities

As we have noted a number of times throughout the book, the virtues must be understood in relationship with one another as distinct from isolated dispositions operating independently, and the same goes for the operations of solidarity. As such, there are practical limitations on the degree of solidarity that can be expected of any given individual, community and the global community as a whole.[35] After all, one could never act out of a position of pure solidarity—prudence must take into account what solidarity has to offer the task of moral reasoning, but it is also charged with the duty of determining how this can be related to the demands of the other virtues in

---

35. I focus below on the solidarity of an individual person to align with the focus of the book, but would suggest that what I develop has implications for understanding of solidarity as a virtue characterizing communities. Indeed, as Lisa Sowle Cahill notes (drawing on the work of the Protestant theological ethicist H. Richard Niebuhr), human relationality, and the solidarity that can arise out of this, is necessarily oriented toward society, "for our actions and interactions form a continuing society." Sowle, "Bioethics, Relationships, and Participation in the Common Good," 209–10. Cahill is drawing on Niebuhr, *The Responsible Self*, 65. I return to this point in the book's conclusion.

the best possible way, all things considered.[36] These include those virtues which are properly agent-focused, such as temperance and fortitude as well as that dimension of the will which is intelligibly directed towards the love of self. As such, prudence must balance the virtue of solidarity with the kind of virtuous attentiveness to one's self that we explored in chapter 3

Furthermore, in view of the anthropological vision of the human person that we developed in chapter 4, it is possible to see that there are certain limitations on the level of solidarity that each person is able to embody because of a number of the dimensions which constitute the human person. In short, this means that it is impossible for the human person to enter into equal solidarity with all other human persons. In the first instance, this is because of our constitution as beings in corporeality. Our embodiment places limitations on whom we can enter into solidarity with, simply because we cannot be in all places at all times, which means that we cannot offer ourselves in solidarity to all people at all times. Our embodiment also implies limitations on the amount of energy that we are able to devote to the capacities which enable the kind of attentive empathy that solidarity requires. Similarly, our constitution as historical beings places limitations on our capacity for solidarity because we exist at a specific moment in history which limits our access to those who lived before us or will live after us.

These factors are compounded by the irreducible complexity of the ethical contexts in which solidarity, and the rest of the virtues, must operate.[37] With some 7.5 billion people currently inhabiting the planet, it would be impossible to allocate the same amount of attentiveness to each, or even many. In addition to this, the sheer infinity of each individual human person would make it impossible to enter into *complete* solidarity with even one person, and also presents the risk of devoting all of one's solidarity to an individual at the expense of all Others, a disposition which would not correspond with the concern for the common good which is also a key component of solidarity, and which we explored in chapter 4. As such, there are times when conflict will be experienced in terms of where the empathetic attentiveness of solidarity should be directed—should I spend time sitting by the bedside of a dying parent or researching ways to assist children who are starving in Africa if my constitution as a person and my unique context makes it impossible to do both?[38] In Roger Burggraeve's words, reflecting

36. Cf. Verstraeten, "Solidarity and Subsidiarity," 134.

37. Cf. Cates, "The Virtue of Temperance," 325.

38. Cf. Pope, *The Evolution of Altruism*, 2. Hutchens notes that one can find a similar issue in Levinasian thought which requires some form of ordering. More specifically, if the "I" is charged with responsibility for the Other, what happens when there is more than one Other to respond to and the "I" cannot possibly respond to both in the same capacity? See Hutchens, *Levinas*, 159.

on this same problem in the context of the Levinasian understanding of responsibility for the Other, the fact that there is more than one Other and that my capacities to respond are limited means that "I must confront and judge, weigh and balance, rank, distinguish, and measure... In other words, priorities must be established."[39] So, the question must be posed: how can prudence prioritize and allocate the empathetic attentiveness of solidarity? More familiarly, this question has been framed by means of the ordering of love: given the complexities of human existence and the necessary limitations on that existence, how can one decide how to order one's priorities and focus one's moral energies in the task of loving others?

The methodological tool that the virtue of solidarity provides in order to assist prudence in responding to this challenge is known as the 'preferential option for the poor,' and it is the task of the next section to explore what this means for our understanding of the virtue, to critique and refine it, and to explain how it can develop our understanding of solidarity.

The Virtue of Solidarity and the Preferential Option for the Poor

A quick glance around our own twenty-first century ethical context reveals that there are many for whom an infringement of dignity, understood with reference to the anthropological vision that we developed in chapter 4, is a more real possibility than for others. Grounding itself in an immediate concern for these persons, CST employs the phrase 'option for the poor' to refer to the special concern that is oriented towards those most at risk.[40] Pope John Paul II specifies this further:

> [The] love of preference for the poor, and the decisions which it inspires in us, cannot but embrace the immense multitudes of the hungry, the needy, the homeless, those without medical care and, above all, those without hope of a better future.[41]

---

39. Burggraeve, *The Wisdom of Love*, 136. Burggraeve goes on to state that "I must therefore conduct myself to the Others, and sit with them at the table, clarifying appointments and agreements meant to reduce the many possible contradictions, obstructions, and interferences opposing or complicating the exercise of my different responsibilities, so as to insure as much balance as possible." Burggraeve, *The Wisdom of Love*, 137.

40. On the connection between solidarity and the preferential option for the poor, see Verstraeten, "Solidarity and Subsidiarity," 143. The phrase "option for the poor" only came into use in official Catholic teaching in the 1970s and was drawn largely from the work of liberation theologians in Latin America. See Curran, *Catholic Social Teaching*, 183–84.

41. *SRS*, no. 42.

The language used to express this concept is especially important and can enhance our understanding still further. In the first instance, we should note that this is a *preferential* option for the poor, not an *exclusive* option for the poor, given that the latter could lead to the undermining of the dignity of those who are not understood as poor.[42] Second, and here we focus especially on John Paul's expression of the concept, the definition of "the poor" is broad and includes both the materially poor (the hungry, homeless and those without medical care) and also those who could be considered vulnerable in the broader sense as anyone "without hope for a better future." One does not need to be in material poverty to experience the conditions of neediness or hopelessness.

This broad definition of poverty can also be found in the work of a number of moral theologians. Ronaldo Zacharias, for example, argues that poverty is manifested in a number of ways, including "the lack of food, housing, work, health care, and basic respect for the dignity of the human person."[43] Laurenti Magesa points towards an 'anthropological poverty,' "which is not merely material but affects the personality itself. It has enormous ethical consequences, one of which is the psychological situation which instinctively obstructs initiative in many areas of personal and social development."[44] In the field of bioethics, Lisa Cahill has pointed out that the tool has been plausibly reframed as a "preferential option for the sick."[45] Finally, Christopher Vogt has taken the concept still further and expressed it as a "preferential option for the stranger," understood as anyone who is in a state of vulnerability as a consequence of their isolation from family, church or community.[46]

Given the breadth of focus that exists here in the preferential option for the poor, it is necessary to ask whether the term 'poor' can encapsulate all that is being asked of it, especially given that in contemporary parlance 'poor' is normally taken to refer to material, and specifically economic, poverty. I would like to propose the argument that the 'preferential option for the vulnerable' is a clearer and more adequate way of defining this tool and will explain why below.

---

42. Curran, *Catholic Social Teaching*, 186.
43. Quoted in Keenan, *A History of Catholic Moral Theology*, 198.
44. Quoted in ibid., 203–4.
45. Cahill, "Bioethics," 137.
46. Vogt, "Fostering a Catholic Commitment to the Common Good," 416, cf. 412.

The Argument Supporting the Move from the Terminology of "Poor" to "Vulnerable" in the Preferential Option

I would suggest that the shift in terminology from *poor* to *vulnerable* is legitimate for the purposes of the book (and perhaps for the field of moral theology more broadly speaking) on a number of levels. First, because it better accounts for the broad definition of poverty noted above whilst still retaining the more common understanding of 'poor' and not relativizing the significance of material poverty; second, because it has the capacity to incorporate actual and potential infringements on human dignity, and third, because it links the preferential option with Levinas's understanding of the essential vulnerability of the human person and the implications this has for considering power, freedom and responsibility. As I will show, this links well with solidarity's concerns to identify structures of sin and with the book's focus on Levinas. We will explore each of these points in turn before returning to the relationship between prudence, solidarity, and the preferential option for the vulnerable.

It is necessary to begin by defining vulnerability and showing its links to poverty. Florencia Luna points out that the word 'vulnerability' derives from the Latin word *vulnerare*, which means 'to wound.'[47] When it comes to moral discourse, she argues that vulnerability can be understood "as a state of destitution that needs to be addressed with sensitivity and that requires protecting individuals from the harm they are prone to suffer."[48] Luna notes that there are at least two dimensions of vulnerability understood in this way. The first of these refers to the sense in which human persons are *persistently* vulnerable in ways which are common to all. That is, there is always a fragility and finitude inherent in the human condition, of the kind that we noted in chapter 4, which carries with it the potential for great harm, a point to which we will return below.[49] The second involves a *variability* of vulnerability which acknowledges that certain individuals or groups may be more or less vulnerable either because of the actions of others or because of circumstance.[50] As such, she suggests there are layers of vulnerability which begin with the level of vulnerability common to all which is then accentuated by factors such as exclusion, material poverty, lack of access to medical care, and so on.[51] It is this point that retains the urgency of material poverty

---

47. Luna, *Bioethics & Vulnerability*, 1.
48. Ibid., 143.
49. Ibid., 1.
50. Ibid.
51. Ibid., 143. Cf. John Paul II's definition of the preferential option for the poor noted above which includes a similar list.

in any appropriation of the preferential option: to suffer from material poverty is to become significantly vulnerable in a variety of ways.[52]

In view of this, it is possible to see how the concept of vulnerability can include those aspects of the broad definition of poverty noted above. Indeed, this link between the two terms has already been implicitly made by a number of authors. The two concepts can be found side-by-side, for example, in a recent review of Catholic bioethics written by Andrea Vicini, and Vogt's article which was noted above suggests that the vulnerability of the stranger is a crucial factor in directing the preferential option for the poor.[53] At the same time, it adds something important to the definition of poverty noted above, in that it can include both the actual and potential aspects of vulnerability. This means vulnerability can refer to the person who is in a situation of vulnerability, for example, the person whose human dignity is prone to harm because he is homeless, as well as the person whose human dignity can be considered vulnerable because she is going through a divorce settlement which threatens to take away her home and the majority of her assets. Whereas 'poor' tends to indicate an actualized state of harm, vulnerability indicates the potential for harm whilst also incorporating the actualized state.

This is significant for approaching ethical issues because it broadens our attentiveness, focusing it on the actual vulnerability of those whose human dignity is currently being infringed and also on the vulnerability to harm of those whose human dignity is potentially at risk. If the adage is true that prevention is better than cure, then this is a positive development. This, too, is reflected in some current thinking in moral theology, although it has not been expressed in this way. For example, Keenan has pointed out that a number of theologians are exploring not only actual poverty, but also the factors that play into vulnerability to poverty, with others exploring vulnerability in terms of access to healthcare for both those who need it now and those who potentially will.[54] Beyond the field of moral theology, this has also been a focus in economics, with recognition that attention *to* vulnerability to economic poverty as well as to economic poverty itself is necessary to provide an adequate response to the issue.[55] In a preferential

---

52. This may help to explain why Francis has placed a renewed emphasis on those who are materially poor in his writings: not at the expense of considering various other forms of vulnerability, but to accentuate how along with material poverty necessarily arises more complex and heightened vulnerabilities.

53. See Vicini, "Bioethics: Basic Questions and Extraordinary Developments," 170, 177; 181, 187; Vogt, "Fostering a Catholic Commitment," 412.

54. Keenan, "Contemporary Contributions to Sexual Ethics," 161–62.

55. Mocduch, "Poverty and Vulnerability," 225.

option for the vulnerable, therefore, our attention is drawn both to responding to actual infringements on human dignity and doing what is necessary to prevent their future possibility. In view of these points, I would argue that 'vulnerable' is a more adequate term than 'poor' for the preferential option.

Beyond the above, from the perspective of the book there is further reason for us to utilize this terminology, and this can be found by returning to our discussion of vulnerability in chapter 4. There we noted, as a consequence of our development of Janssens's 'Human Person Integrally and Adequately Considered,' it was possible to see that human persons are essentially vulnerable creatures who are prone to great harm across a variety of dimensions of their personhood. We explored this point in detail from a Levinasian perspective, noting that for Levinas the term 'face' was practically synonymous with 'vulnerability,' a passivity which is open to the violence of 'totalization' in the presence of the 'I.' As such, from the Levinasian perspective, whenever I encounter the Other I am encountering the *vulnerable* Other.

As noted in chapter 4, this implies that vulnerability is an essential aspect of the human condition, an understanding which links closely with Luna's foundational sense of vulnerability as a persistent feature of human personhood noted above. Furthermore, as we discussed previously, the use of the term 'vulnerability' is particularly provocative in a moral sense because, in highlighting the vulnerability of the Other, it also acknowledges the power of the 'I.' More specifically, an emphasis on vulnerability can acknowledge that the Other is prone to harm precisely because the "I" is capable of doing harm and, in its capacity to choose how it enacts its response to the vulnerable Other, is invested with a freedom for which it can be held responsible. The term can therefore turn the critical attention of prudence both towards the Other who is vulnerable, and towards the one *because of whom* the Other is vulnerable. In other words, it is a term which acknowledges the roles of both victim and perpetrator. In view of this, I would suggest that it is an appropriate addition to the understanding of solidarity developed above, because its broad focus, which considers both those who are vulnerable and those who are responsible for this vulnerability, aligns closely with solidarity's concern for identifying structural sin.

Furthermore, by moving towards the preferential option for the vulnerable, yet another connection is created with Levinas, which has important implications for how the preferential option is understood. We will return to these below when we distinguish between 'vulnerability *as such*' and 'vulnerability *in relationship*.' Having set the foundations for the preferential option for the vulnerable, however, we will now affirm its link with the virtue of solidarity and demonstrate its potential for directing the empathetic attentiveness of solidarity. After this point, we will return to some of the more specific issues arising from the usage of vulnerability and explore their implications for the book's argument.

The Preferential Option for the Vulnerable, Solidarity and Prudence

The 'preferential option for the vulnerable' is helpful in our discussion of solidarity because it provides the basis for a framework from which prudence can direct the empathetic attentiveness of solidarity. On this view, the focus of solidarity should be prioritized and directed towards those who are vulnerable because an infringement of their human dignity is a more immediate possibility for them than for others. On this basis, the preferential option for the vulnerable can begin to inform prudence in choosing how much and to whom solidarity is directed as a priority. In view of the concern for the common good that we developed in chapter 4, the focus of solidarity remains broad here and the virtue at this point must be both general enough to be applicable in all circumstances but also specific enough to yield tangible results.

This combination of prudence, the preferential option for the vulnerable and solidarity will involve an attentiveness to whether or not those goods, which correspond to each dimension of the human person adequately considered and are necessary for flourishing, are available for all others. In view of what we developed in chapter 4, these goods include the material goods required to survive as a person in corporeality (food, shelter, warmth), the opportunity to develop and sustain social relationships, education (in order to ensure an adequate ability to engage with the material world and acknowledge the person's developmental nature), to join social groups, as well as access to and freedom in expressing religious beliefs. Importantly from the Levinasian perspective, this would also involve an avoidance of 'totalization' and allow persons to participate freely and uniquely in the relationships and communities which provide the context in which these conditions can be met.[56] If the empathetic attentiveness of solidarity reveals that these features are not present, this disposition would move towards consistent commitment to transforming the situation to align with the common good. It would do this through further solidarity, and the

---

56. Cf. Hollenbach, *The Common Good and Christian Ethics*, 40. In terms of a system of prioritizing these goods, I would suggest an appeal to Paul VI's *transcendent humanism* as explained in chap. 4.

action which stems from the insights gained from this in dialogue with the virtue of justice.

This is what we could call the foundation for the virtue of solidarity as informed by the preferential option for the vulnerable. Nonetheless, whilst this basis can act as a helpful specification in determining where prudence should direct the empathetic attentiveness of solidarity, it is still beset by similar complications that we noted above regarding the necessary limitations of solidarity: even in view of this more specific focus, the vulnerable are so numerous that it is difficult to imagine a case in which one's solidarity could be directed to all of them equally. This last point is especially important in our discussion, because it stimulates a move to a greater awareness of the complexities involved in human relationships as well as a consideration of the natural inclination we as human persons have, which orients us towards a prioritizing of attention towards those with whom we share the most intimate relationships.

VULNERABILITY AS SUCH AND VULNERABILITY IN RELATIONSHIP

In order to provide the further specification needed to ensure that the preferential option for the vulnerable can direct the empathetic attentiveness of prudence and thus assist in the directing of solidarity, it is necessary to explore vulnerability still further. In this section, I propose that there are two dimensions to vulnerability: 'vulnerability *as such*,' which refers to the kind of vulnerability that is the main focus of the understanding developed above, and 'vulnerability *in relationship*,' which refers to the special vulnerability that occurs within the context of interpersonal encounter and which is closely linked to the philosophy of Levinas. I will explore each of these in turn, but will spend more time on the latter given that 'vulnerability *as such*' has already been defined somewhat.

Vulnerability as such

'Vulnerability *as such*' refers to the vulnerability of an individual considered within the context of her life's situation. As such, it can be determined from the outside, as it were. With the help of a paradigm for justice such as the one developed in chapter 4, one can identify how vulnerable a person is with reference to her human dignity being at risk, actually or potentially. It is the kind of vulnerability that is observed in John Paul II's explanation of the preferential option, in which he refers to the hungry, the needy, homeless, those without medical care and those without hope for a better future. All of these categories of vulnerability can be identified apart from a direct interpersonal relationship: I can watch the evening news and acknowledge the problem of desperate hunger in Africa, or read about the plight of a family on the other side of the country who will soon lose their home. In so doing, the preferential option for the vulnerable requires that my attentiveness and solidarity be directed first of all to those who are most vulnerable and, by implication, whose dignity is most at risk.

At the same time, vulnerability *as such* lacks an awareness of another dimension of vulnerability, which I refer to as 'vulnerability *in relationship*.' In what follows, I will explain what is meant by this term and show how it can further refine the methodological tool of the preferential option for the vulnerable, link it more closely with a natural law approach, and incorporate Levinas's argument regarding the vulnerability that exists in the face when the "I" is encountered by it.

The Nature of Relationships as Linked to Vulnerability

To move to this point, I return to the work of Stephen Pope in his book, *The Evolution of Altruism and the Ordering of Love*. In this book, Pope, whilst recognizing the value of CST and specifically the preferential option of the poor, argues that it needs to be supplemented with a further framework for ordering the attention of prudence akin to what we have been looking for. Pope's reasoning for this builds from the observation that one's preferential concern for those who can be defined as vulnerable according to the definition developed above can, in some instances, find expression at the cost of neglect for those whose vulnerability is no less real, but is perhaps less easily noticed. Pope turns to the character, Mrs Jellyby in Charles Dickens' *Bleak House*, for a literary example of this potential problem:

> Mrs Jellyby is said to possess "telescopic philanthropy" because she could see nothing nearer than Africa, while her own children went dirty, hungry and generally neglected.[57]

Following from what we have developed above, we could say that Mrs Jellyby has understood something of what it means to have a preferential option for the vulnerable, and yet was unable to recognize the vulnerability of her own children—those who are vulnerable *in relationship to her* precisely because she is their mother, and to whom she has a responsibility to

57. Pope, *The Evolution of Altruism*, 41.

act justly which corresponds with the nature of her maternal relationship with them. From this perspective, the *nature* of the relationship is relevant in determining the amount of solidarity that prudence should be directing towards an individual.

As such, there is a need to complement the preferential option for the vulnerable with some way of assessing the *relative* vulnerability of those with whom one is in relationship in view of the *nature* of that relationship. This is not to deny the universal scope of solidarity; as we have seen, this is implied by the understanding of justice that we developed and is an essential part of solidarity. Rather, it is to acknowledge that different types of relationships carry with them different levels of vulnerability and that, if the virtue of justice is concerned with providing each his due, what is due to each human person has something to do with the type of relationship one shares with him and the relative level of vulnerability that is associated with this. Pope has developed a system for ordering moral attentiveness which acknowledges this point and, significantly, re-engages with the natural law tradition in a way that correlates well with Porter's approach.

The Ordering of Love as Foundation for Vulnerability in Relationship

As we have noted above, the preferential option for the vulnerable needs to be complemented with some way of informing prudence on how to focus solidarity so that one can remain concerned for the good of all, while at the same time recognizing the special responsibility one has for those who are especially vulnerable in view of the kind of relationship one has with them. Given our foundational interest in Porter's theory throughout this work, and particularly in her emphasis on the moral relevance of prerational nature as well as the overall intelligibility of the human creature, it is desirable for us to draw on a specifically natural law framework for developing such an ordering. Such a framework can be found in Pope's *The Evolution of Altruism and the Ordering of Love*, in which he develops a systematic argument for what we have been referring to as an ordering of attentiveness which he grounds in Aquinas and modern scientific insights into the nature of the human person.[58]

Pope begins his argument for the need for such a framework on the basis of critiques of personalism and the preferential option for the poor:

---

58. In what follows I draw on Pope's specific conclusions regarding the ordering of love, which arise from his research into Thomistic natural law theory and the contemporary findings of evolutionary science as distinct from the findings themselves.

part of this critique is a demonstration of the need for an ordering of moral attentiveness, to which we have also drawn attention.[59] He finds the resources required for developing such a framework in Aquinas' exploration of the ordering of love in which Aquinas develops an argument for the moral validity of prioritizing attentiveness towards certain persons through a consideration of the nature of the human person. Pope argues that Aquinas, in his observations of human nature, acknowledges a natural priority of attentiveness towards those with whom one shares more intimate relations including one's own family, one's spouse, and beyond these one's friends and associates.[60] Given the broad spectrum of these relationships, Aquinas saw the human person's natural preference for attending to them as a priority as something which goes beyond simple biological links and also includes shared goods which, together, constitute stronger foundational bonds for love than relationships which were grounded exclusively in the kind of universal concern for all persons which we explored above.[61]

As a natural inclination, Aquinas understands this phenomenon as part of the human person's overall intelligibility. After all, as Pope suggests, relational "bonds sometimes exist prior to free choices and they can be said to place a claim on human freedom, prior to autonomous choice, to love and care."[62] Pope goes on to clarify the argument in the following way:

> The most poignant example of these kinds of relations is provided in the familial context, where interpersonal relations are often placed in a broader and more complex context than that which obtains between two free and independent centres of self-consciousness. One does not freely choose one's parents, children, or siblings, yet these people and the relations they involve one in are, for most people, absolutely fundamental to the Christian moral life.[63]

To further this point, Pope demonstrates in dialogue with insights from evolutionary science how such preferences can be linked to our natural constitution as creatures and, indeed, how they have contributed to our survival as a species in general.[64] This provides an argument aligning with

---

59. See Pope, *The Evolution of Altruism*, 32–40. However, it must be acknowledged that Pope does not include solidarity as part of his approach. We return to Pope's critiques of these approaches in the conclusion to the book.

60. Ibid., 63. A similar point regarding the increased vulnerability of intimate relationships is made by Margaret Farley, see Farley, *Just Love*, 217.

61. Pope, *The Evolution of Altruism*, 63.

62. Ibid., 40.

63. Ibid., 40.

64. See ibid., 99–148.

Porter's theory by revealing a natural disposition which draws the human person's attention more closely to others depending on the *nature* of the relationship one has with them. I will develop this argument further in dialogue with the insights of preceding chapters.

Vulnerability in Relationship

In this section, I will develop an argument for the dimension of vulnerability that I refer to as vulnerability *in relationship*. This argument builds on what Pope has argued and addresses some of the complexities regarding the appropriate allocation of prudence's attentiveness which I have noted above, as well as drawing on the approach that has been developing throughout.[65] Vulnerability *in relationship* refers to the relative degree of vulnerability that exists in relationships of different kinds because of the nature of these relationships. The thrust of the argument can be demonstrated by turning to a number of examples. In each case, it is possible to see how the nature of the relationship itself is what defines the degree of vulnerability that exists for each person involved.

For example, a child is vulnerable in a relationship with his parents (or primary care-givers, as the case may be), because it is his parents on whom he relies for both the basic and specific goods required for human well-being and, it would seem, it is natural for him to do so. Not only will the child require food, warmth and shelter from his parents, but also the necessary emotional, psychological and spiritual care as well as schooling in the social and moral skills necessary for his happiness as a whole human person in a given social-cultural context. In view of this, a significant amount of the child's human personhood and subjectivity is bound up with his relationship to his parents, and a lack of due attentiveness on the parents' part is more than likely to have a significantly negative impact on the child's well-being and therefore his capacity for happiness. This is not to say that others are not also responsible for the happiness of the child, only that he will be relatively *less* vulnerable depending on the nature of his relationship with them. For example, a stranger passing in a shopping centre may not stop to feed the child or inquire about his psychological well-being. If the attentiveness of the child's parents is focused appropriately, however, this action would likely not have an impact on the child's well-being or happiness. All things being equal, and assuming the stranger does not actively seek to harm the child, the child is relatively more vulnerable in his relationship with his parents than he is in his relationship with the stranger, and it is the

65. As far as I am aware, this is an original argument.

nature of the relationship between child and parent that determines this vulnerability.[66]

A similar example could be given in terms of a married couple and, indeed, Hollenbach has used such an example in an argument in which he calls for different 'levels' of solidarity in different kinds of relationships.[67] Let us imagine a couple who have been married for ten years, and were in an intimate relationship with one another for a number of years before this. In this marriage, each partner's happiness will be unavoidably tied up with the happiness of the other at a highly specific level.[68] The couple will likely share responsibility for the goods basic to human well-being (food, shelter and warmth) as well as the higher goods associated with human flourishing (social interaction, psychological, emotional and spiritual well-being, and so on). Furthermore, the couple will share their very subjectivity and uniqueness with one another on the most intimate of levels. From a Levinasian point of view, this means that they are opening out their infinity to one another in ever more profound ways and becoming more vulnerable to 'totalization' as a result. In this example, the nature of the relationship means that the couple shares more of themselves with one another and that there is more raw material, as it were, for an infringement of dignity from either side. If we imagine the wife were to pass the child in the shopping centre mentioned in the paragraph above, together with the rest of the child's family, and none of them felt the need to encourage her ongoing emotional, psychological and spiritual development, she would be relatively less vulnerable in her capacity for happiness than she would be if her husband were to act in the same way, consistently ignoring these dimensions of her happiness throughout their relationship.

This demonstration of vulnerability *in relationship*, along with Pope's Thomistic understanding of the ordering of attentiveness, gives us considerable material for developing a framework for informing prudence as to the degree of solidarity which should be displayed in any given relationship. That is, the degree of the solidarity's attentive empathy that prudence will display in a given relationship needs to correlate to the degree of vulnerability that an Other has in that relationship. On this view, the more vulnerable someone's dignity is in my presence, the more responsibility I have to be in solidarity with them and to direct my attention accordingly. In Levinasian language, the closer the Other draws, the more responsible I am for her.

---

66. There are, of course, significant qualifications to this, and we return to these below.

67. See Hollenbach, *The Common Good and Christian Ethics*, 190.

68. Ibid.

Having said this, we should note carefully (as Pope does in his own work) that this is not an argument for some form of "narrow particularism" in which a person could ignore the needs of those with whom he does not share a relationship characterized by a high degree of vulnerability. To do as much would be to ignore the basis on which the virtue is grounded which we explored above. Pope provides illumination on this point:

> Beneficence for all is encouraged insofar as possible. People ought to care for the needs and assist those to whom they are closely connected. The general principle that we ought to do good first to those who are most closely connected with us [or more relatively vulnerable to us] is modified with the proviso, other things being equal (*ceteris paribus*).[69]

In some cases, it is apparent that not all things will be equal and this is where we can see that the ordering of the empathetic attentiveness of solidarity, as with the operations of prudence more generally, is not a mathematical equation for determining who should be accorded what degree of solidarity depending on the nature of the relationship they are in, aside from contextual considerations. As Pope suggests, Aquinas' emphasis on the natural inclination to prioritize the needs of some persons over others was not assigned the category of an *absolute* priority.[70] From this angle, a 'microscopic philanthrophy' which focuses only on those to whom one is closest can be just as damaging as the 'telescopic philanthrophy' of Mrs Jellyby because it ignores what we have said in chapter 4 about the concern that justice implies for *all* people and what we have said above regarding solidarity's affirmation that "we are *all* really responsible for *all*."

Pope uses an example of a stranger in extreme need who could legitimately take priority over one's family in some circumstances. To exemplify this point further, we can return to the dilemma of the father we introduced in chapter 5, who was attempting to decide whether or not the gift of a large sum of money for his son would be an act of generosity, all things considered. Let us imagine, for now, that the father's solidarity with the son has revealed that he will realistically have his well-being secured and be happy *without* the money but that, in the decision-making process, the father has been exposed to the plight of a family on his street who will be made homeless unless someone steps in to assist them financially. In this situation, although the son is relatively more vulnerable in his relationship with his father, yet given that his well-being and potential happiness are secured, the more immediate and threatening plight of the family would legitimately

---

69. Pope, *The Evolution of Altruism*, 64; parenthesis added.
70. Ibid., 64.

prioritize the father's empathetic attentiveness towards them. Significantly, and this is where we return to our considerations from earlier in the chapter, it is the task of prudence to adjudicate which relationship should take priority in this concrete situation, all things considered.[71]

THE VICES ASSOCIATED WITH THE VIRTUE OF SOLIDARITY

Vice and Structures of Sin

In chapter 3, we considered the Thomistic understanding of vice and how it is related to the theological concept of sin. In this section, we will briefly revisit the points made there before moving on to propose three vices that are associated with solidarity. We will begin here with the general category 'structure of sin' and then move beyond this towards a consideration of three specific vices which I would suggest should be understood as deficiencies of the virtue of solidarity as we have developed it in this chapter.

In chapter 3, we spent a significant amount of time exploring the topic of virtue, both as it is expressed in contemporary virtue ethics and as it is understood specifically within Porter's approach to natural law. There, we defined a virtue as a consistent character disposition which enables a person to express themselves in a praiseworthy, admirable or desirable way in the midst of the diversity of complex ethical situations she encounters across a lifetime. We went on to show how Porter integrates this understanding of virtue into her theory of natural law by showing how the virtues are oriented towards achieving happiness for the human person through specifying and focusing his prerational orientation towards goodness. In Porter's approach, therefore, the virtues are praiseworthy, admirable and desirable precisely because they correspond with what counts as flourishing for the human creature, comprehensively considered.

It was out of this understanding of virtue that we introduced the concept of a vice, understood as a consistent character disposition which is lacking in reference to the virtue with which it is associated. For example, the vices associated with the virtue of temperance—which is intended primarily to moderate the consumption of food and drink—are both gluttony and deficiency. These dispositions are understood as vices because the ways of acting that stem from them take away from, rather than promote, the happiness of the human person. Furthermore, we saw how Aquinas links vice with the theological concept of sin by suggesting that, as a vice

71. Ibid.

undermines the natural expression of the good through the virtues, it correlatively weakens the human person's response to the grace of God in the movement towards happiness.

It is here that we can begin to look towards the vices associated with the virtue of solidarity. If the virtue is understood in the way we have developed it above, as a consistent disposition to ensure that the common good is achieved (the concern of justice) by an empathetic attentiveness and commitment to the Other who is encountered, the vice associated with solidarity can be understood—on a general level—as a disposition which is deficient in either of these regards. CST has not been entirely silent on this issue, and has named at least part of the deficiency associated with solidarity as a 'structure of sin.' Recall that CST understands structures of sin as "actions and attitudes opposed to the will of God and the good of neighbor, as well as the structures arising from such behavior" which act as obstacles and impediments in the movement towards the common good and therefore impede, rather that promote, human flourishing.[72] As such, the 'structural sin' vice, as it were, is the consistent character disposition which acts as an impediment for the movement towards the common good, including the flourishing of all human persons.

Whilst helpful, this definition of the vice is rather general and will benefit from further specification. In what follows I would like to suggest three vices, all of which can be understood under the category of the structural sin vice because they act as impediments in the movement towards the common good and the corresponding flourishing of all human persons. I would like to state at the outset that these vices are not exhaustive of the implications of the overarching category of structural sin. Indeed, there is a wide variety of specific ways in which one could embody this vice, and to explore them would likely require another book. Nonetheless, I believe that it is important to name these specifically, given the unique way in which solidarity has been explored above and linked with the thought of Levinas, as well as the original concept of vulnerability *in relationship*. The first of these vices I refer to as the vice of totalization, and this links in with the empathetic attentiveness that the virtue of solidarity requires as well as the Levinasian warning against 'totalization.' The second and third I refer to as microscopic philanthropy and telescopic philanthropy and these reflect, respectively, our discussion of solidarity and its universal scope, as well as the importance of considering vulnerability *in relationship* when directing the empathetic attentiveness of solidarity.

---

72. *CSDC*, no. 193. Cf. the discussion of structures of sin above, and Judith Merkle's article which was used there, Merkle, "Sin," 886–87.

The Vice of Totalization

As we noted in detail above, solidarity requires a form of 'empathetic attentiveness' to an ethical situation in order to be directed appropriately, and the capacity to commit to this attentiveness can inform prudence of the morally salient features in an ethical situation. This is especially the case when the ethical situation one encounters is an Other who is infinitely complex and must be attended to carefully, without pre-conceived judgement or prejudice, if prudence is to have the information required for an adequate response to be made. If this empathetic attentiveness is crucial to the operations of the virtue of solidarity (and therefore important for the operations of the virtue of prudence and, by extension, all other virtues) then it follows that its absence is a deficiency of the virtue. It can therefore be considered a vice and could leave the way open for the further vice of using the Other as a means to an end, in the Kantian sense, rather than respecting her own status as a free and rational 'end.' In a moderate form, this could simply be described as a general lack of due attention to the contextual features of ethical situations that are relevant—and indeed necessary—for the proper functions of prudence. In a more extreme form, it could be described as what Levinas refers to as 'totalization.'

As we noted in chapter 1, Levinas argued powerfully against "totalization," understood as the tendency to assume that the "I" can simply operate out of a position at which it is at home with itself and is open to otherness only inasmuch as it will fit within the walls of the home. Such a tendency, Levinas argued, leads towards a reductionism which attempts to reduce the infinity and uniqueness of other persons into a coherent and limiting philosophical theory over which the "I" can have control. It also rests on the mistaken assumption that the "I" itself is the source of its own constitution, and has no need for what is Other than itself. For Levinas, these were a set of assumptions and attitudes which imply a profound violence which is oriented towards objectifying other persons and the destructive consequences that this encompasses. Indeed, he would go so far as to call such a disregard for the infinity of the Other evil.[73] The disposition which consistently embodies such a disregard we will call the 'vice of totalization.' The vice of totalization would see no need for the kind of empathetic attentiveness that solidarity requires because it acts out of a disposition which suggests that all the "I" needs to operate is contained within the self and that anything external to the self is relevant only in self-referential terms. It leads to what Burggraeve

---

73. Raffoul, *The Origins of Responsibility*, 170. Raffoul is drawing from Levinas, *Entre Nous*, 114.

The Virtue of Solidarity and Attentiveness to Vulnerability 225

describes as "a misunderstanding and even denial of the others."[74] As such, this vice would seek to *impose* or *allocate* a response to a situation without the necessary attentiveness that we have seen is required by solidarity and is necessary for the operations of prudence. As such, it undermines rather than promotes the happiness of *both* the person who has the vice and the Other (or Others) with whom they act it out. An example will help to clarify this point.

Let us return to the father from chapter 5 who is trying to decide whether or not the gift of a large sum of money to his son would be an act of generosity. For now, let us also imagine that the father has the vice of totalization. If this were the case, all the material that practical reason would have to work with to make a decision would come from within the father—his own understanding of the son, his own understanding of what would count as a generous action, his own understanding of the importance of money, and so on. On the basis of these assumptions, the father decides that the gift would be generous and passes the money onto his son, who is in recovery from a gambling addiction. The son suddenly relapses and promptly loses all the money at the local casino. Such an action is vicious rather than virtuous for a number of reasons. In the first instance, it ignores solidarity's call for the kind of empathetic attentiveness that would have given the father relevant information about his son's gambling addiction, which clearly has implications for whether or not the gift of money could be considered generous. In the second instance, because this attentiveness was not present, practical reason cannot be said to be operating out of prudence because dialogue with context did not exist and, as such, it would be impossible for prudence to be able to achieve its function of determining the best course of action, 'all things considered.' As we have noted above, no virtue can operate without prudence, and so this action could not be considered virtuous at all (and this would remain the case even if its effects were more positive). As such, it cannot be said to focus the father's natural orientation towards happiness and thus undermines his flourishing.

Furthermore, the vice of 'totalization' undermines the happiness of the son as well. To explain this point, it is best to focus less on the consequences of the specific action (which in this case obviously undermines his

---

74. Burggraeve, *The Wisdom of Love*, 59. In its *most* extreme form, Burggraeve argues that this disposition manifests itself in the kind of racism and corresponding violent action seen in the Nazi movement. While this manifestation might be relatively rare, Burggraeve points out that Levinas's understanding of "totalization" can help us to see the beginnings of it in what I am referring to here as the vice of totalization. It is a vice, therefore, which should be taken very seriously. See Burggraeve, *The Wisdom of Love*, 60–61.

happiness) and more on the process the vice of totalization engages in leading up to the specific action, which also undermines the son's capacity for happiness, albeit less obviously. Recall that the anthropological vision of the human person we developed in chapter 4 acknowledges the uniqueness of the individual and his subjectivity, and that the virtue of solidarity responds to the latter of these through engaging in action in such a way that the Other is encouraged to be an *active participant in*, rather than a *passive recipient of*, moral decision making. As a consequence, if this is indeed a vice of the father and has been expressed consistently throughout his and the son's lifetimes, it is not difficult to hypothesize that the son's very subjectivity, and therefore capacity for happiness, would be hindered by it.

The Vices of Microscopic Philanthropy and Telescopic Philanthropy

The next two vices which I would like to suggest are associated with the virtue of solidarity relate to the methodological tool of the preferential option for the vulnerable and the concept of vulnerability *in relationship* which we explored above. Recall that the preferential option for the vulnerable is helpful for prudence to determine its priorities in directing the necessarily limited ability for solidarity to be equally attentive to all. Recall also that, to reflect a realistic understanding of human relationships, the concept of vulnerability *in relationship* was necessary to acknowledge that there are some instances in which a person is vulnerable precisely because of the nature of the relationship that she has with another person, and that prudence must take into account the nature of the relationship and the relative vulnerability it carries for it to function adequately. From these two observations we can draw out two vices which represent deficiencies on both counts. I refer to them as the vices of 'microscopic philanthropy' and 'telescopic philanthropy'.[75]

The vice of microscopic philanthropy refers to a disposition which focuses the attention of solidarity narrowly on only a particular person or group of persons without any concern for others who are outside of this.[76] Whilst one might normally focus the attention of solidarity primarily on

---

75. Here I build on Stephen Pope's use of the term "telescopic philanthropy" as used above. See Pope, *The Evolution of Altruism*, 41.

76. Peter Singer critiques a similar disposition, see Singer, *The Life You Can Save*, especially 24–46, 47–65, 139–51. I return to comment on the need to compare and contrast the book's argument more clearly with the arguments of other important moral philosophers and theologians in the book's conclusion.

those with whom one is closest, this must be balanced with the universal scope of solidarity which has as a central feature the common good and a corresponding concern for the dignity of all persons. As we have seen, such a concern has been developed with the methodological tool known as the preferential option for the vulnerable which, put simply, implies that in some circumstances the needs of a vulnerable stranger—someone outside of one's normal focus, as it were—can legitimately be prioritized over those on whom one's attention is normally focused. As such, microscopic philanthropy is a vice because it does not acknowledge the universal scope of human dignity, and the corresponding universal possibility for vulnerability that exists because of this. As a consistent disposition of character, therefore, it is not accountable to the virtue of solidarity, especially in its important emphasis on the preferential option for the vulnerable.

The vice of telescopic philanthropy, on the other hand, can be exemplified in the person who has a serious concern and commitment for the dignity of all persons and is willing to commit the degree of attentiveness that this requires, but is blind to those with whom she is in relationship who are especially vulnerable given the nature of that relationship. The paradigm of such a disposition can be found, as we have seen, in Dickens' Mrs Jellyby whose telescopic focus on the plight of those in Africa comes at the expense of the flourishing of her children who are dirty, hungry and suffer from neglect. The problem with such a disposition is not that it is concerned for the vulnerability of all persons, but that it fails to recognize the vulnerability that exists in certain relationships as part of the nature of those relationships and, as a consequence of this, is unable to engage with the preferential option for the vulnerable in a way which reflects the reality of human relationships. As such, it reduces prudence's ability to order the empathetic attentiveness of solidarity appropriately and is thereby a deficiency of the virtue.

Each of these vices—totalization; microscopic philanthropy; and telescopic philanthropy—represents deficiencies in regard to the virtue of solidarity as it has been developed in this chapter. As such, they reduce the human person's capacity to be attentive to the Other, as well as the morally salient features of any ethical situation, and diminish that capacity for practical reason to make concrete choices which can be described as prudent, and which correspond with the virtue of justice and the understanding of the human person on which it draws. This consideration of the vices associated with solidarity concludes our exploration of the virtue and its relationship with the virtue of prudence and places us at a point where we can bring together the argument of this chapter in a conclusion which will prepare us for the final conclusions of the book.

CONCLUSION

In this chapter, we have built from chapter 5's argument that the disposition known as the virtue of prudence requires a careful attentiveness to the complexity of ethical situations along with the capacity to balance and prioritize a set of diverse concerns in order to be able to facilitate a truly virtuous response. To help the prudent person achieve this, chapter 5 suggested a consideration of the virtue of solidarity as a way of specifying what exactly it means to be attentive, which became the focus of this chapter. Our consideration of the virtue of solidarity drew us into dialogue with Catholic Social Teaching which, we saw, posits solidarity as a disposition that stands with the Other (person or community), empty of pre-conceived judgements, in order to come to an accurate understanding of what would count as a virtuous response to them, all things considered. We have noted, however, that it must be invoked with an awareness of the necessary limitations that all human persons have the capacity to allocate solidarity, and so CST uses the preferential option for the poor (which we suggested be refined to 'vulnerable'), which prioritizes the attention of solidarity towards those for whom an infringement of dignity is a more immediate threat than for others. Drawing from this, we developed the concept of vulnerability *in relationship* to acknowledge the varying degrees of vulnerability which exist relative to the nature of the relationships of which individuals are a part. Finally, we posited three vices that are associated with solidarity: the vices of totalization; microscopic philanthropy; and, telescopic philanthropy.

The chapter has thus explained Porter's understanding of practical reason, its corresponding virtue of prudence, and how the operations of prudence are complemented by the virtue of solidarity through providing the kind of empathetic attentiveness that is required for the proper operations of the virtues (and in order to avoid the vice of totalization). At the same time, the chapter has demonstrated a capacity to avoid the vices of microscopic and telescopic philanthropy through a commitment to the preferential option for the vulnerable, considered in dialogue with the concept of vulnerability *in relationship*. We are now in a position to move to the final stage of the book's argument—the conclusion—in which it will draw together the threads of each chapter and show how the overall argument has demonstrated the plausibility of the hypothesis from which it has been working.

Conclusion

PURPOSE AND STRUCTURE OF THE CONCLUSION

THIS CONCLUSION WILL DRAW together the threads of the book's argument in order to synthesize its findings, both in terms of how these relate to the hypothesis set out at the beginning of the work and some of the original findings that the development of thought has led to throughout. At the same time, it will acknowledge some of the limitations of the book and point to possibilities for future research in light of these. The conclusion begins by reintroducing the hypothesis and revealing, step-by-step, how the book has responded to each dimension of this hypothesis and ultimately demonstrated its plausibility. After this point, the conclusion highlights a number of original findings that the book has made which have arisen from its efforts to demonstrate the plausibility of the hypothesis. The conclusion then looks towards the limitations of the book and links these with possibilities for future research, before finishing with some concluding remarks.

FINDINGS—PLAUSIBILITY OF THE HYPOTHESIS

In this section of the conclusion, I will demonstrate how the book has fortified the plausibility of the hypothesis from which it has been working. To facilitate this process, I have included the hypothesis below, as it was introduced in the introduction to the book, and have broken this section up into subsections which follow the component parts of the hypothesis in order to show how each has been dealt with.

It is possible to develop a set of robust links between the thought of Emmanuel Levinas and Jean Porter. Such links specify the ethical implications of Levinas's thought and develop Porter's theory in an original way. This work required further specification through a developed anthropology, which allows for expansion within the tradition of Catholic theological ethics. Further, the inclusion of Levinas and a focus on the virtue of solidarity allows for an advancement of virtue theory and theological ethics, to the extent that the virtue of solidarity becomes a key aspect of any ethical reasoning.

A Set of Robust Links Between the Philosophy of Emmanuel Levinas and Jean Porter's Theory of the Natural Law

The initial component of the hypothesis suggests that it is possible to develop a set of robust links between the philosophy of Emmanuel Levinas and Jean Porter's theory of natural law, and this section will revisit these links.

The first link between Levinas and Porter appeared in chapter 2, and was framed by both authors' arguments about the foundations of ethics. Here, we noted that both Levinas and Porter argue that an awareness of value, and the ethical concern that arises from this, is a disposition which is natural to the human person and an inherent dimension of consciousness. In relation to Levinas, this was made evident in his argument that ethics is 'first philosophy,' as explained in chapter 1. With regards to Porter, this was expressed in her argument that morality is our natural capacity to act and to reflect on action in such a way as to orient our lives towards the flourishing proper to our kind in a diversity of concrete contexts, as explained in chapter 2. When these perspectives were combined, it was suggested that the moral life is natural to the human person precisely because human persons are prerationally and intelligibly oriented towards the recognition of value, especially the value of other persons. Such an orientation necessarily leads to the discipline of ethical reflection because it underdetermines the operations of reason and therefore stimulates it to achieve a more specific and detailed evaluation of our moral responsibilities.

The second link between Levinas and Porter was closely related to the first, and appeared amidst the discussion of the virtues of temperance, fortitude, and justice in chapter 3. Here, it was demonstrated that, whilst the virtues of temperance and fortitude play a necessary role in the moral life, their self-referential nature requires that they be oriented away from the individual and towards a concern for others. This built on the chapter's observation that the virtues can be understood as aligning the human person's expression of her prerational, natural intelligibilities with happiness and that happiness for the human person is not something that can be bound only to the individual. When it came to the link between Porter and Levinas, this provided the opportunity to draw on the insights of Levinas and Andrew Tallon, as explored in chapter 1, which suggested that, on a prerational level, human persons are constituted in such a way that they can recognize the value of other persons and are motivated to respond. The chapter then proposed an argument which suggested that Porter's observation and the Levinasian insight could be combined to strengthen the argument that it is natural for us to respond to the value inherent in human relationaility. This provided a foundation for understanding the disposition of justice as grounded in the nature of the human person.

The third link between Levinas and Porter arose in chapter 5 within the context of the chapter's discussion about practical and speculative reason. Specifically, it revealed that Porter's suggestion regarding reason's foundation in the prerational intelligibilities of the human creature could be aligned with Levinas's suggestion that ethics is 'first philosophy'. More specifically, the chapter proposed an argument that Levinas was correct in his suggestion that ethics, understood as an optics which sees the human person as always constituted by a relationality that is profoundly affected by the presence of the Other, is always fundamental for the operations of reason. It did so by arguing that, when Levinas and Porter's insights are combined, it is possible to see that any activity of reason always has something to do with our prerational orientation towards being affected by the Other. To further this link, the chapter pointed out that Porter's account of reason, in its framing of the first principles of natural law, builds from the kind of methodology that Levinas proposes. That is, the first principles reflect the constitution of the human person in the same way Levinas argued that the operations of consciousness would be founded in, and reflect something of, the human person's pre-intentional constitution.

The fourth link between Levinas and Porter occurred later in chapter 5, when the need for careful attentiveness was noted in the chapter's examination of Porter's understanding of prudence. Here, the chapter revealed that Porter's approach shows an awareness of the complexity of ethical situations, and the consequent need to pay careful attention to them. Such an awareness, it was noted, has the capacity to avoid what Levinas refers to as 'totalization' inasmuch as it provides an impetus to prevent moral solutions which are simply created within the self (and with no regard for the complexity of what is encountered) from being imposed on situations and, worse still, persons, without the necessary attentiveness required to ensure that their complexity is acknowledged. Whilst their focus is set on different fields of enquiry, Levinas on philosophy and Porter on ethics, it is evident that their concerns are similar and that their observations are congruent with one another in these ways.

Specification of Some of the Ethical Implications of Levinas's Thought

The second part of the hypothesis refers to the fact that, whilst Levinas was concerned with ethics as an 'optics,' he did not seek to develop the practical ethical implications of his phenomenology, a point which was made in chapter 1. This opened up the possibility for the book to introduce Porter's theory as the process of discovering what constitutes the good and, as such, Porter's theory was able to demonstrate some of the practical implications of this fundamental call to goodness.

Moreover, the book did not simply observe the Levinasian insight as the catalyst for a turn to Porter's theory and then abandon any further influence it might have. Rather, it consistently revealed how a consideration of Levinas strengthened and supplemented the argument that ensued. The four dimensions of the Levinas-Porter link, noted above, are examples of this, but there are more: we saw in chapter 2 that Levinasian philosophy can criticize the naturalistic fallacy (a point to which we return below) and that the Levinasian understanding of the 'Saying' and the 'Said' can aid in how we engage with nature as a source of moral insight in Porter's theory of natural law. Furthermore, in chapter 4 we argued that Levinas's understanding of vulnerability constituted an important part of the anthropological vision of that chapter which enabled it to contribute to the book's understanding of justice. The significance of the ethical implications of this point was revealed in chapter 6 when the preferential option for the vulnerable was posited as an essential part of the developed theory. Finally, Levinas's emphasis on the infinity of the Other proved to be essential in highlighting the importance of attentiveness in moral reasoning, something which is at the heart of the approach that the thesis ultimately proposed. Correlatively, his argument regarding 'totalization' was consistently considered in terms of its practical implications throughout the book and assisted in the identification of the vice of totalization in chapter 6. In view of these points, it is possible to see the plausibility of this dimension of the hypothesis.

Development of Porter's Theory in an Original Way

If it is true that some of the ethical implications of Levinas's thought were developed in the theory, then it is equally true that the link between him and Porter has developed Porter's theory in an original way. In the first instance, I would suggest that this has happened by giving further strength to Porter's approach in a number of areas. The link with Levinas's philosophy led to an emphasis on certain parts of Porter's theory which enabled the thesis to move in directions that Porter herself has not yet explored, such as the emphasis on vulnerability and 'totalization' in Levinas which led to the introduction of the virtue of solidarity to counter these problems. Furthermore, I would suggest that Levinas's emphasis on the infinity and uniqueness of the human person gave an impetus to focus on Porter's understanding of prudence and develop this, especially by emphasizing the importance of attentiveness. As such, the book has shown the plausibility of this part of the hypothesis.

Expansion through Catholic Theological Ethics

Further, the book was able to show how Porter's approach allowed for an appeal to developed anthropology and that, as a consequence, it was legitimate to develop an anthropological vision informed by the Catholic tradition. As was noted above, this came about through a consideration of Porter's suggestion that the virtue of justice needs to appeal to a refined understanding of the human person in order to establish more precisely what is 'due' to her. This observation led the book to propose a move to an anthropological vision informed by the Catholic tradition which was developed in chapter 4. Setting its foundation in Catholic teaching on human dignity, the anthropological vision that the book developed drew heavily on Catholic Social Teaching and the personalist moral theology of Louis Janssens, linking also with Emmanuel Levinas's observations about vulnerability and current thinking on the theology of sin.

This anthropological vision found an important touchstone in the introduction of the virtue of solidarity in chapter 6. That is, the virtue of solidarity was defined in dialogue with CST and its emphasis on human dignity and, as such, drew heavily on aspects of the anthropological vision developed in chapter 4. Furthermore, the virtue of solidarity was closely related to the methodological tool of the preferential option for the poor in CST and, as such, was able to provide the context within which the book could argue for a shift from the language of 'the poor' to 'the vulnerable' and develop the preferential option as a core part of its argument.

The Importance of Attentiveness to Vulnerability in Moral Reasoning

Another key dimension of the book's argument is its revelation of the importance of attentiveness to vulnerability in moral reasoning and the link between this and the virtue of solidarity. In order to satisfy this part of the hypothesis, the book moved through several stages of argument. In the first, the possibility for acknowledging vulnerability as an important dimension of the human person was set up by Porter's suggestion that the virtue of justice needs to appeal to a developed anthropology in order to specify what is due to the human person. As noted above, this enabled the book to appeal to an anthropological tradition which was informed by the Catholic tradition. Part of this vision involved Louis Janssens's concept of the human person integrally and adequately considered and his suggestion, which was noted in chapter 4, that such a concept could act as a personalist criterion to inform the operations of justice. Following on from this, the book argued that Janssens's personalist criterion could be improved by acknowledging the Levinasian understanding of vulnerability as an essential dimension of what it means to be human, inasmuch as the human person is a complex and multidimensional creature consistently prone to great harm in a diversity of ways. As such, the book showed that vulnerability is a dimension of the personalist criterion which the person disposed towards justice would need to take into account.

The second stage of the argument was to reveal, and emphasize, the importance of attentiveness to ethical situations in the task of moral reasoning, and this took place in chapter 5. As we have indicated above, this was done through a consideration of Porter's understanding of prudence, whose distinctive character as a virtue is to enable the moral agent to be attentive to the complexity of the ethical situations she encounters. When this was combined with Levinas's and Janssens's observations about the complexity and uniqueness of each human person, the need to be attentive to each individual in order to embody a truly virtuous response to them was emphasized, and it was suggested that such attentiveness should be a priority for the prudent person. However, it was also noted that the human person is, by nature, limited in his capacity to be attentive to all, and that some form of prioritizing would need to take place for this vision of prudence to be realistic.

This led to the third stage of the argument which was the introduction of the virtue of solidarity into the book in chapter 6. As demonstrated therein, the social virtue of solidarity has as its focus the common good, understood as the fulfillment of all human persons, and it seeks to achieve the common good in social contexts by acknowledging situations wherein human dignity is infringed, being attentive to these situations before attempting to respond, and ultimately responding in such a way as to avoid imposing solutions from above, but rather encouraging the active participation of all in the process. We also noted there, however, that the social virtue of solidarity shares the concern noted above of prudence regarding the limitations of attentiveness and, because of this, provides the methodological tool of the preferential option for the poor in order to aid in the prioritization of solidarity towards those for whom an infringement of human dignity is a more immediate possibility than for others.

This led to the fourth, and final, stage of the argument which began with the suggestion that the preferential option could be more adequately termed a 'preferential option for the vulnerable,' as distinct from a 'preferential option for the poor.' This development of terminology had a two tiered advantage—on the first, it provided a broader scope for the preferential option to include those who are vulnerable but might not necessarily be considered 'poor' and, on the second, it enabled the book to link back to vulnerability as a dimension of the human person, and therefore an aspect of the personalist criterion to which a just disposition must attend. Finally, the methodological tool of the preferential option requires that solidarity, and therefore the attentiveness of prudence, be directed first of all to the most vulnerable, thus revealing the importance of attentiveness to vulnerability in moral reasoning and demonstrating the plausibility of this dimension of the hypothesis.

In addition, as was explained in chapter 1, Levinas understood philosophy (and therefore all disciplines which draw on a specific philosophy) as frequently embodying what he referred to as 'totalization.' 'Totalization,' on Levinas's view, is the tendency to ignore the unique mystery that is the Other by attempting to understand her completely, grasp her, and fit her into categories that limit and restrain her. For Levinas, this was embodied in all forms of ontology which posited themselves as fundamental understandings of the human person and which had no capacity for being undone, surprised, or interrupted by the unique presence of the Other. He suggested that such philosophies constituted a profound violence and were indeed the beginnings of all violence: once the Other is 'totalized' in word, it is inevitable that he will be in deed as well.

A desire to avoid creating a 'totalization' has been consistently displayed throughout this work. Whilst it was legitimate, even from a Levinasian point of view, to develop an understanding of the human person in order to facilitate the task of moral reasoning (see chapter 1), there has been a continuing awareness throughout the book of the need to avoid 'totalization.'

This has been expressed by means of an awareness of the limitations of the theoretical framework that has developed. Correlatively, this work remains aware of its need to be inherently open to surprise and transformation in the face of the Other if it is to avoid 'totalization.'

More specifically, however, the inclusion of the virtue of solidarity demonstrates a disposition which has at its heart a concern for avoiding 'totalization,' inasmuch as it is committed to avoiding imposing pre-conceived ideas and solutions by having attentiveness to the Other always as its first movement. Furthermore, the vice of totalization which was identified in chapter 6 reveals that a commitment *to* the disposition of solidarity implies a commitment *against* a disposition of 'totalization.' As such, the book's argument has demonstrated a way to ensure that what Levinas refers to as 'totalization' is avoided.

FINDINGS—OTHER IMPLICATIONS OF THE ARGUMENT

As well as demonstrating the plausibility of the hypothesis, the book has made five important findings that were necessary facets of the argument considered as a whole. I will describe each of these below.

A Unique Response to the Naturalistic Fallacy

The first important finding was proposed in its discussion of the naturalistic fallacy in chapter 2. Here, it was noted that one of the main philosophical criticisms of the naturalistic fallacy has been found in the discipline of phenomenology, especially in the phenomenology of the experience of value in the world. On its own, this observation was not unique, however the book took this foundation and expanded it further by means of the specific Levinasian insight. In view of this, the book was able to show that human persons experience some facts as value-laden such as, for example, the fact of the presence of the Other, and that this observation provides a helpful criticism of the naturalistic fallacy's thesis that all factual observations are value-neutral. Such a criticism is relevant for approaches to morality which take nature seriously and, if expanded, could play an important role in continuing debate about the naturalistic fallacy.

An Argument for the Relevance of the Social Virtue of Solidarity for Interpersonal Relationships

A second important finding of the book was its proposition that the virtue of solidarity which has, up until this point, been largely understood as a social virtue, is also relevant as an interpersonal virtue. This argument was presented in chapter 6, and was founded on the book's argument for the importance of the virtue of solidarity and its capacity to direct the empathetic attentiveness of prudence. It was acknowledged that the virtue of solidarity had been explained with reference to interpersonal relationships by other authors (specifically, David Hollenbach), and the development of this idea in detail made a distinctive contribution to the book's argument. This use of solidarity has the potential to contribute to the discipline of moral theology on at least two levels: first, as an interpersonal virtue which can specify the operations of justice and prudence in those approaches which emphasize the vulnerability and uniqueness of each human person; and second, as a bridge between the methodologies of CST and personalist moral theology which has the capacity to provide a better understanding of the necessary relationship between these two areas and, ultimately, develop both of them.

The Concept of a Preferential Option for the Vulnerable

The third important finding that the book has made is the terminological shift that it proposed between the preferential option for the poor and the preferential option for the vulnerable, which took place in chapter 6. This shift was grounded in the argument that the term 'vulnerable' more adequately captured the focus of the preferential option than did the term 'poor.' Furthermore, the book argued that the inclusion of the word 'vulnerable' would help enable the preferential option to focus more explicitly on all persons who are prone to harm in the great diversity of ways that this can occur, a point which was particularly poignant given the book's discussion of the complexity and multi-dimensional nature of the human person, without losing its necessary focus on those who are materially poor. Furthermore, the use of the term 'vulnerable' highlighted the need for attentiveness to vulnerability as it occurs both in actuality and in potentiality. This reframing of the preferential option also allowed for a more nuanced integration of the virtue of solidarity into the context of interpersonal relationships inasmuch as the focus on vulnerability linked with a dimension of the interpersonal encounter that was emphasized both in chapter 1 and chapter 4. In view of this, the preferential option for the vulnerable that has been proposed here has the capacity both to strengthen the link between CST and personalist moral theology, and to stimulate debate within CST regarding the preferential option and whether its use of the term 'poor' allows for the most adequate use of this tool. These points will be noted as possibilities for further research below.

Vulnerability As Such and Vulnerability In Relationship

The turn to vulnerability in the book led to the development of its fourth important finding. This was developed in chapter 6, in which the book proposed a refined understanding of vulnerability which takes into account the vulnerability that can be understood apart from any specific relational factors (this was referred to as vulnerability *as such*), and the special vulnerability which exists within the context of relationships because of the nature of those relationships (this was referred to as vulnerability *in relationship*). This observation was helpful for the book's argument in specifying what needs to be taken into account when the preferential option for the vulnerable is enacted. Furthermore, in its acknowledgment of the two dimensions of vulnerability, this distinction can help avoid some of the deficiencies which have been noted in regards to the liberation/CST approaches (which typically focus on vulnerability *as such* to the neglect of vulnerability *in relationship*, for which we followed Stephen Pope's use of the term 'telescopic philanthropy') and personalist approaches to moral theology (which typically focus on vulnerability *in relationship* to the neglect of vulnerability *as such*, for which we used the term 'microscopic philanthropy').[1] This developed understanding of vulnerability, it was argued, has the capacity to support a priority of attentiveness towards those with whom one is in relationship, albeit without neglecting vulnerability *as such*, and even prioritizing the latter in certain circumstances.

The Proposition of Vices Associated with the Virtue of Solidarity

The fifth original contribution of the book took the form of the suggestion of three vices associated with the virtue of solidarity in chapter 6, two of which built on Stephen Pope's use of the terminology of 'telescopic philanthropy' in his book *The Evolution of Altruism and the Ordering of Love*.[2]

---

1. See Stephen Pope's critique of these two approaches, Pope, *The Evolution of Altruism*, 32–40. See also chap. 6.
2. Ibid., 41. See chap. 6.

The identification of the vices of totalization, microscopic philanthropy and telescopic philanthropy arose out of the observations that were made in chapter 3 regarding the relationship between virtue and vice, with the latter being a disposition which is deficient or destructive in contrast to the former. The research undertaken for the book revealed a wealth of information on the virtue of solidarity, but no explicit mention of associated vices. As such, these suggestions are original and, whilst it is true that all three arose out of the specific argument in the book, I would argue that they are congruent with current discussions surrounding the virtue of solidarity and that a sustained and critical focus on them could develop our understanding of solidarity and its implications still further. Furthermore, I would suggest that attention to the vices associated with solidarity could reveal further dispositions of character, both for individuals and communities, which are deficient in regards to this virtue.

POSSIBILITIES FOR FUTURE RESEARCH

The book has a number of limitations which have arisen as a consequence of its focus and the approach taken. In this section, I note these limitations, and frame them as possibilities for future research.

The Problem of Anthropocentrism

The first limitation regarding the book is its focus on the vulnerable human person as the focus of ethical concern, something which was also pointed out in regards to the philosophy of Levinas in chapter 1. Such anthropocentrism has been widely, and rightly, criticized in recent years by moral philosophers and theologians who have been reframing the focus of their disciplines to include a concern for the dignity of all other creatures and, indeed, the dignity of all of creation, and our corresponding responsibility to respond to this in an ethical way.[3] Most poignantly in the Catholic tradition has been Pope Francis' 2015 encyclical *Laudato Si'* which also reflects on these themes. Further development of the book's argument would therefore

---

3. In terms of moral philosophy, see for example Low, ed., *Global Ethics & Environment*; Regan, *The Struggle for Animal Rights*; Singer, *Animal Liberation*. The journal "Ethics, Policy and Environment" is also a helpful resource in this area. On the journal's aim and scope, see Hale and Light, "Ethics, Policy & Environment: A New Name and a Renewed Mission." In terms of Christian ethics and moral theology, see for example Jenkins, *Ecologies of Grace: Environmental Ethics and Christian Theology*; Yarri, *The Ethics of Animal Experimentation*.

need to address its relationship to these concerns, and establish whether its focus on the human person is congruent with a concern for all creatures and all creation. This use of natural law theory, given its emphasis on the continuities between the human person and the rest of the creation, may provide a helpful context for this exploration.

The Relationship Between Acquired and Infused Virtues

The second limitation of the book is that it does not develop an understanding of the relationship between the acquired and the infused virtues, something which is an important dimension of Thomistic moral theology. The reason for this is that the thesis, following Porter's *Nature as Reason*, is focused on the life of virtue and the incomplete happiness this constitutes in natural, human life, as was explained in chapter 3. Nevertheless, the infused virtues—understood as those virtues which have as their object more direct union with God—formed an important part of Aquinas' understanding of the virtues and, in order to situate the book more clearly within Thomistic ethics, more critical attention to the relationship between the acquired and infused virtues would need to be developed.[4]

The Relationship Between the Book and Social Ethics

The third limitation highlights the potential for the relationship between the book and the area of social ethics, which remains unexplored. The basic foundation of this relationship already exists, given that the thesis draws heavily on material that is aligned with the area of social ethics. Nonetheless, the book's focus was firmly set on exploring the implications of these areas for interpersonal encounter and, indeed, this was noted in the introduction as one of its limitations. In view of this, future research could explore what implications the book's argument has for social ethics and, indeed, whether its focus on vulnerability and its refining of the preferential option in light of this would be helpful in determining moral responses to complex social situations.[5]

---

4. On some of the work that has already been done in this area, see for example Knobel, "Relating Aquinas's Infused and Acquired Virtues"; Mattison, "Can Christians Possess the Acquired Cardinal Virtues?."

5. The possibility for such a dialogue has been exemplified, at least on a methodological level, by Daniel Daly who has shown that it is possible to take understandings of virtue and vice and apply them to social ethics in terms of social structures of virtue and vice. See Daly, "Structures of Virtue and Vice."

The Relationship Between the Book and Other Approaches to Ethics

Closely related to the third possibility for further research is the fourth, which is that the book's argument requires being situated more clearly in its relationship with other approaches to ethics. In other words, a critical consideration of the argument alongside other approaches within the tradition of Catholic moral theology would help to show how it compares and contrasts with these—what features, for example, does it share with current trends in virtue ethics within the Catholic tradition, with current personalist approaches, and with liberation theology? Furthermore, this kind of analysis could be extended to broader philosophical questions in order to assess whether (or how) the book's argument aligns with proportionalist approaches to ethics, with consequentialist approaches, or with deontological approaches. It is true that the beginnings of this task have been achieved inasmuch as the thesis has been situated within contemporary discussions surrounding virtue ethics and natural law, so an extension of this style of comparison and contrast would not be difficult to envisage and would assist in positioning the book argument alongside other contemporary theories.

The Relationship Between the Book and Specific Moral Norms

In recent times, especially since the promulgation of Pope John Paul II's encyclical *Veritatis Splendor*, there has been considerable debate within Catholic moral theology surrounding the issue of specific moral norms. Typically, this is a debate about the exceptionless character of material moral norms, with some moral theologians (typically referred to as 'traditionalists') strongly supporting the ecclesial magisterium's argument that there are exceptionless material moral norms, frequently those promulgated by the magisterium.[6] On the other side of the debate are moral theologians (typically referred to as 'revisionists') who insist on the universality of formal moral norms, but are hesitant when it comes to proclaiming the exceptionless character of material moral norms, especially when these are founded in understandings of the human person tempered by historical and cultural circumstances.[7] Further compounding the debates between these

---

6. For the outlines of this approach, see Finnis, *Moral Absolutes: Tradition, Revision and Truth*, especially chap. 1.

7. For the outlines of this approach, see Gula, *Reason Informed by Faith*, 283–99. A sustained and critical discussion of both approaches can be found in Salzman, *Catholic Ethical Method*.

two schools (and the many moral theologians who do not align neatly with either of them) is the introduction of virtue ethics and its focus on moral dispositions instead of moral norms and, correlatively, the theory of the fundamental option and its relationship to specific moral actions.[8]

Given that the book arises out of the framework of Catholic moral theology, an important possibility for future research will be to consider what position the thesis argument would lead to within this debate. Such research would likely engage with similar work being done in this area by Catholic moral theologians who have taken an interest in virtue ethics, as well as those working in the personalist and natural law fields (including Porter) upon which the book has relied.[9]

The Relationship Between the Book and Biblical Studies

As was indicated in the Introduction, a limitation of the book was in its lack of detailed attention to Biblical material. This represents the final area of further research which would need to be conducted to ensure the argument became a contribution to Catholic moral theology that aligns with the Second Vatican Council's call for moral theology to be more firmly founded in Sacred Scripture.[10] The development of a relationship between Biblical studies and moral theology is, however, no simple task, not least because there has been a general lack of this kind of work in the past. Compounding this are issues of complexity in regards to exegesis, on the one hand, and the need to avoid using parts of Scripture to 'proof text' specific moral judgments on the other.[11]

Regardless of the above, some promising work has been done in this area, specifically by the moral theologian James F. Keenan and the Biblical scholar Daniel J. Harrington, whose two books linking the Bible and virtue ethics are helpful examples of Biblical studies and moral theology working well together.[12] More recently, Yin Sing Lucas Chan's work has received

---

8. See for example Daly, "The Relationship of Virtues and Norms in the Summa Theologiae"; Lawler and Salzman, "Karl Rahner and Human Nature: Implications for Ethics."

9. For Porter's own discussion of moral norms, see *NR*, 270–308. For a distinctly personalist approach to moral norms, see for example Salzman and Lawler, *The Sexual Person*, 159–61. On virtue ethics and the issue of moral normativity, see chap. 3. For further discussion, see Curran, "Absolute Moral Norms."

10. *OT*, 16.

11. See O'Collins, *Rethinking Fundamental Theology*, 331–32.

12. Harrington and Keenan, *Paul and Virtue Ethics*; Harrington and Keenan, *Jesus and Virtue Ethics*. See also Farley, *In Praise of Virtue*.

widespread critical praise of its advancements in this area.[13] Furthermore, the work of liberation theologians and social ethicists who have engaged seriously with the Bible has shown the power of the Biblical text to transform and provide focus for ethics, especially in terms of following Jesus the Christ's example of preference for the most vulnerable.[14] Finally, the place of Emmanuel Levinas in the argument opens up the possibility for dialogue with his own Talmudic commentaries on Scripture, as well as those of other Jewish commentators, which would make the relationship between the book and Biblical studies a genuinely inter-faith one.[15]

CONCLUDING REMARKS

From the outset, this book has been concerned with creating dialogue amongst a number of different schools of thought with distinct methodologies and areas of focus. It has been based on the conviction that such dialogue is possible and, more importantly, that it will produce results that any one of the conversation partners would not have been able to produce in isolation. This was framed as an attempt to fulfill a personal desire to create links amongst different ideas and, academically, a theoretical concern for moving moral theology towards a global discourse in which it can dialogue with, be challenged by, learn from and integrate insights from a diversity of disciplines as well as with, and from, the diversity that exists within its own discipline. In all these regards, it is submitted as being successful. Not only has it demonstrated the plausibility of its hypothesis and created the dialogue it was concerned with from the beginning, but it has also made some distinctive contributions to the discipline of moral theology, as well as opening up the possibility for further research beyond the confines of this particular study.

The ultimate test of the book's plausibility, however, will not occur within the academy. As a work of scholarship within the discipline of moral theology, its focus is inevitably practical and, if it does not have some practical implications in aiding the navigation of the moral life, then it will be proven to be less than authentic moral theology. As Roger Burggraeve has pointed out, "It is a scandal to confuse love of neighbor with the poetry that

---

13. See Chan, *The Ten Commandments and the Beatitudes*.

14. As an example of this, see O'Neill, "Christian Hospitality and Solidarity with the Stranger."

15. See Levinas, *Difficult Freedom*; Levinas, *Four Talmudic Readings*; Levinas, *Nine Talmudic Readings*; Levinas, *Beyond the Verse*.

sometimes celebrates it."[16] As yet, the book remains only poetry celebrating and seeking to understand what the ethical call of the presence of the Other implies. Its final and most important test will be whether its reflections can be translated into a lived response to the Other which is committed to acknowledging her vulnerability and answering her call to responsibility with solidarity, prudence, justice, temperance and fortitude.

Providentially, between beginning this work as a PhD thesis and now publishing it is a book, my own life's journey has taken me out of the academy and into a role as an ethicist and educator in Australia's largest Catholic healthcare system. I can think of no better place to seek to understand whether the theoretical work contained in this book helps to affirm and guide the work of those who seek to care for the vulnerable each and every day.

---

16. Burggraeve, *The Wisdom of Love*, 182.

Bibliography

CHURCH DOCUMENTS

All translations used have been taken from the online Vatican archives – www.vatican.va

Congregation for the Doctrine of the Faith, *Catechism of the Catholic Church* (1994)
Congregation for the Doctrine of the Faith, *Persona Humana: Declaration on Certain Questions Concerning Sexual Ethics* (1975)
International Theological Commission, *Communion and Stewardship: Human Persons Created in the Image of God* (2004)
Pontifical Council for Justice and Peace, *Compendium of the Social Doctrine of the Church* (2006)
Pope Benedict XVI, *Caritas in Veritate* (2009)
Pope John XXIII, *Pacem in Terris* (1963)
Pope John Paul II, "Address to the Pontifical Academy of Sciences - October 1996"
Pope John Paul II, *Centesimus Annus* (1991)
Pope John Paul II, *Evangelium Vitae* (1995)
Pope John Paul II, *Sollicitudio Rei Socialis* (1987)
Pope John Paul II, *Veritatis Splendor* (1993)
Pope Leo XIII, *Rerum Novarum* (1891)
Pope Paul VI, *Humanae Vitae* (1968)
Pope Paul VI, *Octogesima Adveniens* (1971)
Pope Paul VI, *Populorum Progressio: On the Development of Peoples* (1967)
Pope Pius XI, *Quadragesimo Anno* (1931)
Vatican II Council, *Dignitatis Humanae* (1965)
Vatican II Council, *Gaudium et Spes: Pastoral Constitution on the Church in the Modern World* (1965)
Vatican II Council, *Optatam Totius: Decree on Priestly Training* (1965)

FURTHER RESOURCES

Anscombe, G. E. M. "Modern Moral Philosophy." *Philosophy* 33, no. 124 (1958) 1–19.

Bibliography

Aubert, Roger. *Catholic Social Teaching: An Historical Perspective*. Milwaukee: Marquette University Press, 2003.
Barrow, Robin. *An Introduction to Moral Philosophy and Moral Education*. New York: Routledge, 2009.
Battaly, Heather. "Introduction: Virtue and Vice." *Metaphilosophy* 41, no. 1/2 (2010) 1–21.
Battle, John. "Kevin Kelly and Political Humility." In *Moral Theology for the Twenty-First Century: Essays in Celebration of Kevin Kelly*, edited by Julie Clague, Bernard Hoose, and Gerard Mannion, 263–69. London: T. & T. Clark, 2008.
Beattie, Tina. *The New Atheists: The Twilight of Reason & the War on Religion*. London: Darton, Longman and Todd, 2007.
Becker, Marcel. "Virtue Ethics, Applied Ethics and Rationality Twenty-Three Years after After Virtue." *South African Journal of Philosophy* 23, no. 3 (2004) 267–81.
Benhabib, Seyla. *Situating the Self: Gender, Community and Postmodernism in Contemporary Ethics*. New York: Routledge, 1992.
Blackburn, Simon. *Ruling Passions: A Theory of Practical Reason*. Oxford: Clarendon, 1998.
Bretzke, James T. "Natural and Divine Law: Reclaiming the Tradition for Christian Ethics." *Zygon* 38, no. 1 (2003) 197–99.
Bunch, Wilton H. "Natural and Divine Law (Book Review)." *Anglican Theological Review* 83, no. 3 (2001) 648.
Burggraeve, Roger. "Bioethics." *Theological Studies* 67, no. 1 (2006) 120–42.
Carr, David, and Jan Steutel. "The Virtue Approach to Moral Education." In *Virtue Ethics and Moral Education*, edited by David Carr and Jan Steutel, 247–62. London: Routledge, 1999.
———. "The Holistic Personalism of Professor Magister Louis Janssens." *Louvain Studies* 27 (2002) 29–38.
———. "Violence and the Vulnerable Face of the Other: The Vision of Emmanuel Levinas on Moral Evil and Our Responsibility." *Journal of Social Philosophy* 30, no. 1 (1999) 29–45.
———. *The Wisdom of Love in the Service of Love: Emmanuel Levinas on Justice, Peace, and Human Rights*. Milwaukee: Marquette University Press, 2002.
Cahill, Lisa Sowle. *Sex, Gender and Christian Ethics*. Cambridge: Cambridge University Press, 1996.
Carr, David, and Jan Steutel, eds. *Virtue Ethics and Moral Education*. London: Routledge, 1999.
Cates, Diana Fritz. "The Virtue of Temperance (IIa IIae, Qq. 141–170)." In *The Ethics of Aquinas*, edited by Stephen J. Pope, 321–39. Washington, DC: Georgetown University Press, 2002.
Caygill, Howard. *Levinas and the Political*. London: Routledge, 2002.
Chalier, Catherine. "The Philosophy of Emmanuel Levinas and the Hebraic Tradition." In *Ethics as First Philosophy: The Significance of Emmanuel Levinas for Philosophy, Literature and Religion*, edited by Adriaan T. Peperzak, 3–12. New York: Routledge, 1995.
Chan, Yin Sing Lucas. *The Ten Commandments and the Beatitudes: Biblical Studies and Ethics for Real Life*. Bengalaru: Dharmaran, 2015.
Christie, Dolores L. *Adequately Considered: An American Perspective on Louis Janssens' Personalist Morals*. Louvain: Peters, 1990.

Ciaramell, Fabio. "The Riddle of the Pre-Original." In *Ethics as First Philosophy: The Significance of Emmanuel Levinas for Philosophy, Literature and Religion*, edited by Adriaan T. Peperzak, 87–94. New York: Routledge, 1995.
Clark, Stephen R. *Biology and Christian Ethics*. New York: Cambridge University Press, 2000.
Coffey, David. "Rahner's Theology of Fundamental Option." *Philosophy and Theology* 10 (1997) 255–84.
Cohen, Richard A. "Emmanuel Levinas: Judaism and the Primacy of the Ethical." In *The Cambridge Companion to Modern Jewish Philosophy*, edited by Michael L. Morgan and Peter Eli Gordon. New York: Cambridge University Press, 2007.
Connors, Russell B., and Patrick T McCormick. *Character, Choices and Community: The Three Faces of Christian Ethics*. Mahwah, NJ: Paulist, 1998.
———. *Facing Ethical Issues: Dimensions of Character, Choices and Community*. New York: Paulist, 2002.
Coolman, Boyd Taylor. "Gestimmtheit: Attunement as a Description of the Nature-Grace Relationship in Rahner's Theology." *Theological Studies* 70, no. 4 (2009) 782–800.
Cooper, Bridget. "In Search of Profound Empathy in Learning Relationships: Understanding the Mathematics of Moral Learning Environments." *Journal of Moral Education* 39, no. 1 (2010) 79–99.
Critchley, Simon. "Introduction." In *The Cambridge Companion to Levinas*, edited by Simon Critchley and Robert Bernasconi. Cambridge: Cambridge University Press, 2002.
Crosson, F. J. "Phenomenology." In *The New Catholic Encyclopedia*, edited by Berard L. Marthaler, 11:230–34. Detroit: Gale, 2003.
Crowell, Steven. "Husserlian Phenomenology." In *A Companion to Phenomenology and Existentialism*, edited by Hubert L. Dreyfus and Mark A. Wrathall, 7–30: Blackwell Reference Online, 2006.
Crysdale, Cynthia S. W. "Heritage and Discovery: A Framework for Moral Theology." *Theological Studies* 63, no. 3 (2002) 559.
Curran, Charles. "Absolute Moral Norms." In *Christian Ethics: An Introduction*, edited by Bernard Hoose, 72–83. London: Cassell, 1998.
———. "Catholic Social and Sexual Teaching: A Methodological Comparison." *Theology Today* 44, no. 4 (1988) 425–40.
———. *Catholic Social Teaching 1891-Present: A Historical, Theological, and Ethical Analysis*. Washington, DC: Georgetown University Press, 2002.
———. *Loyal Dissent: Memoir of a Catholic Theologian*. Washington, DC: Georgetown University Press, 2006.
———. "Sin: Don't Lose All That Old-Time Catholic Guilt." In *Reclaiming Catholicism: Treasures Old and New*, edited by Thomas H. Groome and Michael J. Daley, 51–55. Maryknoll, NY: Orbis, 2010.
———. *A New Look at Christian Morality*. Notre Dame: Fides, 1970.
Curran, Charles E., Kenneth R. Himes, and Thomas A. Shannon. "Commentary on Sollicitudo Rei Socialis." In *Modern Catholic Social Teaching: Commentaries and Interpretations*, edited by Kenneth R Himes, 415–35. Washington, DC: Georgetown University Press, 2005.
Curran, Charles, and Richard A. McCormick. *Readings in Moral Theology No. 7: Natural Law and Theology*. New York: Paulist, 1991.

Curren, Randall. "Cultivating the Intellectual and Moral Virtues." In *Virtue Ethics and Moral Education*, edited by David Carr and Jan Steutel, 69–84. London: Routledge, 1999.

Dadosky, John. "The Church and the Other: Mediation and Friendship in Post-Vatican II Roman Catholic Ecclesiology." *Pacifica* 18, no. 3 (2005) 302–22.

Daly, Daniel. "The Relationship of Virtues and Norms in the Summa Theologiae." *Heythrop Journal* 51, no. 2 (2010) 214–29.

———. "Structures of Virtue and Vice." *New Blackfriars* 92, no. 1039 (2010) 341–57.

Damasio, Antonio. *Descartes' Error: Emotion, Reason, and the Human Brain*. New York: Putnam, 1994.

———. *The Feeling of What Happens: Body and Emotion in the Making of Consciousness*. New York: Harcourt Brace, 1999.

Davies, Paul. "On Resorting to an Ethical Language." In *Ethics as First Philosophy: The Significance of Emmanuel Levinas for Philosophy, Literature and Religion*, edited by Adriaan T. Peperzak, 95–104. New York: Routledge, 1995.

Davis, Colin. *Levinas: An Introduction*. Cambridge: Polity, 1996.

Dawkins, Richard. "Accumulating Small Change." In *Philosophy of Biology*, edited by Michael Ruse, 62–68. Amherst, MA: Prometheus, 1998.

———. *The Ancestor's Tale: A Pilgrimage to the Dawn of Life*. London: Phoenix, 2005.

Deck, Allan Figueroa. "Commentary on *Populorum Progressio*." In *Modern Catholic Social Teaching: Commentaries and Interpretations*, edited by Kenneth R. Himes, 292–314. Washington, DC: Georgetown University Press, 2005.

Dent, Nicholas. "Virtue, *Eudaimonia* and Teleological Ethics." In *Virtue Ethics and Moral Education*, edited by David Carr and Jan Steutel, 159–72. London: Routledge, 1999.

Derrida, Jacques. "Living On." In *Deconstruction and Criticism*, edited by Geoffrey H. Hartman, 62–142. London: Routledge, 1979.

———. *Writing and Difference*. Chicago: University of Chicago Press, 1978.

Dill, Jeffrey S. "Durkheim and Dewey and the Challenge of Contemporary Moral Education." *Journal of Moral Education* 36, no. 2 (2007) 221–37.

Dorr, Donal. *Option for the Poor: A Hundred Years of Catholic Social Teaching*. Rev. ed. Marynoll, NY: Orbis, 1992.

Dunne, Joseph. "Virtue, *Phronesis* and Learning." In *Virtue Ethics and Moral Education*, edited by David Carr and Jan Steutel, 51–66. London: Routledge, 1999.

Edwards, Denis. *Ecology at the Heart of Faith*. Maryknoll, NY: Orbis, 2006.

———. *How God Acts: Creation, Redemption and Special Divine Action*. Minneapolis: Fortress, 2010.

Egéa-Kuehne, Denise. "Introduction." In *Levinas and Education: At the Intersection of Faith and Reason*, edited by Denise Egéa-Kuehne, 1–12. London: Routledge, 2008.

Eppert, Claudia. "Emmanuel Levinas, Literary Engagement and Literature Education." In *Levinas and Education: At the Intersection of Faith and Reason*, edited by Denise Egéa-Kuehne, 67–84. London: Routledge, 2008.

Farley, Benjamin W. *In Praise of Virtue: An Exploration of the Biblical Virtues in a Christian Context*. Grand Rapids: Eerdmans, 1995.

Farley, Margaret A. *Just Love: A Framework for Christian Sexual Ethics*. New York: Continuum, 2008.

Fatula, Mary Ann. *The Triune God of the Christian Faith*. Collegeville, MN: Liturgical, 1990.

Finnis, John. *Aquinas: Moral, Political and Legal Theory*. New York: Oxford University Press, 1998.

———. *Moral Absolutes: Tradition, Revision and Truth*. Washington: Catholic University Press, 1991.

Fitzpatrick, Joseph. "Original Sin or Original Sinfulness?" *New Blackfriars* 90, no. 1028 (2009) 458–73.

———. "Original Sin or Original Sinfulness?" *New Blackfriars* 90, no. 1029 (2009) 560–76.

———. "Original Sin or Original Sinfulness?" *New Blackfriars* 91, no. 1031 (2010) 66–82.

Fleming, Daniel J. "Ethics Is an Optics: The Levinasian Perspective on Value as Primary." In *The Routledge International Handbook of Education, Religion and Values*, edited by James Arthur and Terence Lovat, 362–72. London: Routledge, 2013.

———. "Intelligibility in the Natural Law: An Analysis of Jean Porter's Approach." *Australian eJournal of Theology*, no. 15 (2010). http://www.acu.edu.au/__data/assets/pdf_file/0016/225403/Fleming_Natural_Law_GH.pdf.

———. "Primoridal Moral Awareness: Levinas, Conscience and the Unavoidable Call to Responsibility." *Heythrop Journal* 56, no 4 (2015) 604–18.

———. "Understanding Trade in *Populorum Progressio* and *Caritas in Veritate*." *Australian eJournal of Theology* 16 (2010). http://aejt.com.au/__data/assets/pdf_file/0019/272008/AEJT_16-Fleming-Trade.pdf.

Flood, Anne. "Understanding Phenomenology." *Nurse Researcher* 17, no. 2 (2010) 7–16.

Fout, Jason A. "Nature as Reason: A Thomistic Theory of the Natural Law by Jean Porter." *Reviews in Religion & Theology* 13, no. 4 (2006) 590–93.

Frey, William J. "Teaching Virtue: Pedagogical Implications of Moral Psychology." *Science & Engineering Ethics* 16, no. 3 (2010) 611–28.

Gallagher, David M. "The Will and Its Acts (Ia IIae, Qq. 6–17)." In *The Ethics of Aquinas*, edited by Stephen J. Pope, 69–89. Washington, DC: Georgetown Univeristy Press, 2002.

Gascoigne, Robert. *Freedom and Purpose: An Introduction to Christian Ethics*. Mahwah, NJ: Paulist, 2004.

———. "Suffering and Theological Ethics: Intimidation and Hope." In *Catholic Theological Ethics in the World Church*, edited by James F. Keenan, 163–66. London: Continuum, 2007.

Gibbs, Robert. "Height and Nearness: Jewish Dimensions of Radical Ethics." In *Ethics as First Philosophy: The Significance of Emmanuel Levinas for Philosophy, Literature and Religion*, edited by Adriaan T. Peperzak, 13–23. New York: Routledge, 1995.

Gleeson, Gerald P. "Prophecy, Patience and Pardon: Exploring the Context of an Erroneous Conscience." *Australasian Catholic Record* 85, no. 2 (2008) 196–211.

———. "The Scope of the Church's Moral Teaching: A Response to 'Beyond Its Authority?' by Frank Mobbs." *Australasian Catholic Record* 75, no. 3 (1998) 264–70.

Glendinning, Simon. "What Is Phenomenology?" *Philosophy Compass* 3, no. 1 (2008) 30–50.

Goleman, Daniel. *Emotional Intelligence*. New York: Bantam, 1995.

Goodman, Lenn E. "Happiness." In *The Cambridge History of Medieval Philosophy*, edited by Robert Pasnau and Christina Van Dyke, 457–71. Cambridge: Cambridge University Press - Cambridge Histories Online, 2010.

Green, Thomas F. "Voices: The Educational Formation of Conscience." *Studies in Philosophy and Education* 22 (2003) 521–33.
Grisez, Germain, John Finnis, and Joseph Boyle. "Practical Principles, Moral Truth, and Ultimate Ends." *American Journal of Jurisprudence* 32 (1987) 99–151.
Grisez, Germain, et al. "'Every Marital Act Ought to Be Open to New Life': Toward a Clearer Understanding." *Thomist* 52 (1988) 365–426.
Guignon, Charles B. "Introduction." In *The Cambridge Companion to Heidegger: Second Edition*, edited by Charles B. Guignon, 1–41. Cambridge: Cambridge University Press, 2006.
Gula, Richard M. *Reason Informed by Faith: Foundations of Catholic Morality*. Mahwah, NJ: Paulist, 1989.
Hale, Benjamin, and Andrew Light. "Ethics, Policy & Environment: A New Name and a Renewed Mission." *Ethics, Policy & Environment* 14, no. 1 (2011) 1–2.
Hand, Sean. *Emmanuel Levinas*. New York: Routledge, 2008.
Hanigan, James. "Conversion and Christian Ethics." *Theology Today* 40 (1983) 25–35.
Hanson, N. R. *Patterns of Discovery: An Enquiry into the Conceptual Foundations of Science*. Cambridge: Cambridge University Press, 1961.
Haring, Bernard. *Free and Faithful in Christ*. Vol. 1. London: St. Paul, 1978.
Harold, Philip J. *Prophetic Politics: Emmanuel Levinas and the Sanctification of Suffering*. Athens, OH: Ohio University Press, 2009.
Harrington, Daniel J., and James F. Keenan. *Jesus and Virtue Ethics: Building Bridges between New Testament Studies and Moral Theology*. Lanham, MD: Sheed & Ward, 2002.
———. *Paul and Virtue Ethics: Building Bridges between New Testament Studies and Moral Theology*. Plymouth: Rowman & Littlefield, 2010.
Hart, Kevin. "Introduction: Levinas the Exorbitant." In *The Exorbitant: Emmanuel Levinas between Jews and Christians*, edited by Kevin Hart and Michael Alan Singer, 1–16. New York: Fordham University Press, 2010.
Hauser, Marc D. *Moral Minds: How Nature Designed Our Universal Sense of Right and Wrong*. New York: Ecco, 2006.
Heidegger, Martin. *Being and Time*. New York: Harper & Row, 1962.
———. *History of the Concept of Time: Prolegomena*. Translated by T Kisiel. Bloomington: Indiana University Press, 1985.
Henry, Martin. "Original Sin: A Flawed Inheritance." *Irish Theological Quarterly* 65, no. 1 (2000) 3–12.
Hickerson, Ryan. "Neglecting the Question of Being: Heidegger's Argument against Husserl." *Inquiry* 52, no. 6 (2009) 574–95.
Hill, Brennan R. *Christian Faith and the Environment*. Eugene, OR: Wipf and Stock, 1998.
Himes, Kenneth R. *Responses to 101 Questions on Catholic Social Teaching*. New York: Paulist, 2001.
Hittinger, Russell. "The Coherence of the Four Basic Principles of Catholic Social Doctrine: An Interpretation." *Nova et Vetera (English Edition)* 7, no. 4 (2009) 791–838.
Hollenbach, David. *The Common Good and Christian Ethics*. Cambridge: Cambridge University Press, 2002.
———. *The Global Face of Public Faith: Politics, Human Rights and Christian Ethics*. Washington, DC: Georgetown University Press, 2003.

Houser, R. E. "The Virtue of Courage (IIa IIae, Qq. 123–140)." In *The Ethics of Aquinas*, edited by Stephen J. Pope, 304–20. Washington, DC: Georgetown University Press, 2002.

Hume, David. *A Treatise on Human Nature*. Oxford: Oxford University Press, 1973.

Hursthouse, Rosalind. "Virtue Ethics." In *New Dictionary of the History of Ideas*, edited by Maryanne Cline Horowitz, 6:2421–23. Detroit: Scribner's Sons, 2005.

Husserl, Edmund. *The Basic Problems of Phenomenology: From the Lectures, Winter Semester, 1910–1911*. Translated by Ingo Farin and James G. Hart. Dordrecht: Springer, 2006.

———. *The Crisis of European Sciences and Transcendental Phenomenology: An Introduction to Phenomenological Philosophy*. Translated by David Carr. Evanston: Northwestern University Press, 1970.

———. *The Idea of Phenomenology*. Translated by W. P. Alston and G. Nakhnikian. The Hague: Nijhoff, 1964.

———. *Ideas Pertaining to a Pure Phenomenology and to a Phenomenological Philosophy, First Book*. Translated by F. Kersten. The Hague: Nijhoff, 1982.

———. *Logical Investigations*. Translated by J. N. Findlay. London: Routlege, 1970.

———. *Psychological and Transcendental Phenomenology and the Confrontation with Heidegger (1927–1931), the Encyclopaedia Britannica Article, the Amsterdam Lectures "Phenomenology and Anthropology" and Husserl's Marginal Notes in* Being and Time, *and Kant on the* Problem of Metaphysics. Translated by T. Sheenan and R. E. Palmer. Dordrecht: Kluwer, 1997.

Hutchens, B. C. *Levinas: A Guide for the Perplexed*. London: Continuum, 2004.

Hyman, Arthur, James J. Walsh, and Thomas Williams. *Philosophy in the Middle Ages*. Indianapolis: Hackett, 2010.

Irwin, Terence. *The Development of Ethics, 1: From Socrates to the Reformation*. Oxford: Oxford University Press, 2007.

Janssens, Louis. "Artificial Insemination: Ethical Considerations." *Louvain Studies* 8 (1980): 3–29.

———. "Ontic Good and Evil: Premoral Values and Disvalues." *Louvain Studies* 12 (1987) 62–82.

Jeffreys, Derek S. "Nature as Reason: A Thomistic Theory of the Natural Law." *Journal of Religion* 86, no. 3 (2006) 487–89.

Jenkins, Willis. *Ecologies of Grace: Environmental Ethics and Christian Theology*. Oxford: Oxford University Press, 2008.

Johnson, Elizabeth. *Quest for the Living God*. New York: Continuum, 2007.

Johnson, Monte Ransome. *Aristotle on Teleology*. Oxford: Oxford University Press, 2005.

Johnson, Robert N. "Relativism." In *New Dictionary of the History of Ideas*, edited by Maryanne Cline Horowitz, 5:2035–39. Detroit: Scribner's Sons, 2005.

Jones, David Albert. "John Paul II and Moral Theology." In *The Legacy of John Paul II*, edited by Michael A. Hayes and Gerald O'Collins, 79–109. London: Burns & Oates, 2008.

Kane, T. C. "Fortitude, Virtue of." In *The New Catholic Encyclopedia*, ed. Berard L. Marthaler. Detroit: Gale, 2003.

Keenan, James F. "Contemporary Contributions to Sexual Ethics." *Theological Studies* 71, no. 1 (2010) 148–67.

———. "Fundamental Moral Theology: Tradition." *Theological Studies* 70, no. 1 (2009) 140–58.

———. *A History of Catholic Moral Theology in the Twentieth Century: From Confessing Sins to Liberating Consciences.* London: Continuum, 2010.

———. "Natural and Divine Law (Book Review)." *Theological Studies* 61, no. 4 (2000) 777.

———. "Proposing Cardinal Virtues." *Theological Studies* 56, no. 4 (1995) 709–29.

———. "The Virtue of Prudence (IIa IIae, Qq. 23–46)." In *The Ethics of Aquinas*, edited by Stephen J. Pope, 259–71. Washington, DC: Georgetown University Press, 2002.

Kelly, Kevin T. *New Directions in Moral Theology: The Challenge of Being Human.* London: Chapman, 1992.

Kennedy, Philip. *Twentieth-Century Theologians: A New Introduction to Modern Christian Thought.* London: Tauris, 2010.

Kent, Bonnie. "Habits and Virtues (Ia IIae, Qq. 49–70)." In *The Ethics of Aquinas*, edited by Stephen J. Pope, 116–30. Washington, DC: Georgetown University Press, 2002.

Kerr, Fergus. *After Aquinas: Versions of Thomism.* Oxford: Blackwells, 2002.

Kirchhoffer, David G. "Benedict XVI, Human Dignity, and Absolute Moral Norms." *New Blackfriars* 91, no. 1035 (2009) 586–609.

Knobel, Angela McKay. "Relating Aquinas's Infused and Acquired Virtues: Some Problematic Texts for a Common Interpretation." *Nova et Vetera (English Edition)*, 9 (2011) 411–31.

Kopfensteiner, Thomas R. "The Theory of the Fundamental Option and Moral Action." In *Christian Ethics: An Introduction*, edited by Bernard Hoose, 123–34. London: Chapman, 1998.

Kupperman, Joel J. "Virtues, Character and Moral Dispositions." In *Virtue Ethics and Moral Education*, edited by David Carr and Jan Steutel, 205–16. London: Routledge, 1999.

Lamb, Matthew L. "Solidarity." In *The New Dictionary of Catholic Social Thought*, edited by Judith A. Dwyer, 909. Collegeville, MN: Liturgical, 1994.

Lawler, Michael G., and Todd A. Salzman. "Human Experience and Catholic Moral Theology." *Irish Theological Quarterly* 76, no. 1 (2011) 35–56.

———. "Karl Rahner and Human Nature: Implications for Ethics." *Irish Theological Quarterly* 74 (2009) 389–418.

Leahy, Brendan. "John Paul II and Hans Urs Von Balthasar." In *The Legacy of John Paul II*, edited by Michael A. Hayes and Gerald O'Collins, 31–50. London: Burns & Oates, 2008.

Levinas, Emmanuel. *Beyond the Verse: Talmudic Readings and Lectures.* Translated by Gary D. Mole. London: Athlone, 1994.

———. *Difficult Freedom: Essays on Judaism.* Translated by Sean Hand. London: Athlone, 1990.

———. *Entre Nous.* Translated by Michael B. Smith and Barbara Harshav. New York: Columbia University Press, 1998.

———. "Ethics as First Philosophy." In *The Levinas Reader*, edited by Sean Hand, 75–87. Oxford: Blackwell, 1989.

———. *Four Talmudic Readings.* Translated by N. Poller. Bloomington: Indiana University Press, 1990.

———. *Nine Talmudic Readings.* Translated by Annette Aronowicz. Bloomington: Indiana University Press, 1990.

———. *Otherwise Than Being or Beyond Essence*. Translated by Alphonso Lingis. Pittsburgh: Duquesne University Press, 1998.

———. *Totality and Infinity: An Essay on Exteriority*. Translated by Alphonso Lingis. Pittsburgh: Duquesne University Press, 1969.

Linnane, Brian F. "Rahner's Fundamental Option and Virtue Ethics." *Philosophy and Theology* 15, no. 1 (2003) 229–54.

Lisska, Anthony J. *Aquinas's Theory of Natural Law: An Analytic Reconstruction*. Oxford: Clarendon, 1996.

Lovat, Terence J. "Synergies and Balance between Values Education and Quality Teaching." *Educational Philosophy & Theory* 42, no. 4 (2010) 489–500.

Lovat, Terence J., and Neville Clement. "Quality Teaching and Values Education: Coalescing for Effective Learning." *Journal of Moral Education* 37, no. 1 (2008) 1–16.

Low, Nicholas, ed. *Global Ethics & Environment*. London: Routledge, 1999.

Luna, Florencia. *Bioethics & Vulnerability: A Latin American View*. Kenilworth: Rodopi, 2006.

MacIntyre, Alasdair. *Whose Justice? Which Rationality?* London: Duckworth, 1988.

Magidon, Patrick. "Nature as Reason: A Thomistic Theory of the Natural Law." *Heythrop Journal* 47, no. 7 (2006) 662–69.

Manderson, Desmond, ed. *Essays on Levinas and Law: A Mosaic*. Basingstroke: Palgrave Macmillan, 2008.

Marinos, Diamantides. *Levinas, Law, Politics*. Hoboken: Taylor & Francis, 2007.

Markham, Ian. "Faith and Reason: Reflection on Macintyre's 'Tradition-Constituted Enquiry.'" *Religious Studies* 27, no. 2 (1991) 259–67.

Marmion, Declan, and E. Mary Hines. "Introduction." In *The Cambridge Companion to Karl Rahner*. Cambridge: Cambridge University Press, 2005.

Masters, Roger. *The Nature of Politics*. New Haven: Yale University Press, 1989.

Mattison III, William C. "Can Christians Possess the Acquired Cardinal Virtues?" *Theological Studies* 72, no. 3 (2011) 558–85.

McAleer, Sean. "Four Solutions to the Alleged Incompleteness of Virtue Ethics." *Journal of Ethics & Social Philosophy* 4, no. 3 (2010)1–20.

McArdle, Patrick. "Levinas and Responsibility for the Other: A Practical Theological Analysis of the Cases of Nancy Crick and Terri Schiavo." *Australian eJournal of Theology* 13, no. 1 (2009). http://www.acu.edu.au/__data/assets/pdf_file/0009/158454/McArdle_Levinas-and-Responsibility.pdf.

McBrien, Richard P. *Catholicism: New Edition*. New York: HarperOne, 1994.

McCabe, Herbert. *On Aquinas*. London: Burns & Oates, 2008.

McCormick, Patrick. "Review of *Nature as Reason: A Thomistic Theory of the Natural Law* by Jean Porter." *Journal of the Society of Christian Ethics* 29, no. 1 (2009) 251–53.

McCormick, Richard A. *The Critical Calling: Reflections on Moral Dilemmas since Vatican II*. Washington, DC: Georgetown University Press, 2006.

———. "The Gospel of Life." *America* 172, no. 15 (1995) 10–17.

McGrath, Alister E. *A Scientific Theology*. Vol. 1, *Nature*. Edinburgh: T. & T. Clark, 2001.

Merkle, Judith. "Sin." In *New Dictionary of Catholic Social Thought*, edited by Judith A. Dwyer, 883–88. Collegeville, MN: Liturgical, 1994.

Messer, Neil. *Selfish Genes and Christian Ethics*. London: SCM, 2007.

Miller, Hugh. "Reply to Bernhard Waldenfels, "Response and Responsibility in Levinas."" In *Ethics as First Philosophy: The Importance of Emmanuel Levinas for Philosophy, Literature and Religion*, edited by Adriaan T. Peperzak, 53–58. New York: Routledge, 1995.

Mobbs, Frank. *Beyond Its Authority? The Magisterium and Matters of Natural Law*. Alexandria: Dwyer, 1997.

Mocduch, Jonathan. "Poverty and Vulnerability." *American Economic Review* 84, no. 2 (1994) 221.

Moore, G. E. *Principia Ethica*. Cambridge: Cambridge University Press, 1903.

Moran, Dermot. *Introduction to Phenomenology*. Florence: Routledge, 1999.

Morrison, Glenn. "Good Teaching, Spirituality and the Philosophy of Emmanuel Levinas." *Australian eJournal of Theology* 14, no. 1 (2009). https://researchonline.nd.edu.au/cgi/viewcontent.cgi?article=1059&context=theo_article.

Moser, Paul K. "Foundationalism." In *New Dictionary of the History of Ideas*, edited by Maryanne Cline Horowitz, 2:839–41. Detroit: Scribner's Sons, 2005.

Nairn, Thomas A. "Natural and Divine Law (Book)." *Journal of Religion* 82, no. 1 (2002) 140.

Narvaez, Darcia, and Jenny L. Vaydich. "Moral Development and Behaviour under the Spotlight of the Neurobiological Sciences." *Journal of Moral Education* 37, no. 3 (2008) 289–312.

Niebuhr, H. Richard. *The Responsible Self: An Essay in Christian Moral Philosophy*. New York: Harper & Row, 1963.

Njoku, Uzochukwu Jude. *Examining the Foundations of Solidarity in the Social Encyclicals of John Paul II*. Frankfurt: Lang, 2006.

Noonan, John T. *A Church That Can and Cannot Change: The Development of Catholic Moral Teaching*. Notre Dame: University of Notre Dame Press, 2005.

O'Collins, Gerald. "John Paul II and the Development of Doctrine." In *The Legacy of John Paul II*, edited by Michael A. Hayes and Gerald O'Collins, 1–16. London: Burns & Oates, 2008.

———. *Rethinking Fundamental Theology*. Oxford: Oxford University Press, 2011.

O'Connell, Timothy E. *Making Disciples: A Handbook of Christian Moral Formation*. New York: Crossroad, 1998.

———. *Principles for a Catholic Morality: Revised Edition*. New York: HarperOne, 1990.

———. "The Question of Grundentscheidung." *Philosophy and Theology* 10 (1997) 143–68.

———. "The Theology of Conscience." *Chicago Studies* 14 (1976) 103–18.

———. "An Understanding of Conscience." In *Readings in Moral Theology No. 14: Conscience*, edited by Charles Curran, 25–38. Mahwah, NJ: Paulist, 2004.

O'Neill, William. "Christian Hospitality and Solidarity with the Stranger." In *And You Welcomed Me: Migration and Catholic Social Teaching*, edited by Donald Kerwin and Jill Marie Gerschutz, 149–56. Lanham, MD: Rowman & Littlefield, 2009.

Palmer, Clare. *Animal Ethics in Context*. New York: Columbia University Press, 2010.

———. "Animals in Christian Ethics: Developing a Relational Approach." *Ecotheology: Journal of Religion, Nature & the Environment* 7, no. 2 (2003) 163.

Panksepp, Jaak. *Affective Neuroscience: The Foundations of Human and Animal Emotions*. Oxford: Oxford University Press, 1998.

Peperzak, Adriaan T. *Beyond: The Philosophy of Emmanuel Levinas*. Evanston: Northwestern University Press, 1997.
———. "Transcendence." In *Ethics as First Philosophy: The Significance of Emmanuel Levinas for Philosophy, Literature and Religion*, edited by Adriaan T. Peperzak, 185–92. New York: Routledge, 1995.
Peperzak, Adriaan T., ed. *Ethics as First Philosophy: The Significance of Emmanuel Levinas for Philosophy, Literature and Religion*. New York: Routledge, 1995.
Peterson, Anna L. *Being Human: Ethics, Environment and Our Place in the World*. Ewing: University of California Press, 2001.
Pieper, Josef. *Scholasticism: Personalities and Problems of Medieval Philosophy*. London: Faber and Faber, 1960.
Pope, Stephen J. *The Evolution of Altruism and the Ordering of Love*. Washington, DC: Georgetown University Press, 1994.
———. *Human Evolution and Christian Ethics*. Cambridge: Cambridge University Press, 2007.
———. "Overview of the Ethics of Thomas Aquinas." In *The Ethics of Aquinas*, edited by Stephen J. Pope, 30–50. Washington, DC: Georgetown University Press, 2002.
Porter, Jean. "Basic Goods and the Human Good in Recent Catholic Moral Theology." *Thomist* 57 (1993) 28–42.
———. "Chastity as a Virtue." *Scottish Journal of Theology* 58, no. 3 (2005) 285–301.
———. *Ministers of the Law: A Natural Law Theory of Legal Authority*. Grand Rapids: Eerdmans, 2010.
———. "Moral Theology and the Language of Grace: The Fundamental Option and the Virtue of Charity." *Philosophy and Theology* 10 (1997) 169–98.
———. *Natural & Divine Law: Reclaiming the Tradition for Christian Ethics*. Grand Rapids: Eerdmans, 1999.
———. "Natural Law as Scriptural Concept." *Theology Today* 59, no. 2 (2002): 226–241.
———. *Nature as Reason: A Thomistic Theory of the Natural Law*. Grand Rapids: Eerdmans, 2005.
———. "A Response to Martin Rhonheimer." *Studies in Christian Ethics* 19, no. 3 (2006) 379–95.
———. "A Tradition of Civility: The Natural Law as a Tradition of Moral Enquiry." *Scottish Journal of Theology* 51, no. 1 (2003) 27–48.
———. "Virtue Ethics." In *The Cambridge Companion to Christian Ethics*, edited by Robin Gill, 87–102. Cambridge: Cambridge University Press, 2001.
———. "The Virtue of Justice (IIa IIae, Qq. 58–122)." In *The Ethics of Aquinas*, edited by Stephen J. Pope, 272–86. Washington, DC: Georgetown University Press, 2002.
Purcell, Michael. *Levinas and Theology*. Cambridge: Cambridge University Press, 2006.
———. *Mystery and Method: The Other in Rahner & Levinas*. Milwaukee: Marquette University Press, 1998.
———. "The Mystery of Death: Alterity and Affectivity in Levinas." *New Blackfriars* 76, no. 899 (1995) 524–34.
Putnam, Hilary. *Jewish Philosophy as a Guide to Life: Rosenzweig, Buber, Lévinas, Wittgenstein*. Bloomington: Indiana University Press, 2008.
Qureshi, Paul. "Sin, Fundamental Option and Conversion." *Irish Theological Quarterly* 71, nos. 3–4 (2006) 272–84.
Rachels, Stuart. *The Elements of Moral Philosophy*. New York: McGraw-Hill, 2007.

Raffoul, François. *The Origins of Responsibility*. Bloomington: Indiana University Press, 2010.

Rahner, Karl. *Foundations of Christian Faith: An Introduction to the Idea of Christianity*. New York: Crossroad, 1987.

———. "Natural Science and Reasonable Faith." In *Theological Investigations*, translated by Hugh M. Riley, 21:16–55. New York: Crossroad, 1988.

———. "Reflections on the Unity of the Love of Neighbour and the Love of God." In *Theological Investigations*, edited by Karl Rahner, 6:231–49. New York: Crossroad 1969.

———. "Theology of Freedom." In *Theological Investigations*, edited by Karl Rahner, 6:178–96. London: Darton, Longman and Todd, 1965.

Ratzinger, Joseph. "The Church and Man's Calling—the Dignity of the Human Person." In *Commentary on the Documents of Vatican II, Gaudium et Spes*, edited by Herbert Vorgrimler, 5:115–63. London: Burns & Oates, 1969.

Regan, Tom. *The Struggle for Animal Rights*. Clarks Summit, PA: International Society for Animal Rights, 1987.

Rhonheimer, Martin. "Nature as Reason: A Thomistic Theory of the Natural Law (Review Article)." *Studies in Christian Ethics* 19, no. 3 (2006) 357–78.

———. "Sins against Justice (IIa IIae, Qq. 59–78)." In *The Ethics of Aquinas*, ed. Stephen J. Pope, 287–303. Washington, DC: Georgetown Univerisity Press, 2002.

Rigby, Paul. "Levinas and Christian Mysticism after Auschwitz." *Theological Studies* 72, no. 2 (2011) 309–34.

Robbins, Jill. "Tracing Responsibility in Levinas's Ethical Thought." In *Ethics as First Philosophy: The Significance of Emmanuel Levinas for Philosophy, Literature and Religion*, edited by Adriaan T. Peperzak, 173–83. New York: Routledge, 1995.

Rudman, Stanley. *Concepts of Person and Christian Ethics*. Cambridge: Cambridge University Press, 1997.

Russell, Heidi Ann. *The Heart of Rahner: The Theological Implications of Andrew Tallon's Theory of Triune Consciousness*. Milwaukee: Marquette University Press, 2009.

Ryan, Tom. "Aquinas on Compassion: Has He Something to Offer Today?" *Irish Theological Quarterly* 75, no. 2 (2010) 157–74.

———. "By Way of Moral Beauty." *Compass Review* 41, no. 1 (2011) 24–29.

———. "Conscience as Primordial Moral Awareness in *Gaudium et Spes* and *Veritatis Splendor*." *Australian eJournal of Theology* 18, no. 1 (2011) 83–96.

———. "Healthy Shame? An Interchange between Elspeth Probyn and Thomas Aquinas." *Australian eJournal of Theology* 12, no. 1 (2008). http://aejt.com.au/__data/assets/pdf_file/0009/107469/Ryan_Practical_Theol_Conf.pdf

———. "Positive and Negative Emotions in Aquinas: Retrieving a Distorted Tradition." *Australasian Catholic Record* 78, no. 2 (2001) 141–52.

Salzman, Todd A. "The Basic Goods Theory and Revisionism: A Methodological Comparison on the Use of Reason and Experience as Sources of Moral Knowledge." *Heythrop Journal* 42, no. 4 (2001) 423–50.

———. *What Are They Saying about Catholic Ethical Method?* New York: Paulist, 2003.

Salzman, Todd A., and Michael G. Lawler. "New Natural Law Theory and Foundational Sexual Ethical Principles: A Critique and a Proposal." *Heythrop Journal* 47, no. 2 (2006) 182–205.

———. *The Sexual Person: Toward a Renewed Catholic Anthropology*. Washington, DC: Georgetown University Press, 2008.

Schema constitutionis pastoralis de ecclesia in mundo huius temporis: Expositio modorum partis secundae. Vatican City: Vatican Press, 1965.
Scott, Charles E. "A People's Witness Beyond Politics." In *Ethics as First Philosophy: The Significance of Emmanuel Levinas for Philosophy, Literature and Religion*, edited by Adriaan T. Peperzak, 25–35. New York: Routlege, 1995.
Seider, Scott. "The Trouble with Teaching Ethics on Trolley Cars and Train Tracks." *Journal of Moral Education* 38, no. 2 (2009) 219–36.
Sherman, Nancy. "Character Development and Aristotelian Virtue." In *Virtue Ethics and Moral Education*, edited by Jan Steutel and David Carr, 35–50. London: Routledge, 1999.
Singer, Peter. *Animal Liberation*. London: Cape, 1990.
———. *The Life You Can Save: Acting Now to End World Poverty*. Melbourne: Text, 2009.
Skoe, Eva E. A. "The Relationship between Empathy-Related Constructs and Care-Based Moral Development in Young Adulthood." *Journal of Moral Education* 39, no. 2 (2010) 191–211.
Sniegocki, John, *Catholic Social Teaching and Economic Globalization: The Quest for Alternatives*. Milwaukee: Marquette University Press, 2009.
Solomon, Robert C. "Phenomenology." In *New Dictionary of the History of Ideas*, edited by Maryanne Cline Horowitz, 4:1754–1757. Detroit: Scribner's Sons, 2005.
Somit, Albert, and Steven A. Peterson, eds. *Biology and Political Behavior: The Brain, Genes and Politics—the Cutting Edge*. Bingley: Emerald, 2011.
Sowle, Lisa Cahill. "Bioethics, Relationships, and Participation in the Common Good." In *Health and Human Flourishing: Religion, Medicine, and Moral Anthropology*, edited by Carol Taylor and Robert Dell'oro, 207–24. Washington, DC: Georgetown University Press, 2006.
Spohn, William C. "Conscience and Moral Development." *Theological Studies* 61 (2000) 122–38.
———. *Go and Do Likewise: Jesus and Ethics*. New York: Continuum, 1999.
———. "The Return of Virtue Ethics." *Theological Studies* 53, no. 1 (1992) 60.
Steutel, Jan, and David Carr. "Virtue Ethics and the Virtue Approach to Moral Education." In *Virtue Ethics and Moral Education*, edited by David Carr and Jan Steutel, 3–18. London: Routledge, 1999.
Sullivan, Francis A. "The Doctrinal Weight of Evangelium Vitae." *Theological Studies* 56, no. 3 (1995) 560.
Svend, Brinkmann. "Facts, Values, and the Naturalistic Fallacy in Psychology." *New Ideas in Psychology* 27, no. 1 (2009) 1–17.
Sweeny, Eileen. "Vice and Sin (Ia IIae, Qq. 71–89)." In *The Ethics of Aquinas*, edited by Stephen J. Pope, 151–68. Washington, DC: Georgetown University Press, 2002.
Tallon, Andrew. "Can Levinas's Ethical Metaphysics Contribute to Psychoanalysis? The Case for and Against." *Psychoanalytic Review* 94, no. 4 (2007) 657–80.
———. "Levinas's Ethical Horizon, Affective Neuroscience, and Social Field Theory." *Levinas Studies* 4 (2009) 47–67.
———. "Nonintentional Affectivity, Affective Intentionality, and the Ethical in Levinas's Philosophy." In *Ethics as First Philosophy: The Significance of Emmanuel Levinas for Philosophy, Literature and Religion*, edited by Adriaan T. Peperzak, 107–21. New York: Routledge, 1995.

Thornhill, John. "Unravelling the Complexities of the 'Original Sin' Tradition." *Australasian Catholic Record* 83, no. 1 (2006) 25–37.
Trabbic, Joseph G. "The Human Body and Human Happiness in Aquinas's *Summa Theologiae*." *New Blackfriars* 92, no. 1041 (2011) 552–64.
Tullberg, Jan, and Birgitta S. Tullberg. "A Critique of the Naturalistic Fallacy Thesis." *Politics and the Life Sciences* 20, no. 2 (2001) 165–74.
Tuohy, Anne. "Christian Anthropology." In *Foundations of Christian Faith*, edited by Damien Casey, Gerard Hall and Anne Hunt, 93–105. Melbourne: Cengage, 2004.
United Nations. "The Universal Declaration of Human Rights." United Nations. http://www.un.org/en/documents/udhr/.
Van Dyke, Fred. *Between Heaven and Earth: Christian Perspectives on Environmental Protection*. Santa Barbara, CA: Praeger, 2010.
Veling, Terry A. "'For You Alone': A Reading of Transcendence and Relationship in Emmanuel Levinas." *Australian eJournal of Theology* 14, no. 1 (2009) 1–14.
Verplaeste, Jan. *Localising the Moral Sense: Neuroscience and the Search for the Cerebral Seat of Morality*. London: Springer, 2009.
Verplaeste, Jan, et al., eds. *The Moral Brain: Essays on the Evolutionary and Neuroscientific Aspects of Morality*. London: Springer, 2009.
Verstraeten, J. "Solidarity and Subsidiarity." In *Principles of Catholic Social Teaching*, edited by David A. Boileau, 133–48. Milwaukee: Marquette University Press, 1998.
Vetlesen, Arne Johan. *Perception, Empathy, and Judgment: An Inquiry into the Preconditions of Moral Performance*. University Park: Pennsylvania State University Press, 1994.
Vicini, Andrea. "Bioethics: Basic Questions and Extraordinary Developments." *Theological Studies* 73, no. 1 (2012) 169–87.
Vogt, Christopher. "Fostering a Catholic Commitment to the Common Good: An Approach Rooted in Virtue Ethics." *Theological Studies* 68, no. 2 (2007) 394–417.
Waldenfels, Bernhard. "Levinas and the Face of the Other." In *The Cambridge Companion to Levinas*, edited by Simon Critchley and Robert Bernasconi, 63–81. Cambridge: Cambridge University Press, 2002.
———. "Response and Responsibility in Levinas." In *Ethics as First Philosophy: The Significance of Emmanuel Levinas for Philosophy, Literature and Religion*, edited by Adriaan T. Peperzak, 39–52. New York: Routledge, 1995.
Walsh, Michael. "The Myth of Rerum Novarum." *New Blackfriars* 93, no. 1044 (2012) 155–62.
Wang, Stephen. "Aquinas on Human Happiness and the Natural Desire for God." *New Blackfriars* 88, no. 1015 (2007) 322–34.
Ward, Barbara. "Looking Back on *Populorum Progressio*." In *Readings in Moral Theology No. 5: Official Catholic Social Teaching*, edited by Charles E. Curran and Richard A. McCormick, 130–49. New York: Paulist, 1986.
Weber, Elisabeth. "The Notion of Persecution in Levinas's *Otherwise Than Being or Beyond Essence*." In *Ethics as First Philosophy: The Significance of Emmanuel Levinas for Philosophy, Literature and Religion*, edited by Adriaan T. Peperzak, 69–75. New York: Routledge, 1995.
Welch, Sharon D. *A Feminist Ethic of Risk*. Minneapolis: Fortress, 1990.
Welchman, Kit. *Erik Erikson: His Life, Work, and Significance*. Buckingham: Open University Press, 2000.

Werhane, Particia H. "Levinas's Ethics: A Normative Perspective without Metaethical Constraints." In *Ethics as First Philosophy: The Significance of Emmanuel Levinas for Philosophy, Literature and Religion*, edited by Adriaan T. Peperzak, 59–67. New York: Routledge, 1995.

Westberg, Daniel. *Right Practical Reason: Aristotle, Action and Prudence in Aquinas*. Oxford: Oxford University Press, 1994.

Westphal, Merold. "Levinas's Teleological Suspension of the Religious." In *Ethics as First Philosophy: The Significance of Emmanuel Levinas for Philosophy, Literature and Religion*, edited by Adriaan T. Peperzak, 151–60. New York: Routledge, 1995.

White, Kevin. "The Passions of the Soul (Ia IIae, Qq.49–70)." In *The Ethics of Aquinas*, edited by Stephen J. Pope, 103–15. Washington, DC: Georgetown University Press, 2002.

Wieland, Georg. "Happiness (Ia IIae, Qq. 1–5)." In *The Ethics of Aquinas*, edited by Stephen J. Pope, 57–68. Washington, DC: Georgetown University Press, 2002.

Wojtyla, Karol. *Love & Responsibility*. London: Collins Sons, 1981.

Yarri, Donna. *The Ethics of Animal Experimentation: A Critical Analysis and Constructive Christian Proposal*. Oxford: Oxford University Press, 2005.

Zimmermann, Nigel. *Levinas and Theology*. London: Bloomsbury, 2013.

www.ingramcontent.com/pod-product-compliance
Ingram Content Group UK Ltd.
Pitfield, Milton Keynes, MK11 3LW, UK
UKHW022000220326
11408UKWH00003B/403